THE AMERICAN

COMPLETE AND
EASY GUIDE TO
Health Care
Law

Your Guide to Protecting Your Rights as a Patient,

Dealing with Hospitals, Health Insurance,

Medicare, and More

THE AMERICAN BAR ASSOCIATION

COMPLETE AND EASY GUIDE TO
Health Care Law

Your Guide to Protecting Your Rights as a Patient,

Dealing with Hospitals, Health Insurance,

Medicare, and More

 THREE RIVERS PRESS

NEW YORK

Copyright © 2001 by the American Bar Association

All rights reserved. No part of this book may be reproduced or transmitted in any form or by any means, electronic or mechanical, including photocopying, recording, or by any information storage and retrieval system, without permission in writing from the publisher.

Published by Three Rivers Press, New York, New York.
Member of the Crown Publishing Group.

Random House, Inc. New York, Toronto, London, Sydney, Auckland
www.randomhouse.com

THREE RIVERS PRESS is a registered trademark and the Three Rivers Press colophon is a trademark of Random House, Inc.

Printed in the United States of America

Library of Congress Cataloging-in-Publication Data
The ABA complete and easy guide to health care law : your guide to protecting your rights as a patient, dealing with hospitals, health insurance, Medicare, and more / by the American Bar Association.—1st ed.
    1. Medical care—Law and legislation—United States—Popular works.
  I. American Bar Association.
  KF3821.Z9 A22 2001
  344.73'0321—dc21

                                                        2001027350

ISBN 0-8129-2735-4

10 9 8 7 6 5 4 3 2 1

First Edition

THE AMERICAN BAR ASSOCIATION

Lawrence O. Gostin
Professor of Law and Public
Health
Georgetown University, The
Johns Hopkins University
Co-Director, Georgetown/
Johns Hopkins Program on
Law and Public Health
Washington, DC

Charles B. Inlander
President
People's Medical Society
Allentown, Pennsylvania

Ami S. Jaeger
Principal
BioLaw Group
Santa Fe, New Mexico

Timothy Stoltzfus Jost
Newton D. Baker, Baker &
Hostetler Professor of Law and
Health Services
Management and Policy
Ohio State University School
of Law
Columbus, Ohio

John J. Lombard, Jr.
Attorney
Morgan, Lewis & Bockius LLP
Philadelphia, Pennsylvania

Joan Polachek
Attorney
McDermott, Will & Emery
Chicago, Illinois

Robert L. Roth
Attorney
Michaels & Bonner, PC
Washington, DC

Jack A. Rovner
Attorney
Michaels, Best and Friedrich,
LLC
Chicago, Illinois

Salvatore J. Russo
Executive Senior Counsel
New York City Health &
Hospitals Corporation
New York, New York

Charles P. Sabatino
Assistant Director
ABA Commission on Legal
Problems of the Elderly
Washington, DC

Lois Snyder
Director, Center for Ethics and
Professionalism
American College of
Physicians—American Society
of Internal Medicine
Philadelphia, Pennsylvania

Bethany Spielman
Department of Medical
Humanities
SIU School of Medicine
Springfield, Illinois

THE AMERICAN BAR ASSOCIATION STANDING COMMITTEE ON PUBLIC EDUCATION

CONTENTS

FOREWORD

Robert A. Stein,
Executive Director, American Bar Association

The American Bar Association is the nation's premier source of legal information. With more than 400,000 members, representing every specialty and every type of legal practice, the ABA is in a unique position to deliver accurate, up-to-date, unbiased legal information to its members, to the media, and to the general public. The ABA website—www.abanet.org—is an unrivaled database in the legal field.

This book is a good example of how you can benefit from the ABA's network of hundreds of thousands of lawyers.

The ABA Guide to Health Care Law was written with the aid of ABA members from all over the country. Many members of our Health Law Section served as reviewers of the manuscript. The Health Law Section is one of the newest and fastest growing of the ABA's sections. The input of its members was especially valuable because they are experts in their topic and have had considerable experience in dealing every day with health law. They reviewed draft chapters, offering clarifications, suggesting additional topics that would be helpful to readers, and polishing the manuscript to make it even better.

Other ABA members reviewing the manuscript brought a rich range of experience to the project. They included professors of law and of public health, experts on medical ethics, and specialists in the legal problems of the elderly.

Finally, the ABA's Standing Committee on Public Education provided oversight for this project. This committee and its excellent staff contribute the perspective of experts in communicating about the law.

Thanks to all of the lawyers who worked on this book, you can be sure that the information it includes is

- useful,
- helpful,
- unbiased,
- current,
- written in a reader-friendly style that you can understand easily, and
- reflects a national picture, since the ABA's members practice in all jurisdictions.

Public education and public service are two of the most important goals of the American Bar Association. This book shows how the ABA takes an active role in providing the public with information it can use.

The American Bar Association is the largest voluntary association in the world. Besides its commitment to public education, the ABA provides programs to assist lawyers and judges in their work, and initiatives to improve the legal system for the public, including promoting fast, affordable alternatives to lawsuits, such as mediation, arbitration, conciliation, and small claims courts. Through ABA support for lawyer referral programs and pro bono services (where lawyers donate their time), people like you have been able to find the best lawyer for each particular case and have received quality legal help within each budget.

Robert A. Stein is the Executive Director of the American Bar Association. He was formerly dean of the University of Minnesota Law School.

INTRODUCTION

Allan J. Tanenbaum, Chair
ABA Standing Committee on Public Education

Health care in America is better than ever. We are leading longer, healthier lives. Thanks to advances in medicine, we have conquered some of the long-term scourges of humanity.

Unfortunately, health care also costs more than it ever has. Health spending has gone from about 5 percent as a share of the economy to about 14 percent—all in less than forty years. Paying for these health bills is a big issue for politicians (the government pays for about half of our health costs) and a big issue for consumers (who pay the rest, either out of pocket or through their insurance).

This book is designed to help you sort through the maze of health insurance, HMOs, and government programs, while also giving you tips on dozens of other issues where health care and law interact, such as your right to informed consent, new reproductive technologies and the law, and disabilities and the law.

No matter who you are, no matter what your health status is, you probably have plenty of questions about the impact of the law, but you may have no idea where to turn. That's where this book can help. It can help you sort out issues. It provides background information and suggests the pros and cons of various courses of action.

Our main author is an outstanding lawyer and journalist, Cindy J. Moy. Her manuscript was reviewed and approved by health-law experts from all over the country, under the guidance of the ABA's Standing Committee on Public Education. Together, we've worked to provide you with easy-to-understand information that will help you use the laws that affect health care. Our goal is to help you spot problems before they become major—when they're easiest to handle.

In this book you'll find practical, down-to-earth information about everything from guarding the privacy of your medical records to choosing a nursing home. We cover everything from the traditional—such as the licensing of doctors—to the cutting edge, such as research on humans. We get into medical malpractice suits and other possible steps to take when care goes wrong, and we look into the legal side of such end-of-life issues as your right to refuse treatment.

Our authors cover these topics and more in plain, direct language. You won't find legal jargon or technicalities here—just concise, straightforward discussions of how the law affects health care every day.

HOW TO USE THIS BOOK

Most of you will want to keep this book handy, to refer to it at various stages of your treatment. It's clearly organized so you can easily find the help you need as a new issue comes up.

Section One—Patients' Rights gives you an overview of your right to confidentiality and privacy, your right to emergency care, and your right to what the law calls "informed consent"—your right to understand and approve your treatment. In this area especially, knowledge is power. To use your rights you have to realize you have them and understand the steps to take to exercise them. We tell you what you need to know.

Section Two—Paying for Medical Care looks at your options for footing the bill, from private insurance to HMOs and government programs. We help you understand the rapidly changing legal environment, especially of HMOs, look at Medicare and Medicaid, and fill you in on your rights to continue your health insurance for a period when you leave a job—the mysteriously named but popular COBRA legislation. As always, the focus is on *you*—and how this information can benefit you and your family.

Section Three—Reproduction looks at the birds, bees, and deep freeze. It covers everything from the old (midwifery) to the very new, giving you guidance on how law is struggling to catch up with advances in reproductive technology. Other chapters look at some of the legal consequences of failures of reproductive technology—wrongful birth and wrongful pregnancy cases. Sterilization remains a difficult issue, though dwarfed in controversy by abortion. For all these areas, we don't take sides, but rather tell you what the law is, what some of the trends seem to be, and how the legal situation affects people caught up in these difficult circumstances.

Section Four—People with Disabilities covers a wide range of issues dealing with disabilities and the law. We begin by looking at some of the essential protections for people with disabilities, then look at some specific issues. Most of us don't think of pregnancy as a disability, but pregnancy-related conditions are sometimes classified that way under the law, resulting in important legal protections for pregnant women. There are many questions regarding the privacy of persons with disabilities, and we try to give you tips on how the law affects these issues. Vaccinations are covered in this section, as is mandatory testing. We end by taking a look at an old form of disease control, quarantine, and examine some of the legal issues it raises.

All in all, a surprising number of people are affected by the laws regarding disability, and this section will help them, and their families, understand their rights under the law.

Section Five—Nursing Homes is a very practical section that will help you understand such basic matters as how to choose a nursing home, how to pay for it, and what some alternatives are to nursing homes. America's population is aging, and more and more Americans are looking into alternatives to living at home, either for themselves or their aging parents. It's not just your home or the nursing home anymore. We explore assisted living, congregate care, and other alternatives. If you do choose a nursing home, we give you checklists to help you select the right one. We discuss how planning ahead can help you pay for such care, and provide some suggestions on qualifying for Medicaid.

Section Six—Regulating Medical Professionals discusses some of the legal protections in place for patients. We alert you to the protections established by the requirement that doctors be licensed. We also discuss the rapidly evolving area of legal protections for people undergoing experimental procedures. Finally, we look at medical malpractice, an area of law designed both to make medicine safer and to provide a way for patients hurt through negligence to receive compensation for their injuries.

Section Seven—Death and Dying canvasses a number of end-of-life issues. Perhaps the most important of these is your right to refuse life-sustaining treatment, and the tools—living wills, health care advance directives, and the like—that you can use to assure that your wishes will be effective in determining your treatment, even if you can no longer speak for yourself.

The hospice movement is one of the ways the law and medicine are changing regarding end-of-life choices. This form of caring for the terminally ill has proven a comfort for many families. We alert you to some of the legal issues and some ways in which you can try to guarantee that a hospice functions as well as it can.

Organ donation is also growing in importance, and we discuss some of the evolving legal issues it raises. Finally, we look at how the law deals with a highly controversial topic—assisted suicide.

Our final chapter—"Where Do You Go from Here"—gives you websites, books, and other sources of useful information, many just a touch of a computer key or telephone keypad away.

WRITTEN WITH YOU IN MIND

We've made a special effort to make this book practical, by using situations and problems you are likely to encounter. Each chapter is clearly laid out, with a real-life starting situation that shows the practical ramifications of the subject.

Within chapters, brief special sidebars alert you to important points:

- sidebars with this icon ✎ generally give you practical tips that could be of benefit to you or provide interesting additional information;
- sidebars with this icon 🖝 generally give you a warning about a potential pitfall that you can navigate with the right information and help;
- sidebars with this icon 📝 highlight important steps to take; and
- sidebars with this icon 📖 provide clear, plain English definitions to legal or medical terms

A brand-new feature in this series—talking to a lawyer—highlights our experts responding to actual questions from people, giving legal information that may help you as you grapple with similar issues within your own family. It is designated with a telephone icon (☎).

At the end of each chapter, in a section entitled "You must remember this . . ." we highlight the most important points that chapter has covered. In a concluding section of each chapter, entitled "The World at Your Fingertips," we also advise you where to go for more information if you'd like to explore a topic further—usually to free or inexpensive materials that will fill your mind without emptying your wallet.

Sometimes a problem is so complex, or so much is at stake, that you'll want to seek legal advice from someone who knows the facts of your particular case and can give you advice tailored to your situation. But with this book, you'll be able to make informed decisions about a wide range of problems and opportunities. Armed with the knowledge and insights we provide, you can be confident that the decisions you make will be in your best interests.

Allan J. Tanenbaum is Chair of the ABA's Standing Committee on Public Education. He is General Counsel of AFC Enterprises, Inc., in Atlanta, Georgia. He represents the State Bar of Georgia in the ABA House of Delegates.

PART ONE

Patients' Rights

All of us are medical patients, whether our care is for yearly checkups or ongoing illnesses. In the past many of us accepted our treatment without question. Now, patients are taking a more active role in assessing their treatment and their options. Patients are becoming informed as much as possible about their health concerns and are taking an active part in decisions about their health care.

In this section we will discuss the rights that are unique to you as a patient. Chapter 1 deals with your right to confidentiality and privacy. Who gets to see your medical file? What is the difference between your confidentiality and the doctor-patient privilege? We answer these questions as well as many others. Then we will tell you how you can protect yourself from violations of privacy and where to turn if you believe your privacy is violated.

Chapter 2 discusses emergency care. This became an important topic when insurance companies and health maintenance organizations began putting restrictions on your access to emergency services. The state and federal governments took action when patients complained that needed services were not being covered. The question of the services an emergency room staff is required to provide to you is answered in this chapter, too.

Chapter 3 explains informed consent: What is it and what responsibility does it place on you? We provide you with a list of questions to ask your doctor when you are facing an illness or deciding on treatment options. In addition, we will clarify what you should do when your doctor hands you a consent form for your signature and, after signing it, how to let your doctor know you changed your mind.

These three topics are the mainstay of your rights as a patient. Get informed and know your rights as a patient. If you would like more information, please check at the end of each chapter and of the guide as a whole for additional resources and websites regarding these issues.

CHAPTER 1

Confidentiality/Privacy and the Patient's Bill of Rights

Your Guide to the Complicated Legal World of Medical Privacy

Imagine sitting with your friends, enjoying dinner. Your friend Jane tells you that she is taking medication for depression after having an abortion. Jane then turns to another friend and announces that her husband has herpes. She leans across the table to inform another companion that her daughter is being treated for bulimia. She openly tells your hosts that her son is being counseled for substance abuse.

Few of us would discuss our medical problems so candidly. You would not want such information to be readily available to others, and there are laws and regulations that safeguard this information, though your specific rights may depend on the state in which you live and the circumstances of your situation.

WHO HAS ACCESS TO YOUR FILE?

Remember signing all those forms at the doctor's office—the ones that allowed your doctor to share your medical information with the insurance company? Ever wonder who else gets to see that information? As patients, we often have to bare our souls, among other things, in order for doctors to properly diagnose us and to prescribe the correct treatment. Although a thorough medical examination is certainly needed to properly diagnose and treat us, the information it reveals is often very personal, sometimes embarrassing.

The fact is that dozens of doctors, nurses, secretaries, and other professionals in the health care field have legitimate access to this medical information. But what about that accountant at the insurance company? Your spouse? Your children? Your employer? You may be surprised to learn that many of those people have access to an amazing amount of information about you.

There are laws that protect your privacy, especially on the state level, but they vary considerably.

What Is in Your File?

Your medical file contains

- your name, address, and phone number;
- your age, sex, and marital status;
- names and ages of your children;
- your occupation and Social Security number;
- results of lab tests and physical examinations;
- whether you have a living will or a health care power of attorney;
- your family medical history, including risk factors (such as smoking, obesity, or high blood pressure), allergies, immunizations, and any medications prescribed.

The wrong person can do a lot of damage with this information. In one instance, a Maryland banker sat on the state health commission. He got his hands on a list of cancer patients and compared that list with the loan records at his bank. He then called due any loans to individuals whose names were on the list of cancer patients.

RECORDS OFTEN MISUSED

According to one survey, one-third of human resources employees admitted to using medical or insurance records in deciding whom to hire, promote, or fire.

In another case, a company executive found out which employees were taking certain medications and realized that one employee in particular was taking a drug to fight AIDS. The executive then told co-workers. The employee sued the company, but the company won the case. Would you want your employer to know that you are taking birth control pills? Heart medication? Drugs for a sexually transmitted disease? Probably not, but it's all in your file.

HOW THE LAW PROTECTS YOUR INFORMATION

The Federal Government

The United States Constitution

There is no outright guarantee of privacy under the Constitution. There is, though, an *implied right* to privacy under the Constitution that has been consistently expanded throughout the past thirty years. This is the right under which the United States Supreme Court placed a woman's right to obtain an abortion. This privacy right was extended by the Court to individually identifiable medical data. This is any medical data by which someone could find out your name, address, or Social Security number.

A New York law required doctors to report to the state any person taking certain prescription drugs that could be sold by the patient for illegal use by others (such as morphine). The Court ruled that this did not violate the patient's right to privacy because the state took sufficient security measures to protect the data. When deciding whether the state can get access to your medical data, a court will look at

- **whether the intrusion into your privacy is justified by the kind of information requested;**
- **the potential for any harm to you;**
- **the safeguards provided to prevent the unauthorized disclosure of your information to someone else;**
- **the degree to which your information is needed.**

Privacy Laws

There is no federal law at this point that comprehensively and specifically applies your right of privacy to individually identifiable medical information. (However, at present, each state has its own laws governing this information. Moreover, state lawmakers around the country are busily considering an array of proposed new laws, discussed later, to strengthen such protections.) There are also standards that all Medicare and Medicaid facilities must meet. And some federal privacy laws provide some protection of medical data, such as HIV status or psychiatric treatment. These are discussed in later chapters.

The *Privacy Act of 1974* requires that government agencies act fairly when collecting, using, and releasing any information that identifies you. The agency collecting the data is required to notify you that information is being collected and why. You have the right to see this data and to correct any errors within it. The information may not be released to another person without your consent except in certain situations. Your consent is not required if the information is released for a reason that is compatible with the reason for which the information is collected in the first place. Any hospital or health care facility that is operated by the federal government or that maintains records under a government contract must follow the Privacy Act.

The Privacy Act does not protect data that is required to be released under the *Freedom of Information Act*. The Freedom of Information Act, though, grants an exception to some personal medical information. This information will not be released by the government agency if to do so would clearly violate your privacy.

Proposed Legislation

Patient privacy is a major political issue right now, and legislators are in the process of trying to come up with a law that finds the right balance between your privacy rights and the rights of insurance companies, hospitals, and health care providers. These proposed laws typically grant you a clear right of privacy when it comes to your medical information. Some allow you to separate certain portions of your medical records, such as mental health information, from the rest of your record. Many of these proposed laws seek to give you the right to sue in civil court anyone who abuses your personal health information. Other proposals include criminal sanctions for breaches of patient confidentiality or misuse of personal medical information.

Proposed laws such as these will be on the agenda for federal and state legislators to consider for the next few years. The trend is to give you greater rights to privacy, although the penalties for violating your rights are uncertain.

Medicare

Hospitals that participate in the Medicare program must comply with the Medicare Conditions of Participation for Hospitals. These conditions require that hospitals take certain steps to keep your information confidential. The hospital may release copies of your records only to authorized individuals, such as your doctor. The hospital must also take steps to make sure that unauthorized individuals cannot access your records. Furthermore, your original medical records cannot be released by the hospital except by court order, subpoena, or a state or federal law. In most cases where your records are released, the hospital will provide a certified copy of the record, which is accepted in lieu of the original.

State Laws

Current Law

For the most part, health care issues are deferred to each state, including the protection of medical data. The Tenth Amendment to the Constitution gives this power to the states. The result is that your right to privacy regarding your medical information depends in large part on where you live. State law protects your medical data through laws against invasion of privacy and the special duty your doctor has to keep your information confidential.

In short, the law recognizes that a special relationship exists between you and your doctor. Your doctor, as a medical profession, must protect that special relationship by acting in a way that is appropriate for the profession. This includes keeping your information confidential. Breach of patient confidentiality constitutes professional misconduct for licensed health care professionals. National and state medical associations have many guidelines as to what constitutes breach of confidentiality.

The patient-doctor relationship is also regulated by state statutes concerning professional misconduct. Laws against invasion of privacy protect you from a doctor who takes your personal information and gives it to the public. Some state laws provide criminal sanctions for breaches of patient confidentiality. Civil lawsuits for money damages may also be possible.

Some states consider the relationship between you and your doctor to be a contract. These states assume that any time you are treated by a doctor, that doctor enters into an unwritten contract with you and agrees to keep your information confidential unless you grant your permission to do otherwise. Patients are having more success with this contract theory than with invasion of privacy because rarely is medical data released openly to the public. Not all states recognize that a contract exists between you and your doctor, though.

Proposed Legislation

Nearly every state already has laws dealing with privacy of medical records. Many are considering new legislation dealing with medical records, especially when it comes to keeping pace with developments on the information superhighway. The proposed legislation usually contains a common thread—hospitals and health care providers may not disclose your medical information to any unauthorized person. If your information is released, the punishment could be monetary fines or even imprisonment. Approximately ten states already have laws on the books that protect your personal data that is stored in the state's databanks, including medical information. New York requires that insurance companies keep private any medical information received in order to make payments on claims.

Professional Associations

Professional associations are not legal bodies that can make laws. However, they can come up with standards and require their members to adhere to those standards. Those standards are not laws but guidelines for you to use to determine whether your information is as secure as it could be. If a doctor or a hospital violates these standards, they may be subject to professional disciplinary procedures. State and federal laws are still needed to back those standards and to give you an opportunity to seek damages when your privacy is violated.

Hospitals

Many hospital administrators put their own procedures into place to ensure that your information stays private. One lawyer who worked as general counsel to a small Chicago hospital reports that both clinical and administrative hospital staff went to extraordinary lengths to ensure patient confidentiality. On more than one occasion, clinical staff members contacted her to inform her of possible breaches of patient confidentiality—in some instances reporting the behavior of persons who were senior to them.

In addition, a great number of hospitals belong to professional organizations or associations that obligate member hospitals to use caution when dealing with patient records. Additionally, the hospital may face tort liability (discussed in Chapter 17) for breaching patient confidentiality.

The Joint Commission on Accreditation of Healthcare Organizations (JCAHO)

JCAHO furnishes standards to its member hospitals regarding patient confidentiality. The standards require that confidentiality and security of patient information are maintained. The hospital is supposed to design its computer system to allow for easy access to information by doctors and nurses while not compromising the confidentiality of your records. These standards are meant to ensure that your records are accessible when needed but that people who do not need to see your information are denied access. (This is where precautions such as passwords come into play.)

The American Medical Association (AMA)

The AMA released a statement on medical information confidentiality. The statement recommends that only authorized personnel be allowed to enter medical information into a patient's computerized medical record. The AMA also recommends that no information be released from the patient's record without the patient's permission. In addition, the AMA's Code of Medical Ethics requires that doctors treat your information with the most confidentiality possible. The American Nurses Association follows a similar code of confidentiality.

WHEN YOU GO TO THE DOCTOR

Any time you enter a hospital or other medical facility, you automatically agree—whether you know it or not—to let anyone directly involved with your care see your medical record. This includes secretaries, nurses, interns, residents, doctors, nutritionists, pharmacists, and technicians. Obviously, it makes sense that anyone involved with your care have access to your medical information. (Medical researchers generally must obtain permission before getting access to your medical records.)

While providing access is necessary to provide you with the best treatment possible, it can be a bit unsettling to realize just how many people get to see your records.

There are three terms to keep in mind when it comes to medical information:

- confidentiality;
- privilege;
- privacy.

In everyday language these terms might seem interchangeable, but from a legal standpoint, they have distinct definitions.

Confidentiality

Confidentiality means that a doctor should not reveal your personal information to anyone except those people who are caring for you. This duty is rooted in the Hippocratic Oath, which states in part: "Whatever, in connection with my professional practice, or not in connection with it, I see or hear in the life of men, which ought not to be spoken abroad, I will not divulge, as reckoning that all such should be kept secret."

LEARNING THE LINGO

Confidentiality: Doctors should not reveal personal information of patients to anyone except those people involved in the care of the patients.

Confidentiality refers to your expectation that what you tell your doctor will not be repeated to anyone not involved in your treatment. It is your decision as to what other uses may be made of the information. It should be up to you whether your information is released to pharmaceutical companies, other patients, or anyone else not involved in your care.

Privilege

The doctor-patient **privilege** means the doctor cannot disclose the patient's personal information during a legal proceeding without the patient's consent. This privilege is a right held by the patient, but not every state grants patients this right. Privilege can stop a doctor from giving the patient's medical information to the court, but it does not prohibit a doctor from providing the information to the patient's employer, insurance company, or other doctors. That ban comes from privacy and confidentiality rights. Privilege is not absolute. It may be overridden by a court order.

Privacy

The right to **privacy** allows you

- to refuse to see visitors or anyone else not directly involved in your care and to prevent them from seeing your medical records;
- to wear religious medals and your own bedclothes, as long as they don't interfere with your treatment;
- to request to have a person of your sex present during a physical examination by a member of the opposite sex, and not to be required to remain disrobed any longer than is necessary for the medical treatment;
- to insist on being transferred to another room if the person sharing the room with you is unreasonably disturbing to you (for example, with loud music).
  (These examples are drawn from George Annas's excellent *The Rights of Patients*, Humana Press, 1992, page 191.)

Unlike the doctor-patient relationship, in most locations there is no duty on the part of the insurance company to keep your personal information private. One employee of a large insurance company would reportedly look up the names of prospective dates on his computer, although he didn't need access to that information to perform his job. He had access to millions of files. If he saw that a woman asked about or sought coverage for an abortion or for medications used to treat sexually transmitted diseases or substance abuse, he would refrain from asking her on a date. As insurance companies and health maintenance organizations (HMOs) merge and become linked, such renegade employees will have access to more information about more people.

Exceptions That Prove the Rule

It Is in Your Best Interest

In theory, you have the right to dictate which people can and cannot see your medical information. In the real world, doctors, nurses, and other health care workers have considerable discretion in releasing your personal information. For example, your doctor can decide to share your personal information with your spouse and close relatives, but only if the doctor believes in good faith that it is in your best interest.

When is such disclosure in your interest? The **therapeutic privilege** requires that a physician make a reasonable medical judgment that disclosure of the patient's medical condition and obtaining an informed consent would cause an adverse and substantial effect on the patient's medical condition. This is a rigorous standard rarely relied on by physicians.

You Are Unconscious

If you are unconscious or unable to make decisions regarding your care, the doctor has the right to provide your family members with all the information necessary to make an informed decision on your behalf. Otherwise, doctors should use only very general terms, such as "stable," when describing your condition.

Many people have anticipated that at some point in the future they might not be able to make decisions and have written and signed a **living will, health care advance directive,** or **health care proxy.** Through any of these devices, you can appoint a health care agent (sometimes called a health care power of attorney) to make decisions for you. If you have such a document, then that person alone is entitled to information regarding your medical condition. This subject is discussed further in Chapter 26.

Reporting Vital Statistics

Just as the law requires some information to be kept under wraps, it also requires doctors, nurses, and other health professionals to release information in certain circumstances. For instance, most states have laws requiring doctors to file birth and death certificates. Doctors are also usually required to report injuries caused by guns or sharp instruments, such as knives.

When There Is Abuse or Danger to Others

There is a duty to protect that is spelled out by law in many states. For instance, when child abuse is suspected, doctors, nurses, and other health professionals must report the abuse. The same is true for situations when a doctor or a therapist decides that the patient is a danger to others or to himself. If the doctor or therapist feels that disclosing the patient's statements is necessary to protect the patient or a third person, the doctor or therapist must do so.

As an example of what can happen when this information is not shared, a patient told his therapist that he intended to kill his former girlfriend. The therapist believed the patient meant to kill the young woman but did not warn her or confine the boy to a mental institution. After the patient killed the girl, her parents sued the therapist. The therapist claimed the patient's statements were confidential. Although that case was eventually settled out of court, cases such as this and statutes in many states now generally require doctors to warn those who are at risk of the patient's violence or to take other reasonable steps, such as involuntary commitment of the patient or the notification of the police.

When You Have a Communicable Disease

Many states require doctors to report cases of communicable diseases, including (but not limited to) smallpox, tuberculosis, pneumonia, measles, chicken pox, mumps, syphilis, gonorrhea, AIDS, and HIV. AIDS and HIV present a special challenge to patient privacy and confidentiality. This topic is covered more thoroughly in the section on AIDS and disabilities.

In general, confidentiality is needed so that people will be comfortable being tested for AIDS or HIV. That need for confidentiality must be balanced with the desire to protect others from contracting the disease. Although doctors in all states are required to report AIDS cases to state public health departments, states differ in how this information is used.

In Legal Proceedings

Medical information is commonly used in legal proceedings, even when a privilege exists between the doctor and the patient. Any time you make your health or physical condition the focus of a lawsuit, such as in a suit for worker's compensation or for injuries from a car accident or medical malpractice and in some child custody cases, your doctor can be brought into court to testify about your medical condition.

With Other Doctors

A doctor is allowed to discuss a patient with health care professionals that are not involved in the patient's care, but only if the patient consents or if the doctor doesn't reveal the patient's identity. In other circumstances, you have a right to maintain your privacy. For example, imagine that a doctor shows up to examine you—and is trailed by a group of medical students. You have the right to refuse to let the medical students watch your examination.

YOUR CHILD'S MEDICAL RECORD

To a certain extent, you control what goes into your child's medical record, particularly when your child is very young. If you do not tell the pediatrician that your child received medical treatment from an opthamologist or a chiropractor, the pediatrician will not be aware of that treatment.

The situation is very different for older children, who might be able to keep information from you. What happens when your child becomes a teenager? Do you still get to see your child's medical information?

Once again, the law differs from state to state. Overall, states recognize that parents need to be able to give doctors medical information about their children before those children take medication or undergo surgery. In many states, though, such as Illinois, if your child becomes pregnant and asks for an abortion, you may no longer be given access to her medical records. In Montana, however, parents retain the right of access to a child's medical records because her parents are considered to have the right to protect her from decisions she makes as a minor. Some states resolve the issue by letting the doctor decide whether it would be in the child's best interest to let parents see the information.

HOW TO PROTECT YOURSELF

Tell your doctor that you are concerned about who has access to your medical information. Ask her what steps are taken to keep that information confidential. Don't let your concerns be brushed aside.

Take your time and read every form you are asked to sign at the doctor's office or hospital. If you want insurance to pay your claim, you will have to sign the release form allowing the doctor to send your information to the insurance company. On the other hand, you can also specify that the doctor release only the specific information necessary to pay the claim—no more.

For particularly private or embarrassing medical issues, if possible, pay for the visit, medication, or therapy yourself so that the information will not be sent to the insurance company for reimbursement. This may seem unfair after paying insurance premiums, but it is the best way to keep the information out of your insurance company's database.

Ask your doctor for the clinic's or the hospital's policy on discussing patients among the medical staff. Notice whether the staff discusses personal information of patients while at the nurses' station, in the elevator, or in the cafeteria. In one situation, while sitting in a hospital visiting room with her young daughter, an attorney listened as four medical residents discussed in very unflattering terms the personal hygiene of a patient in the maternity ward. Report such breaches to your doctor and ask that the situation be corrected.

Do not discuss your medical concerns while talking on a cellular or cordless phone. A simple baby monitor will allow your neighbors to hear your conversation. Think twice before e-mailing an Internet discussion group and providing information about your medical history. This information can be traced back to you, compiled by the discussion group "host," and sold to marketing companies.

If you believe your medical information is not being treated confidentially by medical staff members, discuss your concerns with your doctor. If you feel your doctor is violating your confidentiality or privacy, report the situation to a managing partner in the clinic or to the chief of staff—even doctors have bosses. You can also report the problem to your state's medical licensing board and the local medical professional association. Both numbers are in your phone book.

WHEN YOU MIGHT WANT TO CONSENT TO RELEASE YOUR INFORMATION

The general rule is that you must consent before your medical information is released to another party, such as your insurance company. Some states have laws that allow your information to be released to any requesting party once you have signed a general release form. In other states your information may only be released to certain parties, such as your HMO or the department of health. Your consent will be required if you plan to submit claims to your insurance company. There are also special authorization forms for HIV and drug-treatment program information, which have further requirements.

What Has to Be in the Release?

Typically a release form will include:

- your name, address, and date of birth;
- a description of the information to be released;
- the identity of the party that will receive the information;
- a statement that you authorize the release of information;
- your signature;
- the time period for which the release will be valid.

What Happens to the Doctor if Your Information Is Released Without Your Consent?

Almost half of the states will take disciplinary action against a doctor if it is discovered that a doctor released confidential information without the patient's consent. This may include revoking the doctor's medical license, though reprimand is the more likely remedy. Remember, though, that the doctor may legally give your information to other health care professionals who are taking part in your medical care or to the state department of health if you suffer a knife or gunshot wound or have a communicable disease.

THE PATIENT'S BILL OF RIGHTS

As part of an ongoing effort to reform managed health care, Congress continues to debate a federal Patient's Bill of Rights. Both Republicans and Democrats agree that a bill of rights is needed, but they cannot seem to agree on what should be included. At a minimum, these proposed bills tend to include

- a requirement that health plans give consumers facts about benefits, exclusions, doctor credentials, and hospital track records;
- direct access to specialists for patients with serious medical needs;
- coverage of emergency services when lack of such care would cause serious harm to the patient;
- a requirement that doctors and health plans provide patients with information on treatment risks, benefits, and alternatives and on any financial arrangements influencing decisions;
- the banning of "gag" clauses, which forbid doctors from disclosing all treatment options (some states already ban these clauses);
- a simplified appeals process that can be accessed quickly.

In 1997, President Bill Clinton appointed the Advisory Commission on Consumer Protection and Quality in the Health Care Industry to research the question of how to provide quality health care for all Americans. To read the advisory commission's report, visit the commission's website at *http://www.hcqualitycommission. gov/*. A summary of the commission's proposed patient's bill of rights is available at *http://www.hcqualitycommission.gov/press/ cbor.html#head1*. This summary goes into greater detail regarding the preceding list of rights.

THE WORLD AT YOUR FINGERTIPS

- For a readable, popular look at your right to privacy regarding medical information, personal computers, voice mail, e-mail, and other property, see *Invasion of Privacy* by Louis R. Mizell (Berkley, 1998).
- Computer-based Patient Record Institute is a nonprofit organization working with health information in an increasingly technological world. To visit their website, go to *www.cpri.org*.
- The Health Law Resource: For a discussion on the need for confidentiality of medical records, see *http://www.netreach. net/~wmanning/cdm.htm*.
- The Center for Democracy and Technology is a nonprofit organization concerned with privacy issues. See *www.cdt. org/privacy/health/960614_testimony.html* for congressional testimony regarding the confidentiality of medical records.

YOU MUST REMEMBER THIS

- Your doctor has a duty to keep your information confidential. The insurance company does not.
- Read all forms thoroughly.
- Ask your doctor how your medical information is protected.
- You need to be open with your doctor in order to receive the best treatment possible. In some instances, however, you should consider paying for the treatment yourself, rather than seeking reimbursement from the insurance company.

CHAPTER 2

Emergency Care

You Have Rights to Emergency Care—
Know How to Use Them

Julie awoke in the middle of the night to the sound of her toddler's cry. Libby's forehead was hot. When Julie took her temperature, the thermometer read 104 degrees. Julie immediately headed for the emergency room of the nearest hospital. The emergency room nurse told Julie that the hospital was too busy with other patients and told her to go to another hospital about fifteen minutes away. Julie drove to the other hospital. The doctor there administered a shot of acetaminophen, which soon brought the fever down. Libby was diagnosed with a viral infection from which she recovered in a few days. Julie's insurance company refused to cover Libby's trip to the emergency room because Julie did not call for prior approval before going to the hospital. Julie is still recovering from the bill.

MANAGED CARE VERSUS EMERGENCY CARE

Understanding Your Policy

Ever read your entire health insurance policy? Did you understand it? Reading an insurance policy can be tedious and confusing. The terms are unfamiliar, and the language seems to be a riddle meant to baffle you. Some health plans do not even give their policyholders the whole policy. Instead they provide you with a shorter outline of your coverage. One man who received such an outline noted that he was covered for "emergency transportation." Later on the man needed to be airlifted to a hospital. The health plan denied coverage, claiming that it only covered ambulances. When the man took the health plan to court, he was able to get the bill for the helicopter covered by the health plan.

When the language in the policy is clear, it will almost always be enforced as it is written, even though doing so may be to your disadvantage. When there are terms such as "emergency transportation," which can be interpreted in several ways, courts will define the terms to protect the reasonable expectations of the insured—you.

Limiting Emergency Care

Emergencies cannot really be managed. By their very nature, emergencies are unexpected, unforeseen, and often frightening—the very qualities that make them difficult to manage.

Originally, however, HMOs did try to manage them, sometimes with disastrous results. When HMOs first became prevalent, many of them limited the use of emergency rooms and services. Patients were required to call the HMO to ask permission to go to the emergency room. Patients would describe their symptoms to HMO personnel who would then approve or deny permission to seek emergency care. Unbeknownst to patients, they were not always speaking with a doctor. Sometimes the decisions were made by customer service representatives with no medical training.

If the patient was denied permission and sought emergency care anyway, the HMO refused to cover the bill. Even if the HMO approved the emergency visit, it would sometimes reverse its decision upon receiving the bill if HMO personnel decided it wasn't an emergency after all. One patient received approval to seek emergency care for severe abdominal pain. He was admitted to the hospital and died within a few hours. His HMO refused to pay the bill, arguing it had not been an emergency.

State Legislatures Get Involved

HMOs argue that instances like these are rare, that most people under managed care give it high marks, and that the procedures that sometimes limit medical care are necessary to contain costs.

However, on the emergency room issue, as more and more horror stories came to the attention of the press and the public, legislators began taking a closer look at how HMOs were operating. Some HMOs required the approval of a doctor to visit the emergency room but did not staff their phone lines outside of normal business hours. Other patients waited hours to receive a call from an HMO doctor, only to be turned down. Still other patients were told by HMO personnel that they were not to call 911 because their problems were not serious enough to warrant ambulances. Some of those patients died before they were able to see their primary physicians.

Public outcry led to state senators and representatives taking on the HMOs, although the outcome varied from state to state. Most states no longer allow HMOs to require that you get preapproval to seek emergency care. Other states require that HMOs offer a telephone number that is staffed twenty-four hours a day, seven days a week, and that a doctor must get back to the patient within a specified period of time, such as thirty minutes.

As patients become frustrated with restrictions on their health care, states are responding by limiting the power of the HMOs to deny coverage. The trend is to require HMOs to provide more coverage, not less. If a patient gets preapproval to go to the emergency room, the HMO cannot later deny coverage for that claim.

ILLEGAL DUMPING—THE EMERGENCY MEDICAL TREATMENT AND ACTIVE LABOR ACT

At one time it was not uncommon for hospitals to "dump" patients that were uninsured, poor, or otherwise considered undesirable. These patients were either turned away or transferred to other hospitals. The result was that patients did not receive immediate treatment. At its worst, it meant the patient died because of the delay.

To deal with this problem, Congress enacted an "anti-dumping" law. The **Emergency Medical Treatment and Active Labor Act (EMTALA)** requires hospitals to

- **give an appropriate examination to you when you go to the emergency room;**
- **decide whether an emergency medical condition exists;**
- **stabilize or transfer you.**

Health care facilities are required to file a report if they suspect that another health care facility is violating EMTALA. If a facility is found to violate EMTALA, that facility could be fined or could even lose its participation in the Medicare and Medicaid programs. In addition, hospitals' own policies may limit dumping. Many not-for-profit hospitals are required to provide some level of charity care beyond EMTALA.

In some instances, though, an unstable patient will need to be transferred. To do this, the doctor must certify that the benefits to the patient of the treatment at the next hospital outweigh the risks of the transfer.

What Is an "Appropriate" Medical Examination?

Courts around the country are struggling with this very issue. One court called the term *appropriate* a "weasel" word used by Congress when trying to reach a compromise. Unfortunately, there is no clear standard in the law as to what constitutes an "appropriate" medical examination. In general, the hospital must give you a medical screening within the hospital's capabilities, although this standard has yet to be tested in most courts.

Usually the court will look at whether you received treatment that was somehow different from treatment received by other patients. For example, you walk into an emergency room with abdominal pains and no health insurance. After waiting four hours to see a doctor, you're given a five-minute examination, told it's probably the flu, and sent home.

To prove that you were not given an appropriate medical examination, you would have to show that other patients with abdominal pain—and health insurance—were given a more thorough examination. You do not have to prove that you were treated differently because of your race, sex, political beliefs, religion, or some other improper motive. It doesn't matter *why* the examination was inappropriate. It only matters that it was not appropriate.

 WHY PATIENTS LOSE EMTALA CASES

Hospitals win most cases brought under EMTALA. Usually the patient loses because he or she is unable to provide enough evidence that the medical examination given was not appropriate. In other cases the patients lost because they could not prove they ever actually went to the emergency room or because the transfer was proper, although the paperwork regarding the transfer was filled out incorrectly.

What Is an "Emergency Medical Condition"?

An **emergency medical condition** means the symptoms are so severe that any delay in medical treatment could reasonably be expected to seriously harm you. In the case of a pregnant woman, it also means any serious harm that could come to the unborn child. In fact, any woman in labor is considered to have an emergency medical condition.

When Is a Patient Stabilized?

A patient is **stabilized** when it is unlikely that his or her condition will significantly worsen during, or because of, the transfer. Under the EMTALA, a pregnant woman is not considered "stabilized" until she delivers the baby.

It is quite possible for the hospital to provide an appropriate medical examination and not find an emergency medical condition. It is also quite possible that you are stable and, against all medical odds, you suddenly get worse. In that case, the hospital might unwittingly transfer or discharge an unstable patient. The court will take into account the medical judgment of the doctor who treated the patient.

There are times when transferring a patient is simply the best possible course of treatment. In one case a new mother collapsed in the emergency room of a children's hospital where her newborn was being treated. The pediatric staff got the woman onto a bed and started an IV. The woman's life was in no immediate danger, so the doctors, all pediatricians, had the woman taken by ambulance to a hospital a block away where she could be seen by doctors who regularly treat adults. The woman agreed to the transfer. She received emergency care and was brought back to the children's hospital to be with her child after doctors determined she was well enough to do so.

TALKING TO A LAWYER

Ongoing Treatment under the EMTALA

Q. When my mother was brought to the ER because of respiratory distress, the doctors managed to get her stabilized. Does the EMTALA require that the hospital provide ongoing treatment to the patient after the patient is stabilized?

A. The EMTALA requires that the hospital provide treatment to stabilize patients, but it does not require the hospital to provide treatment after stabilization. The EMTALA is a limited "antidumping" law. It is not a malpractice law.

Answer by Cindy J. Moy, attorney and author, Golden Valley, Minnesota

When and How May a Patient Be Transferred?

The hospital may transfer the patient if:

- **the patient requests the transfer in writing; or**
- **the doctor certifies that the benefits of transferring the patient outweigh the risks.**

When a patient is transferred, the method of transportation must be sufficiently equipped to get the patient to the next hospital. In one case a woman with high blood pressure was in labor when the hospital transferred her to a hospital three hours away. In the woman's condition, it was possible that a cesarean section would have needed to be performed during the transport. The ambulance had neither the equipment nor the staff to perform such an operation. A court found that the transportation was not adequate.

When the hospital transfers the patient:

- **the transport, such as an ambulance, must have adequate equipment and personnel;**
- **the hospital to which the patient is being transferred must agree to accept the patient;**

- **the first hospital must give all the patient's medical records to the second hospital.**

A transfer to another hospital does not need to be done in an ambulance. The patient's own car may be adequate, depending on the patient's condition. One court found it acceptable when a young man had to be taken by his own car to a hospital two hours away, even though his pain medication wore off and he needed to keep his arm elevated.

As the patient, you may choose to:

- **refuse treatment;**
- **refuse to agree to the transfer;**
- **request the transfer yourself.**

Which Hospitals Must Comply with EMTALA?

The EMTALA applies only to hospitals that have emergency rooms and that receive federal Medicare funds. This does not mean that you, as a patient, need to be on Medicare. It means that *the hospital* participates in the Medicare program. Nearly every hospital in the country with an emergency room partici-

A CATCH-22

Hospitals are only liable under the EMTALA if the patient actually comes into the emergency room, though there is some leeway on this factor that is discussed later in this chapter. In one case an injured boy in Louisiana was brought to a small hospital that was unable to properly treat him. The doctor called another hospital to arrange for a transfer. The second hospital refused to take the boy after learning he was uninsured. The boy's parents sued the second hospital under the EMTALA and lost because the court determined that the boy had never "come" to the emergency room at the second hospital.

pates in the Medicare program, which ensures that most patients will receive the care needed. Hospitals that do not participate in Medicare are not subject to the EMTALA but may be subject to state laws.

How the Medicare Program Affects Your Emergency Care

In 1998, a group of teenage boys tried to bring one of their friends, who had been shot, to an emergency room in Chicago. The wounded boy went into shock half a block from the emergency room. His friends ran to the emergency room and asked for help. The staff called 911 but refused to leave the emergency room, in accordance with hospital policy. The hospital staff was severely criticized in the community and the media. The hospital administrators explained that the policy was in place to protect the staff from violent situations on the street and because the staff needed to take care of the people who were already in the emergency room waiting for treatment.

The Health Care Financing Administration (HCFA) fined the hospital $40,000, claiming the hospital violated the EMTALA. It also told the hospital that it had to either change its policy or the HCFA would take away the hospital's Medicare program. The hospital changed its policy, even though there is no state or federal law that requires the hospital to give emergency care to people that are not on hospital grounds.

The HCFA does not have the authority to make laws, but it does have the authority to decide who gets Medicare funding. Medicare programs make up millions of dollars of a hospital's budget and no hospital would realistically be able to stand up to the HCFA and refuse to change its policy. Thus, the HCFA's decision to force the hospital to change its policy affects the treatment you may receive in an emergency room.

Though the new policy was popular, it may well have unforeseen harmful consequences. In making health care policy, even good intentions can have bad results. For instance, the emergency room staff must now leave the hospital to assist people within the immediate vicinity of the hospital. Right now there is no way for the hospital to know when staff will be required to leave the hospital. That means the patients within the emergency room may have to wait longer or will not receive the treatment they need. There is also the question of what qualifies as the "immediate vicinity"? Half a block? One block? Two blocks? Is that measured from the emergency room or from the property line of the hospital as a whole?

Another problem is deciding how the emergency room staff is supposed to take care of the person outside. Does the staff have to carry oxygen tanks or other medical equipment when they leave the hospital? Are the emergency room nurses required to pick up the patient and carry the person into the emergency room? Many states require that nurses be specially trained and certified before they can transport patients. Will this put nurses in jeopardy of losing their licenses?

What about the safety of the emergency room staff? The incident that began this debate involved gunfire from a gang. How will inner-city hospitals recruit qualified employees if emergency doctors and nurses know that they could be forced to put themselves at risk on the streets? Is the hospital required to hire security to escort emergency personnel when they leave the hospital to help someone on the street? What does the staff do if, when they are helping a person on the street, violence erupts?

These are questions that are currently unanswered. Hospitals will be trying to deal with the policy implications of HCFA's actions for the next several years.

MALPRACTICE AND MANAGED CARE

Managed Care and the EMTALA

Taking on an HMO for malpractice used to be a daunting task. It's a bit easier now because more and more states are allowing lawsuits against HMOs, particularly in light of the U.S. Supreme Court ruling in June 2000 that patients cannot sue an HMO under federal law when doctors ration medical care in order to receive cash bonuses. However, in many states the basic rule remains that you can sue a hospital or a doctor for malpractice, but not an HMO.

This puts the doctor between a rock and a hard place. The HMO can tell the doctor that you are to be transferred to another hospital. Under the EMTALA, however, the doctor may not be able to authorize a transfer. In such a case, the doctor has to choose between getting paid and transferring an unstable patient. Lately, state legislators have gotten wind of this dilemma. Some states now require HMOs to cover the medical bills at the hospital where the patient seeks emergency care, leaving the issue of whether the patient should be transferred up to the doctor and the patient.

Although the EMTALA claims are different from medical malpractice claims, most lawsuits contain claims on both these legal issues. A medical malpractice claim is one in which the doctor who treated you acted negligently or recklessly and you were injured as a result. In an EMTALA claim, you must prove that the hospital is required to comply with the EMTALA, that you went to the hospital seeking treatment, and that the hospital either did not properly screen you or that the hospital sent you away before stabilizing your condition. You can recover the same personal injury damages under the EMTALA as you would under

 AVOIDING THE DAMAGES CAP

In recent years, a number of states have passed laws limiting how much plaintiffs can be awarded in medical malpractice damages. The jurisdictions disagree on whether these damages caps in malpractice laws apply to EMTALA damages. One court held that malpractice damage caps do apply to EMTALA claims, whereas a California court came to the opposite conclusion. There, the damages cap was held to not apply in a lawsuit under the EMTALA and the plaintiffs could recover more than the $250,000 allowed under the cap. This makes an EMTALA claim more lucrative to the plaintiff than traditional malpractice claims.

the medical malpractice laws of your state. (Medical malpractice is discussed further in Chapter 24.) However, unlike other medical malpractice claims, the majority of courts hold that the EMTALA creates a private right of action against the hospital only. Therefore money damages are usually not obtainable from the doctors.

In addition to money payable to you, the hospital may also be fined as much as $50,000, payable to the government.

Malpractice and the ERISA Curse

Few malpractice cases manage to be brought against health plans because most are preempted under a federal law called the Employee Retirement Income Security Act (ERISA). (See Chapter 4 for more discussion on ERISA.) This law bars you from bringing a claim against your employer's health plan because it denied you benefits. One family, though, managed to take on their health plan and win. A mother in Georgia called her health provider to get approval to take her six-month-old son to the emergency room. She was told to take her son to a hospital forty-two miles away from her home. The plan received a 15 percent discount for patients treated at this hospital.

On the way to the hospital, the baby's heart stopped. He was revived at another hospital but developed gangrene. Both of the baby's hands and legs had to be amputated. The boy's parents sued their health plan and won a $45 million judgment. The family later settled for an undisclosed amount when the health plan appealed. The family was able to sue the health plan because they were not insured through their employers. Because they were not insured through their employers, their claim was not preempted by ERISA.

Why the Law May Change

The public is growing increasingly upset at what they see as abuses by HMOs, and lawmakers are beginning to take notice. Whether or not the ERISA block should be removed and people should be allowed to sue HMOs is now at the forefront of the political arena. So far legislation that would remove ERISA protection has passed only in Texas, but the gap is narrowing and the public outcry is getting louder. Look for more states to make the change and for more people to take on their HMOs in court and win. For more information on this topic, see Chapter 4, Insurance and Managed Care.

Getting Your Medical Bills Covered

ERISA does not bar claims for economic loss based on the denial of benefits. In other words, you can sue your health plan to try to get them to cover your medical bills. Any amount you are awarded is limited to the amount of the medical services that are disputed. If you have a bill for $2,900, that is all you are allowed to recover from your health plan. To win coverage for medical bills, you will have to show that you complied with your health plan contract. If you go to the emergency room for a migraine at a time when your doctor is holding office hours, even though this is clearly not allowed under your policy, you may not be able to get coverage for those medical bills.

THE WORLD AT YOUR FINGERTIPS

- The American Hospital Association website addresses many issues faced by hospitals today. To see how they are facing concerns about emergency care, go to *http://www.aha.org* and search for "emergency."
- The American College of Emergency Physicians offers a comprehensive site discussing all aspects of emergency care, including how it is affected by managed care. See *http://www.acep.org.*
- For a directory of websites for specific hospitals throughout the country, take a look at the listings on *http://smi.bih.harvard.edu/EM.bookmarks.html*, a site maintained by the

Division of Emergency Medicine at the Beth Israel Deaconess Medical Center in Boston.

YOU MUST REMEMBER THIS

- Emergency room doctors are required to examine you, to determine whether there is an emergency, and then—if there is an emergency—to either stabilize you or transfer you to another hospital.
- An "appropriate" medical examination is one that a doctor would give to any patient presenting your symptoms, vital signs, and complaints, regardless of your race, gender, religion, insurance status, or income level.
- You can request to be transferred to another hospital. You can also refuse to be transferred to another hospital.
- Hospitals are not required to transfer patients in ambulances. The type of transportation required depends on the distance to be traveled and on the condition of the patient.

CHAPTER 3

Informed Consent

*How to Understand—
and Approve—
Your Treatment

Carol was nervous about her upcoming surgery to have her ovaries removed. Her doctor assured her that everything would be fine. When she woke up after surgery, Carol was shocked to learn that the doctor removed her uterus as well.

Carl was suffering from an enlarged prostate. His doctor discussed with him all the treatment options, and Carl decided to undergo a new outpatient procedure that would allow him to avoid surgery while shortening the recovery period. The procedure worked wonders. Carl, however, was upset to learn that while he was under anesthetic, several officials of the company that invented the procedure were allowed into the room to watch the procedure being performed.

WHAT IS INFORMED CONSENT?

What It Means

In a nutshell, **informed consent** means that a doctor cannot treat you until he explains the procedure to you and you agree to the treatment. Informed consent protects your freedom to make decisions about your body. It allows you—rather than your doctor—to decide whether to undergo a particular treatment, despite your doctor's expertise and medical training. With informed consent, the patient makes the decision about treatment—and is the one who has to live with the decision, whatever the outcome.

You might assume that your doctor would automatically inform you of all the options available to you. You must realize that informed consent is, in effect, a dialogue between you and your doctor. It is not simply a piece of paper. Only when you are armed with all available information can you make an informed choice as to your options.

LEARNING THE LINGO

Informed consent: Your agreement to undergo a medical treatment or procedure after your doctor informs you of all the facts needed to make an intelligent decision. It gives you more control over your medical destiny.

Disabled and Non-English-Speaking Patients

Informed consent is the right of all patients, including those who are physically disabled or tourists visiting the United States and immigrants who do not speak English. The law requires that doctors and facilities take steps to ensure that these people are fully informed as to their treatment options before the treatment begins. For example, a deaf person has the right to have someone communicate with her using sign language. If the person does not speak English, an interpreter will usually be used to ensure that the patient understands the illness or injury and the treatment options. The interpreter that is most commonly used today is a phone service that provides interpretation in dozens of languages.

How It Came About

Informed consent came about so patients could better share in decisions about their treatment. One of the earliest cases, in 1914, dealt with a woman who claimed a doctor operated on her, without her consent, to remove a lump from her stomach. The woman sued her doctor and won. As the judge in that case put it: "Every human being of adult years and sound mind has a right to determine what shall be done with his own body; and a surgeon who performs an operation without his patient's consent commits an assault, for which he is liable in damages" (*Schloendorff* v. *Society of New York Hospital,* 105 NE 92, 93 [NY APP 1914]).

Despite the legal requirement that you be informed about all aspects of your treatment, there are still instances, even today, of patients whose rights to consent were violated. A 1995 study by the Food and Drug Administration (FDA) found that dozens of doctors had implanted experimental medical devices in their patients. Those doctors either did not tell the patients the device was being implanted or failed to tell the patients that the device was experimental.

Any implantation of an experimental device is supposed to be discussed with the patient, as well as reported to the FDA. Yet the same study found that in one hospital, doctors implanted an experimental prosthetic device that had a chemical coating in 258 patients, although the doctors reported only 37 of the implantations to the FDA. It is unknown how many of the patients were not told the device was experimental.

 YOUR RIGHT TO CHOOSE

Informed consent is not a guarantee of a particular outcome. It is a method of allowing you to make a rational and educated decision regarding medical treatment.

HOW DO I KNOW IF I'M PROPERLY INFORMED?

How to Be a Consenting Patient

You are properly informed when the doctor explains to you all the facts necessary to make a knowledgeable decision regarding your medical care. This information should be given to you when you are calm, sober, and preferably not medicated. There are times, of course, when you will have to make a fast, nerve-wracking decision about treatment for yourself or a family member. When time is of the essence, the doctor should give you as much information as possible in order for you to make a sound decision, but this information will no doubt be less comprehensive than it would be in other, nonlife-threatening situations.

It is difficult for patients to make rational decisions right after they receive shocking news or when they are under pressure to make a decision quickly. Sometimes a doctor may give you an overview only of the diagnosis and the treatment options in order to let the information sink in and to give you a chance to digest what you've learned. Then, at a later time, your doctor will go more in depth into your alternatives. This gives you time to let your head clear so that you can participate more fully in decisions about your medical care.

When you can think clearly, you have to actually understand the information the doctor gives you. If your alternatives are couched in medical jargon that you do not understand, you cannot legally consent to the treatment because, in effect, you have no idea what your doctor is talking about. To be informed, you need to be given the information in terms you can understand. In some cases, a patient will not be able to understand the information, such as when the patient is a child or is mentally incompetent. In those situations, a guardian or a surrogate (someone who is legally authorized to make decisions for you) will need to gather the information and either consent to or refuse the treatment.

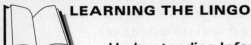

LEARNING THE LINGO

Understanding Informed Consent

Informed consent gives you more power in decisions about your medical care, but it also gives you more responsibility. You cannot force your doctor to step outside the boundaries of good medical judgment, to violate medical ethics, or to perform alternative treatment the doctor considers too risky.

When Informed Consent Must Be Requested

You do not have to give informed consent for every medical procedure performed. Informed consent is generally reserved for those situations when:

- **there is a risk of death or injury;**
- **drugs are given;**
- **diagnostic tests (such as angiograms) are going to be performed;**
- **a surgical procedure is going to be performed.**

Regular examinations or the taking of blood samples do not usually require informed consent, unless an HIV test is going to be performed. Informed consent applies to elective procedures, such as plastic surgery and vasectomies, as well.

What Exactly the Doctor Has to Tell You

In most cases on informed consent, the patient consented to the treatment but argues that he did not have enough information about the treatment to make the consent effective.

There are several pieces of information that a patient needs in order to make a choice about treatment:

- a description of the proposed treatment or procedure in terms the patient can understand (even the brightest among us can get lost when wading through medical jargon);
- the benefits, the risks, and the side effects of the treatment;
- the risks of *not* treating the ailment;
- any alternative treatments that are available, along with the risks of those alternative treatments;
- the rate of success for the treatment, as well as how "success" is defined;
- a description of the recuperation period, including a time frame and possible complications;
- conflicts of interest—patients need to know if the doctor has something to gain financially by referring the patient to a particular facility or by recommending a specific treatment.

This does *not* mean that the doctor has to tell you of every conceivable ache, pain, or minor side effect that may occur. It *does* mean that the doctor has to tell you about any facts that might cause a reasonable person to decide not to agree to the treatment. For example, a reasonable person might decide to not have surgery after she finds out it carries a 50 percent risk of paralysis. The doctor needs to tell her of this risk in order for her consent to be "informed."

In most states, a jury will consider four questions to determine whether a patient's consent was informed.

1. Did the patient understand enough of the information to give an effective consent?
2. Was the patient given the same information as other patients in the same situation?
3. If the patient had been given sufficient information, would he have consented to the treatment?
4. Was the patient warned about the complication(s) that later arose?

Even if the patient did not give an informed consent, the patient cannot bring a lawsuit if the patient was not injured. In other words, if there is no harm done, the doctor cannot be punished in a court of law. You are still entitled to file a complaint with the state licensing agency against the doctor for professional misconduct, regardless of whether an injury resulted. The doctor may then face some form of discipline from that agency.

What You Should Ask Your Doctor

There are several questions you can ask your doctor in order to make sure your consent is informed:

- **What is the problem?**
- **How serious is it?**
- **How accurate are the test results?**
- **When does treatment have to begin in order to be most effective?**
- **Describe the treatment?**
- **What are the risks involved in the treatment?**
- **What are the odds that the treatment will be successful?**
- **What if treatment is not successful?**
- **What are the side effects of a treatment?**
- **What are the risks in not treating the problem?**
- **What alternative treatments are available?**
- **Will medical students or residents be involved with my treatment?**
- **Will students or residents be practicing any procedures on me that are unrelated to my care?**

Consent Forms

Written informed consent forms vary from doctor to doctor, hospital to hospital. Some are so vague that they seem to cover every imaginable situation that might arise. With forms this vague, many courts have concluded that the patient did not consent at all. Other forms may be so detailed as to inform the patient, for example, as to how bodily tissues or organs will be disposed.

In years past, some doctors and hospitals asked patients to sign a consent form that had patients agree to not sue for malpractice. These forms are of little use today. Courts have ruled that such consent forms are not valid. On the other hand, consent forms that require malpractice claims to be **arbitrated** are valid. In arbitration, a neutral third party holds a hearing with you and the doctor and then renders a decision. Arbitration is usually much less expensive than a lawsuit because it avoids the formalities and the delays of a courtroom. In other words, they can't stop you from suing, but you may end up in arbitration rather than a courtroom.

 ## LEARNING THE LINGO

Arbitration: When both sides have an opportunity to be heard by a neutral third party, who then renders a decision by which both parties must abide.

TALKING TO A LAWYER
Losing in Arbitration

Q. If my claim ends up in arbitration and I do not like the outcome, can I still sue?

A. Yes, but your grounds for appeal are very limited.

Answer by Cindy J. Moy, attorney and author, Golden Valley, Minnesota

Does Consent Have to Be in Writing?

No. *Informed* consent does not mean *written* consent. Informed consent means you have all the information necessary to make an informed decision, regardless of whether you sign a form.

Many consent forms are in writing simply to keep in the medical record for the doctor's and your protection.

Do I Have to Sign the Form?

No. You are not required by law to sign any kind of consent form. Keep in mind, though, that the doctor can then choose not to treat you. The whole purpose of informed consent is to give you enough information so that you can share in the decisions regarding your health care. Your decision as to whether to sign an informed consent form should be secondary to your decision as to whether you want to agree to the treatment.

Do I Have to Agree to Everything in the Form?

No. You have the option to cross out any clauses with which you do not agree or to which you do not consent. Just take a pen and put an "X" through the clause. The doctor must explain the risks of putting those restrictions on the treatment, if any. The doctor may require that the restrictions be noted in your medical record. If the restrictions are so strict as to make the procedure unsound, the doctor can choose to not proceed with the treatment.

When Informed Consent Is Not Necessary

There are times when it simply is not possible for a doctor to explain a medical treatment or procedure to you. There are also times when it is not necessary for a doctor to provide you with such information.

Doctors are not required to obtain informed consent from you when:

- it is an emergency situation;
- the risks are minor or are well known to the average person;
- the patient doesn't want to know the specific details;
- the doctor can show that telling the patient would cause the patient psychological harm or make the patient so upset that

the patient would not be able to make a rational decision. In the rare situations that this happens, the doctor is required to tell a person of the patient's choosing.

WHEN YOU CHANGE YOUR MIND

You can withdraw your consent at any time, but this may affect your treatment. Obviously it is best to change your mind *before* the doctor begins a surgical procedure. Changing your mind can put both you and your doctor at risk. Once you withdraw your consent, the doctor has to discuss with you the effects of not proceeding with the treatment.

In Wisconsin, a woman went into labor and was admitted to the hospital. She had planned on, and was prepared for, a vaginal delivery. During delivery she changed her mind, and three times asked her doctor to perform a cesarean. The doctor continued to prepare for a vaginal delivery. When complications arose during delivery, the doctor delivered the baby by cesarean section. The baby was paralyzed from the neck down.

The woman sued the doctor because he did not acknowledge that she withdrew her consent to a vaginal delivery. The doctor argued that once the vaginal delivery began, the patient could not withdraw her consent. The woman won the case. Because a cesarean delivery was a viable medical alternative to a vaginal delivery, the woman had the right to withdraw her consent to a vaginal delivery. When she withdrew her consent, the doctor was obligated to discuss with her the consequences of her withdrawal and her options at that point.

Although the woman won in Wisconsin, the law varies from state to state. In every state, though, you have the right to withdraw your consent. Your doctor should discuss with you the effects this will have on your treatment, but the ultimate decision is generally up to you.

THE RIGHT TO REFUSE TREATMENT

After being informed of your diagnosis, as well as of the treatment options and the risks involved, you can choose to not undergo treatment. You can refuse any treatment, as long as you are an adult, unless perhaps you are mentally incompetent and have lost your ability to make informed decisions. Although you have the right to refuse treatment, the public health department has the right to isolate you if you have a contagious disease and are a danger to others. For more on the right to refuse life-sustaining treatment, see the section on Death and Dying (Chapters 26–29).

THE WORLD AT YOUR FINGERTIPS

- The following doctor's website will provide you with more information on informed consent and provides a sample informed consent form for cataract surgery: *http://www.informed consent.com/*.
- For the physician's point of view of informed consent, see the American Medical Association's advice at *http://www. ama-assn.org/physlegl/legal/infcons.htm*.
- For a discussion of informed consent and psychotropic medication, see Health Promotion and People with Developmental Disabilities: *http://www.dcs.wisc.edu/pda/hhi/hpp/ pmedic/index.html*.
- Want to know what doctors really think about informed consent? Take a look at the discussion at *http://www-hsc.usc. edu/~mbernste/ethics.informed_consent.html*.

YOU MUST REMEMBER THIS

- **Informed consent** means that your doctor must explain the treatment or procedure to you, along with all of the risks and any alternatives. You must then agree to be treated before the doctor may proceed.

- Informed consent is not necessary for every procedure. It is usually limited to cases where surgery or medication is required.
- Consent does not require a written form. If you are given a form, you are not required to sign it, although the doctor can choose not to treat you if you do not sign it.
- You can withdraw your consent at any time.
- You can refuse to be treated. The question of whether there is a right to die is treated elsewhere in this guide.

PART TWO

Paying for Medical Care

Your Options: From Insurance to HMOs

and Government Programs

Few of us realize the value of good medical coverage until it is gone. Then we are faced with finding new insurance or joining a health maintenance organization or paying those medical bills out of our own pockets. Sometimes it might even seem as though we spend less on medical care than we pay in insurance premiums.

In this section we will explore the various options out there to cover our medical expenses. First we will explain the difference between insurance and managed care and how that difference affects your legal rights. Then we will clarify Medicaid: what is it and when do you qualify? We will discuss what property you are allowed to keep in order to receive benefits. Then we'll discuss Medicare, covering all the basics of this important program.

Next we cover the Consolidated Omnibus Budget Reconciliation Act, also known as COBRA. This chapter tells you how much you will have to pay for your COBRA coverage and the reasons why you might not be able to get coverage. It will explain which companies are not required to offer COBRA and when your company must inform you that you qualify.

Most of us will use a combination of these methods to pay for medical care as we age. If you would like more information, please check at the end of the guide for additional resources and websites regarding these issues.

CHAPTER 4

Insurance and Managed Care

A Quick Guide to the Rapidly Changing World of HMOs

Dale is at work for the first day at his new job. His supervisor keeps bringing paperwork for him to sign. In one folder is the information on the company benefits. There are three health plans from which Dale can choose. Dale skims through the policy books for each plan but they all look the same to him. The only difference that he can see is the price. Dale does not want to spend the rest of the day—or night—wading through pages of boring legal and medical jargon. He figures that all health plans are similar, so it does not really matter which one he chooses. He fills out the form for the least expensive health plan and gives it to his supervisor. Did Dale make the best choice?

HEALTH CARE TODAY

It's Harder Than It Used to Be

It wasn't that long ago that insurance was fairly straightforward. You paid your premiums and a deductible. When you reached your deductible, your insurance began paying your medical bills. There were no lists of doctors that you could or could not see. Your doctor did not get paid based on how much medical care you did *not* receive. Today, many of us are covered by some form of managed care.

What Is Managed Care?

Managed care refers to a method of keeping down the costs of medical care by managing your health care through preventative medicine and patient education and by utilizing resources in the best way possible. That does not mean that managed care is bad or wrong. It simply means that you must follow more rules when you go to the doctor in exchange for paying less for your health care.

What Are the States Doing to Ensure That Patients Get the Care They Need within the Managed Care System?

Each state makes its own laws as to the benefits that health insurance (which includes managed care) must provide. There is also some federal law on level of coverage required for specific situations, such as childbirth.

The state laws are often similar to one another. For example, in most states there are laws that limit the preexisting conditions that health care plans may put into their policies. Usually a health care plan is required to renew health coverage for all members who pay their premiums, even if the member has become ill and requires expensive treatment. Almost every state now requires that new mothers be allowed to stay in the hospital for at least forty-eight hours after giving birth. More than half the states require health plans to pay for visits to the emergency room.

Some states expanded their laws to include minimum hospital stays for mastectomy patients and to give women the right to see an obstetrician-gynecologist without going through a primary care doctor first. Some states require health care plans to cover treatment for mental illness and substance abuse, as well as for prenatal care and minor surgery. A few states require health plans to cover chiropractic and hospice care. Other states require that if a health plan covers prescription drugs, then it must also cover contraceptives that are prescribed by a doctor. Less than a dozen states require that health plans offer in vitro fertilization as part of their health plans.

The most recent wave of legislation gives patients the right to appeal the health plan's decision to not pay for treatment to an independent reviewer that has the power to order the health plan to pay for treatment. This is a big change from the days when the health plan's decision was final and the patient had no other recourse.

MANAGED CARE AND YOU

The Ultimate Goal

The purpose of managed care is to provide you with the best medical care possible while keeping that medical care within your price range. Consumers and lawmakers are trying to find ways to balance quality health care for you with the health plan's right to make a profit.

The Ultimate Problem

The biggest criticism and concern about managed care is that your doctor is no longer given the final say on what type of treatment is covered. Now the managed care organization gets to make—or at least influence—that decision. The problem is that the doctor's opinion on what is needed may differ from the health plan's opinion of what it should cover. Bear in mind that the person at the health plan who is influencing your care may not be a doctor or nurse. That person may not have any medical training whatsoever.

How Does It Affect Me?

The insurance company influences your doctor's decision by limiting the care for which the company will pay. What used to be a decision between you and your doctor is now a decision among you, your doctor, and your health plan. You either must abide by your managed care policy or pay for the treatment out of your own pocket. Let's assume, for example, that your health plan allows you to stay in the hospital for 48 hours after giving birth, unless there is a medical necessity for a longer stay. Not every woman is physically ready to be on her own within 48 hours after childbirth. Yet you may either have to leave the hospital or pay for any further treatment yourself.

How Is the Law Dealing with This Change in the Patient-Doctor Relationship?

One of the biggest questions surrounding health plans is whether the health plan or the doctor is responsible for the actions of its doctors when you are injured. The law is not settled, yet nearly every state is trying to come up with an answer. In California, the law states that your health plan is responsible for its actions and that your doctor is responsible for his or her actions. In other words, you cannot necessarily sue your health plan when your doctor makes a mistake. Another California law, though, states that in some cases you could sue the health plan when your doctor is negligent and you are injured. Exactly when this could happen, however, is not clear at this point. In some cases you may be able to sue the health plan for not checking the credentials of its doctors. (The next section goes into more detail on this topic.) You may also be able to sue based on the information the health plan put in its brochures, although this is a difficult hurdle to jump. As more cases move through the courts, this area of law will become clearer.

Does That Mean I Can Sue My Health Plan When It Does Not Live Up to the Promises in the Health Plan's Brochure?

Not exactly. Most of the information in your health plan's brochure is considered to be general marketing, which is sometimes called "puffery." In one case some people sued their health plan over the health plan's brochure that claimed that the health plan would provide "high standards" of medical service. The patients did not receive what they considered a high standard of medical care. The patients lost their lawsuit because the court decided that the health plan brochure was puffery and not a contract to provide a certain type of medical care. Although the patients lost in that case, it is possible that if a health plan provided more specific details about the care provided to patients, you might be able to win in a negligence case against a health plan, such as when a health plan provides little access to medical specialists.

What Other Ways Can I Sue My Health Plan for Negligence?

There are three main theories of law under which you could sue your health plan. They are the respondeat superior, apparent authority, and corporate negligence liability. Not every state recognizes these theories. Your state might not recognize any of them. Lawsuits against health plans are becoming more popular, though, so the odds are that your state will allow patients to sue under at least one of the following legal theories.

Respondeat Superior
Respondeat superior, for our purposes, says that a health plan is responsible for the actions of the doctor when the health plan controls the work of the doctor. To decide whether the health plan is responsible for the doctor's actions through respondeat superior, a court will look at the contract between the doctor and

the health plan, the day-to-day interaction between the doctor and the health plan, and the amount of control the health plan exercises over the doctor's decisions. In one case a court found that the doctors were under the control of the health plan's medical director, who policed the medical services provided to patients and whose decision as to whether the health plan would cover certain treatments was final. In that case the health plan was responsible for the actions of the doctor under respondeat superior.

Apparent Authority

Apparent authority says that a health plan is indirectly responsible for the acts of its doctors because patients consider the doctors to be representatives of the health plan. This is sometimes known as **ostensible agency** or **agency by estoppel.** This is different from respondeat superior because in apparent authority the doctors are not employees of the health plan. But the key here is that the public is led to believe that the doctors represent or are employed by the plan, thus giving patients the impression that the plan's doctors are capable of giving qualified medical care.

Corporate Negligence Liability

Corporate negligence liability, as it applies to health plans, holds that the plan owes you, as its member, a duty:

- **to take reasonable care in making sure that its doctors are qualified to provide proper treatment; and**
- **to draft and enforce rules and policies to see that you get quality medical care.**

This type of liability was used by a woman who was injured by the health plan urologist to whom her primary care provider referred her. The health plan did check to make sure the doctor was licensed, but the health plan's background check of the doctor was cursory. The court held that the health plan had a duty to its members to make sure that its doctors were qualified and to drop from its network any doctors that the health plan found posed a foreseeable risk of harm to its members.

Texas Takes the Lead

Texas was the first state to pass a law permitting health plan members to sue their health plans for malpractice when the health plans did not use ordinary care in making medical-treatment decisions. It also made it illegal for health plans to throw doctors out of their health plans when the doctors help the patients appeal health plan decisions or prescribe treatments the health plans do not want the doctors to prescribe. This law was partially overturned by a court decision. Even so, other states are now considering similar legislation.

Is Suing My Only Option When My Health Plan Refuses to Cover the Treatment I Need?

No. Your health plan should provide you with the process you need to follow to appeal the health plan's decision. In some health plans the only thing you will need to do is to get your doctor to write a letter stating why the treatment is necessary. It can be useful to get the opinion of another doctor, in writing and probably at your own expense, and submit that to the health plan. In a few states the law gives you the right to complain to an independent reviewer that will make its decision and, if it decides in your favor, has the authority to make the health plan cover your treatment. Regardless of the law in your state, you will need to go through the health plan's appeal process before you can consider taking your health plan to court.

MANAGED CARE AND YOUR DOCTOR

If My Plan Includes a Certain Doctor, Then That Doctor Is Qualified to Treat Me, Right?

This is another hot issue for health plans. A few years ago health plans were not required to check a doctor's credentials at all. This is changing now that lawmakers and courts are more sympathetic to the claims of patients. At the present time there are no clear guidelines as to how in-depth a health plan must be in checking on the credentials of its doctors. What is clear is that health plans are beginning to develop their own procedures for determining whether doctors are qualified before they are admitted to the health plan. This is the only way that health plans can avoid being held responsible for the doctors' negligence when it is shown that the doctors are unqualified.

What Are the Qualifications for Which the Health Plan Will Check?

At a minimum, your health plan should confirm that the doctor has:

- a valid license to practice medicine;
- professional liability and malpractice insurance;
- board certification or eligibility;
- any other appropriate credentials for the specific area of practice.

You will have to ask your health plan how it checks the credentials of its doctors and how often this information is updated. For example, the plan should do checks of the federal database on physicians to determine as much information on them as possible.

What the plan does—or does not do—to check out physicians would be important evidence in cases brought under the corporate liability theory, discussed earlier.

If My Health Plan Does Not Check
Credentials, Does That Mean I Can Sue
If I Am Injured?

This is a relatively new theory of law, but most states are now allowing patients to sue their health plan for negligent credentialing when:

- the patient is injured through the doctor's negligence; and
- the health plan did not have a good credentialing policy in place; and
- an adequate credentialing policy would have caused the health plan to decide not to select or retain the doctor as one of its providers.

Can My Doctor Take into Account the
Cost of Treatment When Deciding
How to Treat Me?

Yes. There is no law that stops a doctor from considering the cost of your medical care when deciding how to treat your illness. The courts, though, generally require that your doctor base his decision on what is best for you within the standard of care, regardless of how much it would cost.

A Conflict of Interest

The problem with managed care is that it puts your doctor between a rock and a hard place. The doctor may feel you need a particular treatment, but your health plan will not approve it. Your doctor can either decide to not offer you the treatment or to prescribe the treatment and bill you directly. If your doctor decides to bill you directly, there is the chance that the doctor will not be paid.

The health plan may also offer your doctor financial incentives to keep costs low. In some plans, the doctors get a percentage of the money they save the health plan. Those doctors make money by *not* providing care. In some cases health plans will kick doctors out of their plan if the doctors try to push for more expensive medical treatment for their patients. Getting kicked out of a health plan can ruin a doctor's practice. Would that money encourage your doctor to decide against giving you medical care? Good question—and one you should ask your doctor.

Although many angry consumers are trying to make it illegal for health plans to offer doctors financial incentives to limit care, that change will have to come through the legislature rather than through the courts. In a case recently considered by the Supreme Court, a woman went to her health plan's clinic with abdominal pain. The health plan made her wait eight days before she had an ultrasound test. In the meantime her appendix burst, causing infection and requiring surgery. The woman won a medical malpractice lawsuit against the clinic in state court. She also wanted to sue her health plan in federal court. The woman asked the Supreme Court to ban financial incentives that influence health care decisions. The U.S. Supreme Court declined to invade the legislature's territory by ruling that the practice is unlawful. Instead, the Court ruled that the woman could not sue her health plan in federal court.

IT PAYS TO ASK

Ask your doctor how she is compensated by your health plan. If your doctor gets a percentage of any money she saves the health plan, you should keep in mind that your doctor has a conflict of interest when it comes to your health care. If your doctor refuses to answer, you may wish to look into other health providers.

MANAGED CARE AND FEDERAL LAW

How Is Congress Facing the Managed Care Debate?

As with the states, the federal government is taking a close look at how patients are being treated. Both of the major parties have introduced bills that would give consumers more protection from managed-care abuses. Already Congress requires health plans to allow women to stay in the hospital at least forty-eight hours after giving birth vaginally and ninety-six hours for cesarean-section births.

What Is ERISA?

The Employee Retirement Income Security Act of 1974 (ERISA) is a federal law that controls how your employee benefit plan is administered. Part of the law protects the health plan offered by your employer from being sued for interfering in your health care. This is a powerful tool for health plans facing litigation. To illustrate, in a number of cases patients sued health plans for paying doctors bonuses for not performing certain expensive tests, for refusing to refer patients to other doctors, and for not following the opinion of an outside specialist to provide certain treatments. These cases are typically thrown out due to ERISA.

Is This Fair?

The managed care organizations think it is fair, but many patients and doctors do not. State lawmakers, Congress, and the courts are beginning to side with patients and doctors. A woman in California sued her health plan after her husband died of stomach cancer. She believed that his death was caused in part by the health plan's delay in approving treatment for him. A jury awarded her $120 million. The health plan asked for a new trial, but the judge denied the health plan's request. The case reflects the changing attitudes we have toward managed care.

How Did the California Woman Sue If ERISA Says You Can't Sue a Health Plan?

ERISA only protects health plans that are offered by employers. If you purchase your health plan on your own or through some other type of organization, ERISA does not apply. In one case a woman's doctor admitted her to the hospital because she required total bed rest for a high-risk pregnancy. Her health plan decided that bed rest was not necessary and would only approve home nursing care for the woman for ten hours a day. The woman's baby died in utero during a time when the nurse was not with the woman. The woman had health coverage through her employer, and when she brought a lawsuit against her health plan it was blocked by ERISA. If you buy your health plan on your own or through some other type of group, you may still be able to bring a lawsuit against your health plan.

How Much Can I Get If I Sue?

Despite that huge award in California, it is unlikely you would recover that kind of money. The states do not agree on how or when you can sue a health plan and on what kind of damages you can recover. In another state the California woman's lawsuit might have been thrown out of court. In some states you can only recover the cost of the treatment or test. If a prostate exam costs $200 in your state and your health plan refuses to pay for a prostate exam, you could sue your health plan for $200 if the exam would have turned up the fact that you have prostate cancer. It does not matter if you die because of the health plans refusal to pay for the test. All you can recover is the $200.

Upcoming Changes to ERISA

ERISA's affect on health plans is a hot topic. Stories about patients dying because their health plans denied treatment angered the public and lead to an outcry for changes in the law. Medical care and health plans are on every political candidate's platform—although not always on the same side. The managed care industry and some politicians argue that letting patients sue their health plans will drive up the cost of health care. Nevertheless the trend appears to favor holding health plans responsible for their decisions regarding medical care.

THE WORLD AT YOUR FINGERTIPS

- *Outsmarting Managed Care: A Doctor Shares His Insider's Secrets to Getting the Health Care You Want* by Bruce A. Barron (Times Books, 1999). Barron, a doctor, was at one time an adviser to one of the largest health insurers in the country. In this book he shows you some techniques for getting the treatment you feel you need from managed care.
- *Health against Wealth: HMOs and the Breakdown of Medical Trust* by George Anders (Houghton Mifflin, 1996). Anders, a reporter for the *Wall Street Journal,* highlights cases in which managed care wreaked havoc on the lives of its patients. Anders shows how managed care has changed the medical priorities of doctors and hospitals and proposes solutions for how to deal with that change.
- *The Complete Idiot's Guide to Managed Health Care* by Sophie M. Korczyk and Hazel A. Witte (MacMillan, 1998). Explains in easy-to-read form how to get the most care out of managed care.

YOU MUST REMEMBER THIS

- Managed care is a way of keeping health care costs lower and thus more accessible to you.
- Managed care saves you money but may affect the kind of medical care you receive.
- If your health plan is through your employer, your health plan is protected from lawsuits under ERISA.
- Be sure to read your health plan closely to know exactly what coverage you have for medical care.

CHAPTER 5

Medicare and Medicaid

*Government Programs to the Rescue—If You
Qualify and Know How to Use Them*

*Ben just turned 65 years old. He knows he's eligible to be covered under
Medicare, but he does not remember signing up for it. Does he have to pay to
be covered by Medicare? Will Medicare make him change doctors? What is the
difference between Medicare and Medicaid?*

MEDICARE AND MEDICAID

What Is Medicare?

Medicare is a health insurance program funded by the federal
government. It is part of the Social Security Act. Originally,
Medicare would cover you only if you were 65 years of age or
older. Later Medicare was expanded to include people with long-
term disabilities and people with permanent kidney failure who
need dialysis or a transplant. Medicare is not based on your
income or whether you can afford health care.

What Is Medicaid?

Medicaid is also a health insurance program, jointly funded by
the state and federal governments. This program works with
each state to pay for health care for people with low incomes.
Medicaid takes a large part of the budget in most states. It is
a form of welfare and, as such, is always subject to political
pressure.

How Do Medicare and Medicaid Differ?

Medicare is not based on your income or your assets, as Medicaid is. Medicare is based only on your age or disability. The two

programs are different in the types of health care they cover and in the amount of money they will pay for your care. *Remember that Medicare offers several different types of health plans and your coverage will depend on the plan you choose.*

MEDICARE OVERALL

Does Medicare Pay My Entire Medical Bill?

No. There is a deductible that you are required to pay. After that, Medicare pays for part of your care, such as 80 percent, and you are responsible for the rest of the bill.

 SAVE THESE NUMBERS

If you lose your Medicare card or you change your address, call the Social Security Administration at 1-800-772-1213 or, for the hearing and speech impaired, at 1-800-325-0778.

Do I Have to Go to a Certain Group of Doctors?

No, unless you enrolled in a Medicare managed care plan, which is explained in another section of this chapter. Otherwise you only need to find out if your doctor or hospital accepts Medicare.

What Is Medicare Assignment?

If a physician or other provider charges you more than the Medicare-approved amount, the amount of your liability depends on whether the provider accepts **assignment.** Going to a doctor who accepts assignment will help you avoid excess charges. Accepting assignment means that the provider agrees to accept the **Medicare-approved amount** as payment *in full.* Your liability is limited to a coinsurance payment of 20 percent of the

Medicare-approved amount. So if the approved amount for a procedure is $100, you would owe only $20 to a physician who accepts assignment.

What If My Doctor Does Not Accept Medicare Assignment?

Your doctor can require you to pay the whole bill for your health care services at the time you receive them, though he or she cannot charge more than 15 percent over the Medicare-approved amount. Medicare may then reimburse you for the part of the bill it considers appropriate.

What If I Am Covered by the Railroad Retirement Act?

The Social Security Administration administers Medicare, but it doesn't cover quite everybody. Railroad workers are covered by a separate federal program, **Railroad Retirement,** which is integrated with Social Security. Your Railroad Retirement Board administers some parts of your Medicare program. When you have Medicare questions, your first call should be to your local Railroad Retirement Board. Call 1-800-808-0772 to find your local office. You can also get Medicare information for railroad retirees on the Internet at *http://www.rrb.gov.*

MEDICARE: PART A AND PART B

What Do I Need to Know About Medicare?

The key to Medicare is understanding that it is divided into two parts: Part A and Part B. The type of coverage you have depends on whether you are enrolled in Part A or Part B. This will determine how much money you will end up paying out of your own pocket. You are normally enrolled in both Part A and Part B, unless you decline Part B coverage (if, for example, you had employer-based group coverage that already covers what Part B would).

What Is Part A?

Part A is your *hospital* insurance. It helps you pay for your care in a hospital or a skilled nursing facility. It also pays for some home health and hospice care. You do not pay to be covered by Part A. Your Medicare bills are handled by a **fiscal intermediary.**

LEARNING THE LINGO

Fiscal intermediary: A private insurance company that contracts with Medicare to process your bills for Part A health care services.

When Do I Qualify for Part A?

You qualify for Medicare Part A when:

- **you turn 65 years old and you are eligible for retirement benefits from Social Security or the Railroad Retirement Board;** *or*
- **you are under 65 years of age but receive Social Security disability benefits for 24 months; or**
- **you are under 65 years of age and suffer permanent kidney failure.**

What Is Covered Under Part A?

Under Part A, benefit limits and costs are based on a **benefit period.** At the beginning of each benefit period, a new cycle of benefits, deductibles, and coinsurance starts anew. A benefit period begins the first day you receive in-patient hospital care. It ends when you have been out of a hospital and have not received skilled nursing care services for sixty days in a row. A subsequent hospitalization begins a new benefit period.

In general, Medicare Part A covers:

- a semiprivate hospital room and hospital services, except for private duty nursing or a television or telephone in your room. The percentage you are required to pay will vary according to the length of your hospital stay. After 150 days per benefit period, you pay for all hospital costs.

- a semiprivate room in a skilled nursing facility, along with meals, skilled nursing, and rehabilitative services—*as long as you meet certain conditions.* Your condition must require, on a daily basis, skilled nursing or skilled rehabilitation service that as a practical matter can only be provided in a skilled nursing facility. You must be admitted within a short time— usually no more than 30 days—after you leave the hospital, and your hospitalization must have been for at least three days. Finally, the skilled care you receive must be based on a doctor's order. If you meet these conditions, you do not pay anything for the first 20 days. After that you are required to pay up to $95.50 per day for days 21 to 100. After 100 days you pay all costs.

- certain home health care if a number of conditions are met. *If* you are under the care of a physician who determines your need for home health care and sets up a plan; *if* you are homebound; *if* the care you need includes part-time or inter- mittent skilled nursing, physical therapy or speech therapy; and *if* your care is provided by a Medicare-approved home health care agency, *then* Medicare will cover part-time or intermittent skilled nursing care, physical therapy, occupa- tional therapy, speech therapy, home health aide services and other services. "Intermittent" means less than 28 hours a week. Medicare pays the full cost for these services, though it won't pay for medications for patients living at home, nor does it cover general household services or ser- vices that are primarily custodial.

- hospice care for terminally ill patients, including physician or visiting nurse services, individual and family psychologi- cal support, short-term in-patient care, home health aide services, drugs, and respite care—short-term in-patient care in a facility to give family caregivers some relief—on an occasional basis.

- blood from a hospital or skilled nursing facility, as long as your stay is covered by Medicare. Medicare only pays for blood after you pay for the first three pints.

What Comes Out of My Pocket?

These amounts change from year to year. As of January 2001, however, for each benefit period that you are covered under Part A, you will pay:

- **$792 total for days 1 to 60 of a hospital stay per benefit period;**
- **up to $198 per day for days 61–90 of a hospital stay per benefit period;**
- **$396 per day for days 91 to 150 of a hospital stay (these are the 60 "lifetime reserve days"; if you've used them up you must pay the full costs); and**
- **all costs for each day beyond 150 days of a hospital stay;**
- **up to $99.00 per day for days 21 to 100 of skilled nursing care in a facility;**
- **all costs beyond the 100th day within the benefit period for skilled nursing care in a facility;**
- **the cost of the first three pints of blood from a hospital or a skilled nursing facility during a stay that is covered by Medicare Part A.**

What Is Part B?

Part B is your *medical* insurance. It covers your doctor visits, out-patient hospital care, physical therapists, and other health care services that Part A does not cover. ***You must pay a monthly premium to enroll in Part B.*** Your Medicare bills are processed by a **Medicare carrier**.

How Do I Qualify for Part B?

You qualify for Part B if:

- you qualify for Part A; *or*
- you are a United States citizen or permanent resident age 65 or older.

How Do I Pay My Premiums?

Your premium either is taken out of your Social Security check or Civil Service Retirement check or is billed to you directly by Medicare every three months.

What Is Covered Under Part B?

Part B covers

- doctors visits, in-patient and out-patient medical services and supplies, physical and speech therapy, diagnostic tests, and durable medical equipment; you pay a $100 deductible once per year plus 20 percent of the Medicare approved amount if the physician takes assignment, probably more if the physician does not take assignment;
- 50 percent of out-patient mental health treatment;
- blood tests and urinalysis; Part B will usually cover 100 percent of the cost;
- intermittent skilled care and home health aide services if you do not have Part A;
- durable medical equipment; you pay 20 percent of the

Medicare approved amount if the supplier takes assignment; if the supplier does not accept Medicare, you may end up paying more of the costs yourself;

- blood, you pay for the first three pints, plus 20 percent for each additional pint.

Part B may pay up to 80 percent of the charge for:

- x-rays,
- speech language pathology services,
- artificial limbs,
- kidney dialysis and kidney transplants,
- emergency room visits,
- ostomy bags, surgical dressings, splints, casts, and braces,
- breast prostheses after a mastectomy,
- some ambulance services,
- one mammogram per year for female Medicare recipients 40 years old or older,
- one pap smear, pelvic examination, and breast exam every three years for all female Medicare recipients,
- diabetes monitoring, and
- one flu shot each year.

What Comes Out of My Pocket?

If the provider accepts Medicare assignment, you will pay

- the $100 deductible once every year;
- 20 percent of the approved amount of your medical care;
- 50 percent for most out-patient mental health care;
- 20 percent of the first $1,500 for physical therapy services and 100 percent thereafter;
- 20 percent of the first $1,500 for all occupational therapy services and 100 percent thereafter;

- **20 percent of the approved amount for durable medical equipment;**
- **the costs of the first three pints of blood received as an outpatient, plus 20 percent of the approved amount for any additional pints.**

MEDICARE HEALTH PLAN CHOICES

Why Would I Want to Change Medicare Plans?

Recently Medicare began offering its recipients more choices. You are not required to sign up for any of these other options. Not all options are available in every part of the country. Some of these health plans, however, may offer you more benefits than Part A and Part B. In some cases this could save you money. For example, some Medicare health plans will pay for prescription drugs, dental care, or eyeglasses. Keep in mind that the premiums for these health plans may be more than what you pay for Medicare Part B. You will need to compare the costs and make the best choice for you.

How Do I Qualify for the Other Health Plans?

You qualify for the other plans if you:

- **are currently enrolled in both Part A and Part B;** *and*
- **are not suffering from kidney failure at the time of the switch; and**
- **you live in the geographic area of the health plan.**

What If I Switch to a Medicare Health Plan and at Some Point I No Longer Qualify for That Plan?

Then you are automatically covered under Medicare Part A and Part B again.

What Are My Options?

- *Stay where you are.* Your first option of course is to simply stay with Medicare Part A and Part B. You are not required to join a Medicare health care plan.

- *Buy a supplemental (Medigap) insurance policy.* There are ten standard supplemental insurance policies available through various insurance companies. These policies are designed to give you more benefits than Medicare alone. You still pay your Part B premium, plus you pay the supplemental insurance policy premium. There are two types of supplemental insurance policies. With a Medigap policy you are free to go to any doctor or hospital that accepts Medicare. With a Medicare SELECT policy you are required to go to a specified list of doctors or hospitals.

Medigap policies do not cover long-term care. You do not need a Medigap policy if you are already covered by Medicaid because Medicaid covers the gaps in Medicare. If you get retiree health coverage through a former employer or union, you might not need Medigap insurance either. Your retiree coverage may or may not provide the same benefits as Medigap insurance. You will have to take a look at your coverage, costs, and the stability of the program to decide whether it is a better option than Medigap.

You do not need a supplemental insurance policy if you enroll in a Medicare managed care plan. A managed care plan is usually very comprehensive. If you can afford it, however, keep your Medigap policy long enough to make sure that you are satisfied with your managed care plan. If you do not like your managed care plan, you can disenroll at any time. If you give up your Medigap coverage, though, you may not be able to get it back at the same price.

The best time to get a Medigap policy is when you first become covered by Medicare. During the first six months that you are 65 (or older) *and* enrolled in Part B, insurance companies must accept you regardless of your health condition. During this time they cannot charge you more than they charge other people of the same age. Buying a Medigap policy during this time can save you a lot of money because you will be charged much higher premiums after the six-month period is over. If you don't join during your original six-month window, your Part B premiums will be permanently higher.

- *Enroll in a Medicare Managed Care Plan.* Managed care plans refer to health maintenance organizations (HMOs) and preferred provider organizations (PPOs). Depending on the plan you choose, you may or may not be required to pay premiums other than your Part B premium. You may be required to go to only those doctors and hospitals within your health plan. You can disenroll from a managed care plan at any time by calling the Social Security Administration at 1-800-772-1213 or, for the hearing and speech impaired, at 1-800-325-0778.

- *Purchase a Private Fee-for-Service plan.* This is essentially a private insurance policy that you purchase on your own. You must still pay your Part B premium, plus any premium charged by the plan and an amount set by the plan for each visit or service. Your policy, not Medicare, will determine how much you will be reimbursed for your medical bills. In the end you may wind up paying more for medical services in this type of plan than with Medicare, but you have the benefit of being able to see any doctor you want. Don't forget, though, that Medicare also allows you to see any doctor as long as she accepts Medicare.

- *Choose a Medicare Medical Savings Account (MSA) Plan.* A Medicare MSA plan is currently a test program and is available only in select parts of the country. It has a high deductible, and you must stay in the program for one full year. Medicare will deposit money directly into your Medical Savings Account. You use that account to pay for your medical expenses. If you do not use all of the money in your account, it carries over into the next year. If you use all the money in your MSA, you must pay the full cost of your medical care until you meet the deductible. If you take money out of the MSA for nonmedical expenses, it will be taxed as income. For more information on Medicare MSA plans, call 1-800-318-2596.

MEDICARE RIGHTS AND APPEALS

What Are My Rights?

The laws, rules, and regulations on Medicare grant you several rights as a Medicare patient:

- You are protected against unethical practices, and you are assured access to needed health care services.
- You do not need to get prior approval for emergency care.
- You are entitled to receive emergency care anywhere in the United States.
- You are entitled to appeal most decisions regarding payment for your medical services.
- You are to be given information about all of your health care treatment options.
- Your doctor may not refuse to tell you about certain treatment options even if those options are more expensive and would place a greater cost on your health plan.
- Your Medicare health plan must provide you, in writing, information on how it pays its doctors if you request that information.
- Your doctor must tell you whether he has a financial interest in a health care facility to which you are referred if you specifically ask your doctor to give you that information.

How Do I Complain About My Medicare Benefits?

If you believe that Medicare should not have refused to pay for a medical service you received or if you believe that your hospital is discharging you too soon, you have the right to appeal the decision. The telephone number for your State Health Insurance Assistance Program is listed in Appendix A. Call that number and tell them you need to make a complaint about your care or to appeal a denial of payment.

When you are admitted to a hospital, you should be given a notice entitled *An Important Message from Medicare: Your Rights While You Are a Medicare Hospital Patient*. This notice explains

Peer Review Organizations (PROs), which are groups of doctors and other health care professionals that review care given to Medicare patients in the hospital. It will also describe how you can appeal your discharge from the hospital or the denial of payment for a hospital stay.

Appealing Through Your Medicare Managed Care Provider

If you've chosen to join a Medicare managed care program, your option is to go through the appeal process that the provider has set up. Your Medicare managed care plan is required to give you written instructions on how you may appeal a coverage decision. After you file your appeal, the health plan is required to review its decision. If your health plan does not decide in your favor, the decision automatically goes to an independent review organization that contracts with Medicare. This review organization will make a decision and send you a written notice of its decision. If your health would be seriously harmed by waiting out the process, you can request a decision within 72 hours. If you do not have a copy of your health plan's appeal process, call your health plan and request the instructions.

If the cost of the service is at least $100 you can request a hearing. The next step, if the cost of the service is at least $1,000, is to request a review by the Appeals Council of the Social Security Administration. The step following that, if the cost of the service is at least $1,000, is to file for review in federal district court.

How Do I Appeal a Decision Regarding Nursing Home, Home Health Agency, or Hospice Costs?

When Medicare denies coverage, it must give you a written notice explaining the denial. This is not the same as an official Medicare determination that you are not covered. Tell your provider to file the claim. If Medicare decides that the service is not covered, it will send you a notice explaining the decision and how to appeal. If the cost of the service is at least $100, you can request a hearing. If the cost of the service is at least $1,000, you can request a review by the Appeals Council of the Social Security Administration. You also have the option of filing for review in federal district court if the cost of the service is at least $1,000.

What Do I Do If There Are Medical Services on My Bill That I Did Not Receive?

While charges for services not provided may be an innocent mistake, Medicare fraud is a serious problem. The best way to keep your health care affordable is to make sure that Medicare is not paying for services you did not receive. On your bill there will be the name, address, and telephone number of your Medicare carrier. Call the carrier immediately and tell the person that you did not receive the services that are listed on your Medicare statement. Medicare will take the investigation from there. Medicare will not reveal your name in this type of situation if you ask that it keep your identity confidential.

MEDICAID

What Is It?

Medicaid is a program run by both the state and federal governments to help people get medical care. It offers basic assistance to people with lower income levels. Medicaid is part of the welfare program. Each state must follow federal Medicaid guidelines, as well as put its own Medicaid laws into place. Because of this, Medicaid rules are different in each state, and each state has different eligibility standards. All states require that adults without dependent children must be at least 65, blind, or disabled *and* that they meet **income** and **asset tests.**

The **income tests** are linked to the federal Supplementary Security Income (SSI) program or, for younger applicants, to Temporary Assistance to Needy Families (TANF). In most states, persons eligible for SSI or TANF are automatically covered. These are **categorically eligible** individuals.

Asset or resource tests are explained further later. Basically, they say that you must own very few assets to qualify, but they permit you to not count as assets your home, car, and other important items of property.

Who Is in Charge of Medicaid in My State?

Each state puts one agency in charge of its Medicaid program. This agency is usually called the social services department, public welfare department, public aide department, human services, or something similar. You can call your local agency on aging or senior center for information. Appendix B of this book lists phone numbers of state Medicaid offices.

 THE PAPER TRAIL

The application you submit for Medicaid must be an original, not a photocopy. Always, ALWAYS, keep photocopies of every paper you send to the Medicaid office.

What Should I Bring with Me When I Apply for Medicaid?

You will need documents such as your driver's license, Social Security card, birth certificate, and marriage or divorce certificate. At some point in the process the Medicaid office will want to take a look at your bank statements and appraisals for any property that you own. This topic is covered in more detail in Chapter 21 on Medicaid planning for nursing homes.

How Long Does It Take to Qualify?

The Medicaid office must decide whether you qualify for coverage within 45 days of your application. If the office requests more information from you, the clock stops ticking on that 45 days until you provide the information. Therefore, it is in your best interests to provide the information they need as soon as possible. Remember to photocopy *everything* you send to the Medicaid office. If they lose your papers, the burden will be on you to resend the documents.

How Does It Work?

If you qualify for Medicaid, it will pay your medical bills. To find out if you are "poor enough" for Medicaid, the state will look at your monthly income and the fair market value of your resources. A **resource** is the term for the property that you own. To qualify for Medicaid in most states, your resources must not be valued at more than $2,000 for an individual or $3,000 for married couples.

Is Everything I Own a Resource?

No. There are certain things that are not considered "countable" resources for Medicaid purposes:

1. your home;
2. basic items in your day-to-day living, such as clothing, furniture, and household appliances;
3. one motor vehicle, although some states limit how much the car can be worth;
4. one wedding ring and one engagement ring, regardless of value;
5. prepaid funeral expenses totaling $3,000 or less (including burial plots, gravesites, caskets, headstones, and maintenance of the gravesite);

6. property that is essential to earning a living;

7. property that cannot be sold without creating an undue hardship;

8. reparation payments such as those made to victims of Agent Orange or the Holocaust;

9. cash value of life insurance, if the face value is less than $1,500 (if the face value is higher, the cash value is counted as an asset).

Will Medicaid Pay the Full Cost of Medical Care?

In general, yes, though it may not pay the full cost of nursing home care. See Chapter 21.

What Is "Medical Neediness"?

Most states also cover some people whose income falls below a certain level after they "spend down" a portion of their income on medical bills. These are called **medically needy** individuals.

What Does Medicaid Cover?

In general, the majority of Medicaid programs will pay for:

- **hospital stays,**
- **laboratory and x-ray services,**
- **out-patient hospital services and some health clinic services,**
- **family planning services and supplies,**
- **some dental care,**
- **some care by podiatrists, chiropractors, and optometrists,**
- **home health services,**
- **physical therapy,**
- **medications,**
- **dentures,**

- prosthetic devices,
- eyeglasses, and
- hospice care.

Can I Appeal a Medicaid Decision?

Yes. You may appeal any decision that affects your Medicaid eligibility or services. You should receive prompt written notice of any decision about your coverage. This notice will explain how you can appeal. The appeals process differs slightly from state to state, but it always includes a right to a fair hearing. You are not required to hire a lawyer for this hearing, but it is a good idea to get help from either an attorney or someone familiar with Medicaid.

Will Medicaid Pay My Medicare Premiums?

In some cases Medicaid will pay your premiums and deductibles for Medicare or Medicare Supplemental Insurance policies. If your employer offers a group health plan, Medicaid may pay for you to be enrolled in that program. Essentially Medicaid will decide whether it is most cost-effective for you to be on Medicaid or for Medicaid to pay your premiums for you to get coverage elsewhere.

Will I Lose My Medicaid Coverage If I Move to Another State?

If you move, you will be required to follow the Medicaid rules in your new state. You must be a resident of the state to qualify for Medicaid. You are considered a resident if you are living in the state and intend to stay there permanently or for a long period of time.

Will I Be Notified Before My Medicaid Coverage Is Taken Away?

Yes. Federal law requires that the state give you a fair hearing, if you request it, before the state agency prior to your Medicaid coverage being terminated. Typically you will get a notice in the mail at least 10 days before your Medicaid is to be cut off. You can then request a hearing (usually within 90 days). In some cases your Medicaid will be continued until the hearing. It is recommended that you consult an attorney or find a person who, although not an attorney, is familiar with Medicaid hearings to help you.

THE WORLD AT YOUR FINGERTIPS

- To get detailed information about Medicare or to see a list of free publications, visit *www.medicare.gov* on the Internet.
- The Health Care Financing Administration (HCFA) is the overall administrator of Medicare and Medicaid. Their website is at *www.hcfa.gov.* This site includes the laws and regulations on Medicare and Medicaid.
- Medicare and Medicaid are part of the Social Security Act. You can call the Social Security Administration at 1-800-772-1213 or, for the hearing or speech impaired, 1-800-325-0778. Or visit their website at *www.ssa.gov* to get more information on Medicare and Medicaid.
- *Prescription for Profit: How Doctors Defraud Medicaid* by Paul Jesilow and Gilbert Geis (University of California Press, 1993) offers examples of how easy it is for unscrupulous doctors to abuse the Medicaid system and how U.S. taxpayers end up paying for it.
- The American Medical Association offers advice to doctors on how to comply with Medicare and Medicaid regulations. This may be of interest to patients as well. This information may be accessed online at *http://www.ama-assn.org/physlegl/legal/hlthcare.htm.*

YOU MUST REMEMBER THIS

- For questions about Medicare or Medicaid, call the phone number for your state listed in Appendix A or Appendix B of this book.
- Medicare is a federal health insurance program for people age 65 years or older.
- Medicaid is a federal and state welfare program to provide health care to people with lower incomes.
- You must pay to enroll in Medicare Part B.
- Medicare health plan options differ widely in the services covered.

CHAPTER 6

COBRA

Keeping Your Benefits for a While After Your Job Is Gone

Louise works for a manufacturing company. Her employer provides a health plan to all of its employees, including Louise. She is also covered by her husband's insurance. Now it appears that Louise is going to be laid off. Her husband's insurance is not as good as her health plan, and she does not want to rely on his insurance alone. Her human resources administrator tells her that under COBRA she can keep her insurance for a time, giving her an opportunity to find another job with a health plan. Louise is not exactly sure what she has to do under COBRA to keep her health plan. Is she still eligible to keep her health plan even though she is covered by her husband's insurance? How long can she keep her health plan under COBRA?

IN GENERAL

What Is COBRA?

COBRA is the acronym for the Consolidated Omnibus Budget Reconciliation Act of 1985. COBRA is a federal law that amends the Employee Retirement Income Security Act of 1974 (ERISA). ERISA is a federal law that controls how your employee benefit plan is administered. COBRA is a complex law that courts, employers, and employees struggle to understand. In short, COBRA lets you and your dependents continue your group insurance coverage for a specific period of time after your employment status changes.

Why Is COBRA Important?

It is important that you be able to keep your group insurance if you quit your job or are fired. Group insurance costs a lot less than buying an individual policy. With group insurance the health risks are spread among many people, which makes your premiums lower.

In addition, you probably did not have to get a physical before getting your group insurance policy. With an individual insurance policy a physical examination may be required of everyone in your family that would be covered. If you or any of your dependents have preexisting conditions, that may not be included in your individual policy, and you could be left with a big medical bill to come out of your own pocket.

A BIG BENEFIT

COBRA lets you continue your insurance for about the same cost until you can get group insurance somewhere else.

COBRA AND YOU

To Whom Does COBRA Apply?

COBRA applies to private employers and local and state governments that:

- **employ 20 or more people on a typical business day, *and***
- **sponsor group health plans for their employees.**

COBRA applies to all group health plans regardless of whether the plans are self-insured or HMOs. It also applies to dental and vision plans.

What Terms Do I Need to Know?

COBRA offers "**continued coverage**" to "**qualified beneficiaries**" whose group insurance is terminated because of a "**qualifying event**." When you decide to keep your health plan under COBRA, you "**elect**" to be covered.

You are a **qualified beneficiary** when you have group insurance through your employer. Your spouse and dependents are also qualified beneficiaries. COBRA allows you to **continue** your insurance **coverage** until you get group insurance someplace else. A **qualifying event** is when you lose your insurance coverage because you lost or quit your job or your hours were reduced. If you are fired because of gross misconduct, you are not entitled to COBRA. Your spouse or dependents qualify for COBRA when they lose insurance coverage because:

- **you die;**
- **you are fired (unless you were fired for gross misconduct) or quit your job;**
- **your hours are reduced;**
- **you and your spouse are divorced or legally separated;**
- **you become eligible for Medicare; or**
- **your child is no longer considered a dependent under your health plan.**

How Long Do I Have to Choose COBRA Insurance?

You have 60 days from the date of your qualifying event. COBRA is retroactive to the day of your qualifying event. Hence, if you elect COBRA on day 60, your health plan will also cover those first 59 days after your qualifying event.

Do I Have to Pay for COBRA Insurance?

Yes. Your employer can charge you up to 102 percent of the total cost for your benefits. The total cost for you must be calculated the same way it is calculated for other people with the same type of benefits under your health plan.

Do I Have to Undergo a Physical Examination to Get COBRA Coverage?

No. You do not need to do anything more than any other person with the same health plan as far your insurability is concerned.

Will My Benefits Be Different Under COBRA?

Your benefits must be the same as employees with the same health plan. If the coverage is changed for all the employees, it is changed for you, too.

COBRA AND YOUR EMPLOYER

How Will I Find Out About COBRA?

COBRA only applies to companies with twenty or more employees. With most companies that size, there will be either a human resources person or an administrator in charge of your health plan and benefits. That is the first place to start when you have a question about your health plan or COBRA.

Does My Employer Have to Tell Me About COBRA?

Yes. There are three different stages at which your employer must educate you about COBRA. An initial notice will be sent to you—usually in the form of a letter—telling you that you can choose to continue your coverage under COBRA and what you must do to make that choice. An event notice will be sent to you when you leave your company or when your hours are reduced or when something else happens that would terminate your health insurance. Finally, you will receive a termination notice telling you when your COBRA coverage is about to end.

When Can I Expect the Initial Notice?

The health plan administrator for your company has 14 days to notify you of your right to elect to continue your coverage under COBRA. You then have 60 days to decide whether you want to elect to continue your coverage.

LIMITS ON COBRA

How Long Will My COBRA Coverage Last?

If you lose your job or your hours are reduced, your continued coverage lasts for 18 months or until you get other insurance. If you die, your coverage ends, but your spouse and dependents may pay for continued coverage for 36 months. If you are divorced or your child is no longer a dependent, continued coverage lasts for 36 months or until your spouse or child finds other insurance.

My State Offers Continued Coverage, Too. Can I Add That to the COBRA Coverage?

No. Some states offer insurance laws similar to COBRA. If your state requires your employer to offer you continued coverage, that coverage runs at the same time as COBRA. You cannot tack one onto the end of the other.

When Can My COBRA Insurance Be Taken Away?

You can lose your COBRA coverage when:

- **your employer stops offering a health plan to its employees;**
- **you do not pay your premiums;**

- you qualify for Medicare (although your dependents may still qualify for COBRA); or
- you become insured under another group health plan.

What If My Employer Goes Bankrupt?

In most cases you will lose your insurance. If you retired from your company before it filed for bankruptcy, you can continue your insurance coverage under COBRA. Your dependents can continue their coverage only if your employer took away your coverage within a year before or after filing for bankruptcy.

What If My New Insurance Does Not Cover as Much as My Other Policy?

Generally your COBRA coverage ends when you enroll in a new health plan. The exception to this is when your new policy excludes or limits your coverage for a preexisting condition. In that case you might be able to keep your COBRA coverage for the full 18 or 36 months.

What If I Get Married and I Am Put on My Spouse's Health Plan?

This is considered a new health plan, and your COBRA coverage will end.

COBRA'S PAST—AND WHAT IT MEANS FOR YOUR FUTURE

Confusion in the Courts

COBRA is a very complex law that was enacted at the end of a Congressional session. Many commentators complain that it is a group of piecemeal amendments strung together with no rhyme or reason. The result is that the part of COBRA that concerns your insurance is confusing, at best, for you, your employer, and any court that ends up hearing your court case.

The Big Question

When it comes to COBRA, courts struggled with one question more than any other: What happens when you are covered by a spouse's health plan as well as your own? Do you still qualify for COBRA? The U.S. Supreme Court says yes, ending years of debate among lower courts throughout the country. The debate is not over yet though. The Supreme Court left several questions. To understand the controversy you will need to know a little of COBRA's background.

- *In the Beginning* . . .   In the 1980s, lawmakers realized that a growing number of Americans did not have health insurance. At the same time hospitals were refusing to treat people who were not covered by insurance. Congress enacted COBRA to provide you with affordable private health insurance. It lets you keep your group health plan from your former employer while you find insurance from another employer.

- *The Phrase That Causes Most of the Trouble* . . .   COBRA states that your continued coverage under your old plan ends on the day you "first become[ ], after the date of election" covered under any other group health plan. That means that after you decide to continue your health plan under COBRA, your COBRA coverage ends on the first day that your new health insurance begins. What does that mean for you if you are also covered under your spouse's insurance? Technically you are covered by health insurance the entire time. Should that count for COBRA purposes? For years the courts could not agree.

- *The First Line of Thought* . . .   One line of reasoning is that coverage under a spouse's plan does not affect COBRA because it was in place before you left the company. Thus you did not "first become" covered under your spouse's policy after you became eligible for COBRA. The law says "first become" plain and simple. This is the reasoning that the Supreme Court later adopted.

• **_The Other Line of Thought_ ...** The opposing point of view is known as the "significant gap" line of reasoning. This states that preexisting coverage under a spouse's plan makes you ineligible for COBRA because COBRA is only for those people who would have no insurance at all. Because you have insurance, you do not require COBRA—unless there is a significant gap in the coverage you had under your health plan and the coverage you would have under your spouse's plan. For example, your health plan covered medical expenses for pregnancy, but your spouse's does not. If you are in your childbearing years, to rely on your spouse's health plan alone would leave you without significant coverage. This gap could have entitled you to COBRA coverage.

• **_Why the Significant Gap Theory Did Not Hold Up_ ...** When is a gap in insurance significant? Courts were stuck trying to figure out the answer to that question, and each court came up with a different answer. Is there a significant gap when your policy puts a $1,000,000 cap on medical costs for newborns and your spouse's policy puts a $100,000 cap on newborn costs? Is there a significant gap if your policy covers bone marrow transplants but your spouse's does not? The courts said no. But how is an employer or an employee supposed to know when a court will say yes? There simply was no clear-cut rule to follow.

The Outcome

The Supreme Court decided that you cannot be disqualified from COBRA if you are covered under your spouse's health plan before your qualifying event (such as being fired from your job). Employers considered this decision to be unfair because they said it allowed former employees to get double insurance. The Court disagreed, stating that most of us do not want to pay for more insurance than we need. If we are covered under a spouse's policy as well, then we probably need both insurance plans.

TODAY'S COBRA PROBLEM: THE PREEXISTING CONDITION RULE

The Supreme Court decided that even if you get a new health plan, your COBRA insurance cannot be canceled if your new insurance does not cover a preexisting condition. The problem is that the Court did not explain what it meant by preexisting condition. It also did not explain how big the gap in coverage must be in order for you to keep your insurance under COBRA. This issue will begin to appear in the courts in the near future.

THE WORLD AT YOUR FINGERTIPS

- For an online booklet explaining COBRA, visit the website for the Department of Labor's Pension and Welfare Benefits Administration at *http://www.dol.gov./dol/pwba/public/pubs/COBRA/cobra95.htm.*
- Business owners who want more information on how COBRA affects their company should check out the CCH Business Owner's site at *http://www.toolkit.cch.com/text/P05_4835.asp* as well as the FindLaw™ Small Business site at *http://sbiz.findlaw.com/text/P05_4835.stm.*

YOU MUST REMEMBER THIS

- COBRA lets you and your dependents continue your group insurance coverage for a specific period of time after your employment status changes.
- Your employer must inform you within 14 days of a qualifying event that you have the right to continue coverage under COBRA.
- You must choose whether you want to elect COBRA coverage within 60 days after your qualifying event.
- Coverage under a spouse's health plan does not make you

ineligible to continue your health plan under COBRA, as long as you were covered before your qualifying event.

- If your new health plan does not cover a preexisting condition, you might still be able to continue your former health plan under COBRA.

PART THREE

Reproduction

The Birds, the Bees, and the Deep Freeze

When and how we have children is changing on practically a monthly basis. Today couples who want to conceive may choose from a number of high-tech methods to help them get pregnant. Then they may choose the high-tech or low-tech way in which they wish to give birth. We can choose to terminate a pregnancy or to undergo a procedure so that we will not become (or cause someone else to become) pregnant. With all these choices comes questions as to who is responsible for what, and when. This section will answer some of those questions.

We will explore issues raised by some of the current forms of assisted reproductive technology: Who owns your frozen embryos—you or the fertility clinic? Are surrogacy agreements enforceable within your state? What should be included in a surrogacy agreement? When a man donates sperm, is he entitled to paternity rights? After that we will take a look at wrongful birth and wrongful pregnancy claims. We will explain the difference between these two types of claims as well as your doctor's duty to act according to your wishes when it comes to your reproductive choices.

Sterilization is considered next, particularly as applied to hospitals run by religious organizations and to the rights of the mentally disabled. At one time the mentally disabled were sterilized as a matter of course. Today that is no longer the case. The mentally disabled are now recognized as having reproductive rights, too.

We will cover the choices available for giving birth. You do not have the absolute right to choose where and how you have your baby; for instance, not every state allows the practice of midwifery. We will take a look at the different approaches taken by the law toward midwifery and how that affects your choices. We will also discuss one of the most controversial topics of our time—abortion. This chapter will explain how abortion became legal and the laws surrounding abortion today. It will also go into detail on a minor girl's right to an abortion and whether her parents must be notified.

These chapters cover some of our most personal choices. If you would like more information on these topics, please check at the end of the guide for additional resources and websites regarding these issues.

CHAPTER 7

Assisted Reproductive Technology

Having Babies Ain't What It Used to Be—and the Law Is Struggling to Catch Up

> *Molly and Peter sitting in a tree*
> *K-I-S-S-I-N-G*
> *First comes love*
> *Then comes marriage*
> *Then comes Molly with a baby carriage.*

HIGH-TECH BABY MAKING

The Brave New World of Conception

Life is a bit more complicated than the nursery rhymes of our childhood days. In 1978, the first "test tube" baby was born through in vitro fertilization. Although love and marriage were never absolute necessities for producing a baby, only one woman and one man were required. That is no longer the case. True, it still takes the genetic materials of one man and one woman; but with cloning experiments being conducted in several countries, we may someday find biological reproduction obsolete.

The benefit of all this technology is that people who may not be able to conceive on their own are able to have children. The downside is that this technology is creating situations with which the courts and the legislatures have never had to deal. Consider this: Baby making used to involve two nontechnical terms—mother and father. Now a baby can be made using **in vitro fertilization** (with either pronuclear-stage embryo transfer or trancervical embryo transfer), **gamete intrafallopian transfer (GIFT)**, donor oocytes, donor sperm, microsurgical epididymal sperm aspiration, intracytoplasmic sperm injection, assisted hatching of oocytes, and anonymous embryo donation. It is no longer the birds and the bees, but the birds, the bees, and the deep freeze.

When Does the Law Come into Play?

When the intended parents use their own gametes with assisted reproductive technology, the baby-making process may be unusual, but it is relatively free of legal worries. When third parties participate as gestational carriers or donors, the law is less clear on balancing the rights and interests of all the parties. Although some may question whether we should be using this technology at all, the courts have consistently decided that we have a right to privacy when it comes to having children. It is not the court's role to decide whether we should or should not be able to use a particular form of technology. That role is left to legislatures, which so far have taken a range of approaches, from banning technologies to providing a legal framework for parents, doctors, and judges.

DO YOU OWN YOUR BODY PARTS?

Controlling Embryos

Traditionally, only renewable body parts, such as blood and sperm, have been sold. The commercial sale of body parts has not been based on property rights. The use of gametes and embryos, because of their tremendous potential to create a child with a genetic connection to the parents, gives the intended parents the legal ability to direct and to control their use under a theory that the parents have quasi-property rights.

In Virginia, a couple asked their fertility clinic to give them their frozen embryos so that they could try a different doctor.

The clinic refused. The couple sued the clinic and won. The court found the couple did have a quasi-property interest in their embryos. Not all courts are comfortable with declaring embryos as "property." Nevertheless, you have a good chance of getting to your embryos when third parties try to interfere. Courts tend to provide parents with some form of property rights to their embryos, such as the right to possess, use, or donate. Things become much more difficult when the fight is between you and your spouse. Control battles over embryos are discussed later in this chapter.

IT'S *YOUR* GENETIC MATERIAL

In California, three doctors took eggs and embryos from patients who sought fertility treatments. The doctors then used these eggs and embryos for other patients. In most cases the doctors did not have the consent of the original patients to do this. California now makes it a felony to take human embryos and use them without the patient's consent.

What Happens to the Eggs, Sperm, or Embryos You Don't Use?

Whether you succeed in having all the babies you desire or decide to stop fertility treatments, there will usually be embryos or sperm left over. (There may be eggs, too, though it is still experimental to freeze eggs.) You can keep this genetic material frozen for possible future use by you, donate it to another patient, donate it for research, or have it destroyed by the clinic. Regardless of your decision, the clinic should ask you—before you start treatments—what you want to do with any remaining genetic material. This is an important step. Unless you decide what you want done with it, the clinic will be unsure how to treat this material. Even if you later amend your written agreement, it is important to have one in place before any procedures are initiated. Clinics may or may not keep genetic material on hand indefinitely. You want to make sure it is not destroyed, used, or donated without your consent.

A problem arises when a couple divorces and cannot agree on what to do with the remaining embryos. Potential human life is not mere property. This kind of dispute raises complex emotional, legal, and ethical issues.

If there is no agreement, the court will have to balance the interests of the people fighting for control. A New York couple had five frozen embryos remaining when they divorced. The wife asked for sole control of the embryos. The husband wanted to donate the embryos to the clinic. When they began their fertility treatments, the couple had signed an agreement stating that they would donate the embryos to the clinic. The court ruled that the agreement was valid and the embryos were to be donated. Other courts have invalidated written agreements if they are unclear or if they force a person to become a parent against that person's will.

Who Is Daddy?

When **artificial insemination** is performed using anonymously donated sperm, the woman's husband is considered the legal father as long as:

- he consented to the procedure, *and*
- a doctor or other medical professional supervised the insemination.

On the other hand, if no doctor is involved, a donor may be granted paternity rights. Only forty-two states have laws regarding artificial insemination, and only thirty-five of those clarify parental rights in cases of artificial insemination. In California a man donated his sperm to a lesbian couple. The woman was inseminated with the man's sperm at home. There was no assistance from medical professionals, and the man was not present when the woman was inseminated. Later the man decided he wanted paternity rights, including visitation. Because no medical professional was involved in the actual insemination of the mother, the father was granted paternity rights.

SURROGACY

Traditional or Gestational

There are now two types of surrogacy. In a **traditional surrogacy,** a woman (the surrogate) undergoes intrauterine insemination with sperm from the man who wants to be the legal father. The baby is produced by genetic material from the father and from the surrogate mother. Traditionally, once the baby was born, the father's wife had to adopt it through stepparent adoption. In a **gestational carrier surrogacy,** an embryo is transferred to the gestational carrier. The baby has no genetic material from the carrier. Here is where it gets confusing: the gametes can come from either the intended parents or from one or more gamete donors. If the embryo is transferred from a donor, then the baby has three mothers: the genetic mother, the gestational mother, and the intended mother. Is it any wonder that weighing the legal rights of the three women, the child, and the father(s) is confusing?

LEARNING THE LINGO

Traditional carrier: A woman who gestates (is pregnant with) an embryo to whom she has a genetic relation but for whom she does not intend to be the legal mother.

Gestational carrier: A woman who gestates (is pregnant with) an embryo to whom she has no genetic relation.

Is It Legal?

Whether a surrogacy agreement will stand up in court depends on the state in which you live. Both legislatures and courts are suspicious of any contract that involves fees in exchange for a baby. Some states will uphold the arrangement if there is a contract clearly outlining the responsibility of the parties. Some states require the intended father's wife to adopt the baby as though she were the baby's stepparent. Some states refuse to recognize any type of contract that transfers parenthood from a surrogate to the couple who contracted with her.

Who Is Considered the Parent?

In a gestational surrogacy, courts lean toward giving parenthood to the genetic parents. In those cases the person who "intends" to parent is considered the "legal" parent. The courts have considered the surrogate's claim to the child as weaker because she does not share any genetic material with the baby. In order to make its decision, the court looks at the human relationships involved rather than at the way the baby was conceived.

In a traditional surrogacy, the surrogate is almost always considered to be the "legal" mother. In custody disputes, though, joint custody with the father and his wife is the norm. The most famous traditional surrogacy case is the "Baby M" case from the late 1980s. A New Jersey court decided that the surrogacy contract was void because it required the surrogate to give up the baby in exchange for money. Nevertheless, the court granted custody to the father and his wife. The surrogate was granted visitation rights. The court in that case stated that a noncompensated surrogacy agreement, which would not involve any type of payment to the surrogate and would not require the carrier to turn over the child until after the statutory waiting period for adoption, would be legal.

What About Other States?

Despite the ruling in New Jersey, other states do allow surrogacy contracts, including the payment of money to the surrogate for carrying the child.

The most common terms (which continue to evolve) in a surrogacy agreement are that:

- the intended parents want to be included in prenatal doctor visits,
- the intended parents will be present in the delivery room,
- the carrier will refrain from smoking and drinking alcohol during the pregnancy,
- the carrier will surrender her "rights" to the child.

Who Decides Which Parents
Are to Keep the Baby?

A judge has to decide who gets to keep the baby when the "parents" start fighting over custody. That's exactly what happened in an unusual case in California. An embryo from two anonymous donors was transferred into a gestational carrier. The carrier gave birth to the baby and turned the little girl over to the couple who had hired the carrier to carry the child. The husband filed for divorce before the baby was born and refused to pay child support because, he claimed, the child was not "his."

The trial court sided with the father and ruled that the baby did not have any parents at all. The intended mother was not allowed to adopt the girl because there was no one for her to adopt the girl from. (The carrier did not want to keep the baby. The anonymous donors did not come forward to claim the child either.) In essence, the court made the child an orphan.

The mother appealed, though, and the trial court's decision was reversed. The higher court reasoned that the baby would not have been born if the mother and the father had not agreed to have the embryo transferred into the carrier. It was the intent of the mother and the father to have a baby. Thus, the father had to pay child support, and the mother was granted custody of the little girl.

What About Children Conceived
After a Parent Dies?

Through the use of assisted reproductive technology, children can be conceived months—even years—after one or both of the parents die. If a couple freezes their embryos, the wife can have the embryos transferred after her husband's death. If both parents die, the person who "inherits" the embryos could have them transferred to a carrier, thus creating a child whose parents are deceased.

The question then becomes whether the child is a "survivor" of the parent(s). This can affect the child's right to inherit from the estate of the parent(s), to receive Social Security benefits, or to collect on a life insurance policy. Assisted reproductive technology creates a new class of children whose rights and status need to be protected. Most federal and state bureaucracies simply are not equipped to handle the implications of nonconventional conceptions and births.

In one case a woman in Louisiana was impregnated with her husband's sperm three months after he died. One year later she applied for Social Security survivor's benefits for her daughter. These benefits are based on a deceased parent's earnings at the time he died. Initially her claim was denied because the law required the daughter to either be alive at the time of her father's death or born within 300 days after it. It took several appeals for the mother to finally receive benefits for her daughter.

TALKING TO A LAWYER

Including Embryos in a Divorce Settlement

Q. My first wife and I divorced, and I received control of the embryos in the settlement. My second wife and I want to use the embryos to have children. Can my ex-wife stop us?

A. Yes. Even where a husband and a wife sign a clear agreement giving one partner control of the embryos, courts are reluctant to enforce the agreement because it forces one person to become a legal parent against his or her will. Therefore, as a matter of public policy, a court would most likely allow your ex-wife to step in and prevent you from using the embryos with your second wife because your first wife would be the child's genetic mother.

Answer by Cindy J. Moy, attorney and author, Golden Valley, Minnesota

Social Security Benefits

Under the Social Security Act, survivor's benefits are disbursed in order to support children who were dependent on the wage earner at the time of his or her death. Children conceived after the parent's death are not dependent on the wage earner at the time of death. Whether those children should still collect benefits is a question with which the courts are struggling right now. At the time of this writing, this situation has occurred when the mother became pregnant through technology, using frozen sperm or embryos, after the death of the father. Conceivably, however, this situation could also arise if the wage earner who died was the mother, and the father hired a surrogate to carry a frozen embryo through pregnancy after the mother died.

The Act is broadly interpreted by the courts so as to grant benefits to qualified applicants whenever possible. Some commentators predict that as Social Security funds begin to dwindle, courts will become more conservative in deciding who qualifies for those benefits. For now, these children usually receive benefits.

Inheritance Laws

State inheritance laws generally require a child to be conceived before the parent died in order for the child to inherit from the parent's estate. This is because at the time these laws were written the technology did not exist for a child to be conceived after one parent was deceased. These laws permit the state to distribute the estate among the heirs without wondering who might come along down the road. It also protects the courts from having to investigate suspicious claims from people claiming to be heirs conceived after the parent died.

The state has to balance those concerns with the goal of keeping children off public assistance when they could be taken care of through the deceased parent's estate. It also does not want to punish children for the way in which they were conceived.

A few states simply ban children conceived after the parent's death from inheriting from the estate, unless the parent specifies otherwise in his or her will. This goes hand in hand with other states that require children to show that the dead parent intended to have more children. If the children cannot prove that the parent intended to have more children, they cannot inherit from the estate.

If there are children in your family who have been or might be born as a result of assisted technologies, you should have specific provisions for these children in your will, whether you want them to share in your estate or not. If you don't handle the matter in your will, the courts will have to sort out the results in particular cases. Whenever there is a legal proceeding regarding the right of possession of embryos or other genetic material, the court should address the inheritance rights of the child along with the right of possession of the genetic material itself.

INSURANCE AND INFERTILITY TREATMENTS

Few insurance plans directly cover treatment for infertility, although policies may cover treatment for illnesses (such as endometriosis) that contribute to infertility. Some policies will cover infertility treatment if the couple has been trying to conceive for a year or more. Consumers are fighting to get more coverage for infertility treatment. Eleven states now mandate that insurance companies include infertility treatment in their plans.

Is Infertility a Disability?

A few years ago courts began seeing lawsuits in which men and women claimed that infertility was a disability under the Americans with Disabilities Act (ADA). If infertility is a disability because it interferes with a major life event, employers are discriminating against persons with a disability by not providing an accommodation such as time off from work for doctor visits.

Employers argue that infertility is not a disability under the ADA because it does not prevent people from performing their job duties. They also argue that to be a disability, it would have to affect a major life activity. Reproduction, according to their theory, is not a major life activity. Instead, major life activities are caring for yourself, performing manual tasks, walking, seeing, hearing, speaking, breathing, learning, and working.

The Supreme Court held that having children is a major life event and that infertility is a disability. Likewise, legislatures are increasingly requiring insurance companies to cover infertility treatment, including prescription drugs and surgery. The types of assisted reproductive technology that will be covered and the extent to which they will be covered remain to be seen.

THE WORLD AT YOUR FINGERTIPS

- The Fertile Thoughts website contains helpful information about infertility, assisted reproductive technology, and adoption. It also has links to other useful sites. *www.fertile thoughts.com*.

- Resolve is a consumer group that provides education, support, and advocacy on assisted reproductive technology issues. Its website address is *www.resolve.com*.

- The American Society for Reproductive Medicine is a nonprofit group that studies infertility issues. Here you can research state insurance laws to find out what level of coverage is required for infertility treatments and to obtain patient education booklets; go to *www.asrm.org/*.

- The website for the Center for Advanced Reproductive Care (CARC), University of Iowa Hospitals and Clinics (UIHC), *http://www.uihc.uiowa.edu/pubinfo/arc.htm,* will tell you everything you ever wanted to know—and a few things you didn't—about the different forms of assisted reproductive technology available.

- *The Clone Age: Adventures in the New World of Reproductive Technologies* by Lori B. Andrews (Henry Holt & Company, Inc., 1999). Andrews is a law professor and attorney specializing in genetic and reproductive technologies. She takes a look at how technological changes affect how people are having babies and at how the law must change to keep up with the times.

YOU MUST REMEMBER THIS

- You have the right to control how your gametes or embryos are used.
- Before beginning infertility treatments, make sure you have a written agreement with the clinic as to how your eggs, sperm, or embryos will be taken care of once you end your treatments.
- In a traditional surrogacy, although the carrier is considered the "legal" mother, the father and his wife will almost always get shared custody of the baby.
- A child conceived after a parent dies may not be able to inherit from the parent's estate.
- Legislatures are beginning to require that medical plans cover infertility treatments, although the practice is not yet widespread.

CHAPTER 8

Wrongful Birth and
Wrongful Pregnancy

Cases Raise Difficult Issues, Including the Monetary Value of a Child

Angela and Adam are the parents of two beautiful children. They agreed that Adam would get a vasectomy so that they would not have any more children. A year after a doctor performed a vasectomy on Adam, Angela found out that she was pregnant.

Ben and Marti, a couple in their forties, were excited about the birth of their fourth child. They were concerned about the higher risk of birth defects because of their age, but the doctor assured them the baby would be fine. The doctor told them there was no need to test for birth defects, even though such tests are routine for pregnant women over the age of 35. Ben and Marti's baby was born with severe birth defects that would have been detected by the routine tests.

WRONGFUL PREGNANCY

What Is It?

Wrongful pregnancy occurs when someone undergoes a sterilization procedure, such as a vasectomy or a tubal ligation, but the procedure does not preclude pregnancy and the birth of a child. Another common term for this is **wrongful conception.**

Can I Sue for Wrongful Pregnancy?

It used to be that parents were not allowed to bring lawsuits for wrongful pregnancy or conception. That has changed over the past couple of decades. Now most courts agree that parents can bring a claim for wrongful pregnancy, but courts continue to disagree as to what costs the parents can recover.

Some states allow parents to recover only those costs associated with pregnancy and delivery, such as:

- **prenatal and postnatal medical expenses,**
- **pain and suffering during pregnancy and delivery,**
- **cost of a second sterilization,**
- **loss of wages, and**
- **any permanent injury resulting from pregnancy or delivery.**

For years doctors and hospitals have argued that when a woman becomes pregnant in this situation, she should have an abortion or give the child up for adoption in order to lessen the cost. So far this has not worked in court, and it is doubtful it ever will.

Does Wrongful Pregnancy Apply Only
When the Baby Suffers Birth Defects?

No. Most wrongful pregnancy cases involve the unplanned birth of a healthy child. The majority of states allow claims for wrongful pregnancy. Parents can usually get reimbursed for the ordinary medical expenses directly associated with the pregnancy and the birth of the child. A few states let the parents sue the doctor for all of the expenses in raising the child. These states look at the financial burden a child can place on a family of limited means.

A few other states believe that it is not possible for parents to be harmed by the birth of a healthy child, so parents are not allowed to sue for wrongful pregnancy. Some courts say that the value of life outweighs any costs to the parents. They believe that a newborn should not be looked at as property, with costs and benefits assigned to it. There are also courts that believe that allowing parents to recover the costs of raising a child creates emotional harm by making the children feel they are not worth the cost of being raised.

What Is the Monetary Value of a Child?

Some states allow parents to get reimbursed for the costs of raising the child, minus the beneficial value of having a child. Deciding how much monetary value to assign to having a child is a difficult task, though. How much is a child worth? Courts continue to struggle with deciding on the value of a child's aid, companionship, and comfort to parents. Still other courts warn that allowing actions for wrongful conceptions will make doctors decide to stop performing sterilizations altogether.

Is Wrongful Pregnancy the
Same as Wrongful Life?

Wrongful pregnancy claims are different from claims for **wrongful life.** In a wrongful life claim, the baby brings the claim by arguing that, but for the doctor's negligence, "Mom would not have become pregnant and I [the baby] would not exist." Very few states will allow wrongful life claims. Courts consider it against public policy to agree that life is less desirable than nonlife. The legal theory is that the doctor owes a duty to the mother, but not the fetus, so the baby cannot claim wrongful life.

LEARNING THE LINGO

Wrongful life: A type of medical malpractice claim brought on behalf of a child that argues that the child would not have been born but for the negligent advice to, or treatment of, the parents.

WRONGFUL BIRTH

What Is It?

There are two main situations in which parents bring claims for wrongful birth. First, the father or the mother underwent a sterilization procedure that is somehow faulty, and the couple becomes pregnant again. This claim is rooted in medical malpractice law. In the second situation, a pregnant woman is not informed that her child may be born with birth defects, thereby losing her choice as to whether to continue the pregnancy.

The theory behind a wrongful birth claim is that parents should be given reimbursement for some of the economic costs of raising the child. It is not an attempt to make the child feel unwanted.

The First Wrongful Birth Cases

In 1934, in one of the first wrongful birth cases, a Minnesota husband underwent a vasectomy because the wife's doctor told them she might not survive another childbirth. His wife later became pregnant. When the husband sued the doctor for wrongful birth, the court ruled that the vasectomy was to protect his wife's life, not his, and that the husband should feel fortunate to be blessed with the fatherhood of another child.

In 1957, a Pennsylvania father lost his claim for the wrongful birth of his child. The court stated that to let the father make the doctor pay for the costs of raising the child would force the doctor to pay for the fun, joy, and affection that the father would have in rearing and educating the child.

When a Baby Is Born with Birth Defects

Health care providers have a duty to give you any significant information about tests that will tell you the likelihood of your future child being born with mental or physical defects. They also have a duty to perform the tests accurately. You have the right to prevent the birth of a baby with mental or physical defects, either by not conceiving in the first place or by terminating the pregnancy. This right is granted to a woman for the most part by the constitutional provisions that allow her to have an abortion.

As you can well imagine, this is a hotly contested issue among abortion rights advocates and foes. On one side is the right to be fully informed about the well-being of the child you are expecting. On the other side is the doctor who may be opposed to abortion. Keep in mind that wrongful birth laws do not require doctors to perform abortions. These laws simply require that doctors give you information on tests that measure the genetic health and the status of the fetus. The decision is then up to you.

It is not the doctor's right not to decide to tell you about possible problems with the child you are expecting. You need that information in order to make choices for you, your family, and your baby. When the doctor does not give the information you need to make that choice—either by not telling you about routine tests or by failing to tell you the results—that is the basis for a **wrongful birth.**

What Do Parents Need to Prove a Wrongful Birth Claim?

To bring a wrongful birth claim for a baby born with birth defects, you will have to show that:

- a duty existed between you and the doctor;
- there was a breach of that duty because the doctor failed to perform her duty to you with reasonable care; and
- the doctor caused you to lose your option to terminate the pregnancy.

Do All the States Allow Wrongful Birth Lawsuits?

No, not all states allow you to bring claims for wrongful birth. Only a handful ban wrongful birth claims outright. About half the states have considered banning such claims. Some states require the parents to prove that the doctor "caused" the birth defects. Of the states that do allow wrongful birth claims, few agree on what you should receive if you win your claim.

The majority of states will not allow you to be reimbursed for *all* the expenses involved in raising a child. They allow you to recover only those costs that come about from raising a developmentally disabled child. The public policy concern is that developmentally disabled children will be treated differently by their families as well as the law, making them feel as though they are inferior. This concern has to be balanced with the fact that medical treatment for a developmentally disabled child is so costly that it can financially ruin a family. It is a terrible stress for a family when they are forced to go on public assistance because they have lost their home and savings to pay the medical costs of one child.

In Florida, parents sued for wrongful conception of their twins. One child was born with birth defects. The other child was healthy. The parents were not allowed to recover the costs of the healthy baby. The parents were granted reimbursement of the extra costs of raising the child with birth defects.

ARTIFICIAL LIFE SUPPORT FOR PREMATURE BABIES

With the constant advances in technology, more and more premature babies are surviving because of new medications and machines. The question is whether surviving is the same as thriving, or, in other words, whether being alive is the same as living. In Houston, Texas, a woman went into labor only 22 weeks into her pregnancy. There was little chance that the baby girl would survive. The baby's parents told the doctors that they did not want artificial life support put on their child.

The doctors, following standard procedures at the hospital, placed the baby on artificial life support. At seven years old, the girl was severely retarded, suffered from cerebral palsy, and could not see, walk, talk, roll over, or feed herself. The parents sued the doctors, claiming that by ignoring their wishes to keep their daughter off life support, the doctors caused the girl's wrongful birth.

This is a unique wrongful birth claim. Regardless, a jury awarded the family a multimillion-dollar award, finding that the doctors should have obeyed the family's wishes to keep their daughter off life support so that, in essence, nature could run its course. Whether a jury in another part of the country would reach the same conclusion is unknown.

THE WORLD AT YOUR FINGERTIPS

- An organization called Attorney Advantage put together a website that provides current medical and legal information, community resources, and financial planning for parents of neurologically impaired children: *www.whymychild.com.*
- This site, *www.apfelgreene.com/medinfo.html,* operated by a Maryland law firm, offers comprehensive information on the legal theories surrounding medical malpractice claims involving pregnancy and delivery.
- As genetic testing for birth defects and other illnesses becomes more available, groups such as Genetic Alliance may prove to be a useful resource. Their website is at *www.geneticalliance.org.*

YOU MUST REMEMBER THIS

- Wrongful pregnancy cases mostly involve the unplanned birth of a healthy child.
- Courts differ widely on how much parents can be reimbursed for the costs of raising a child that results from wrongful pregnancy.
- Your doctor has a duty to give you any significant information as to the chances of your future child being born developmentally disabled.
- You have the right to prevent the birth of a developmentally disabled baby, either by not conceiving in the first place or by terminating the pregnancy.

- At least one couple succeeded in bringing a wrongful birth claim after doctors went against their wishes and put their premature baby on artificial life support. It is too soon to determine whether couples in other parts of the country would win on this type of claim.

CHAPTER 9

Sterilization

Difficult Issues Involve Religion and Involuntary Procedures

Camille and her husband Rob are the parents of two children. Rob wants to undergo a vasectomy so that the couple will not have any more children. Camille and Rob do not want to use contraception because of their religious beliefs, but they believe that a vasectomy is not contraception. Their health plan offers them a choice of three hospitals, but only one is located near them. This hospital is affiliated with a religious organization and refuses to perform vasectomies or tubal ligations, claiming that the law does not require the hospital to perform procedures that violate its religious covenants. Can the hospital refuse to perform certain procedures based on religious beliefs?

RELIGIOUS HEALTH CARE FACILITIES

Catholic Hospitals

Although there are many religious organizations that provide health care in some form, the most prominent denomination is the Roman Catholic Church. Catholic hospitals, which are non-profit, control more than twice the market than that of the largest private health care organization. There are more than 600 Catholic hospitals in the United States, although that number is shrinking as hospitals merge with one another and become more profit oriented. Catholic hospitals generated more than $35 billion in net patient revenues in 1997. Currently four of the ten largest health care systems in the United States are Catholic.

When religious organizations provide health care, those organizations must deal with federal and state regulations governing hospitals and managed care plans. Some of these regulations conflict with the religious beliefs of some religions. For example, the Catholic Church runs its hospitals according to the Ethical and Religious Directives for Catholic Health Care Services. This directive spells out the church's objection to abortion, sterilization, and family planning. The directive states that direct sterilization of either men or women is not permitted in a Catholic hospital. Procedures that result in sterility are allowed when the direct effect is the treatment of a serious illness and a simpler treatment is not available.

The directive conflicts with state and federal laws that require health care providers to provide "sensitive" services, which include abortion, sterilization, family planning, and access to the morning-after pill for rape victims. This conflict affects you when you go to a religiously run hospital for treatment that does not comport with the religious organization's beliefs.

The Church Amendments

In 1973 Congress enacted the Church Amendments. This law allows health care facilities to refuse to perform certain procedures if those procedures violate the religious organization's moral or religious beliefs. The Church Amendments were enacted after a Montana court ordered a Catholic hospital to perform a tubal ligation on a woman, in violation of the church's beliefs against sterilization. Before the hospital appealed the case, Congress acted. The law states that no court or public agency can require any doctor or hospital to perform any procedure that would violate that person's or hospital's religious or moral beliefs. The law also makes it illegal for private hospitals to discriminate or to refuse to hire personnel who refuse to participate in abortions or sterilizations because of their religious beliefs.

Medicaid and Medicare Managed Care Plans

In 1998 the Church Amendments were expanded to cover Medicaid and Medicare managed care plans. If those plans are run by religious organizations, the plans may refuse to provide for, reimburse for, or provide coverage of treatments if the organization objects to those services on religious or moral grounds. If the plans refuse to cover treatments on those grounds, the plan must inform enrollees of these restrictions before or during enrollment or within 90 days of the date the restrictive policies are adopted by the plan.

Congress was concerned that by expanding the Church Amendments Medicaid patients' access to health care would be too limited. As a result, the law requires that if you are enrolled in a managed care plan that is unwilling or unable to provide a particular service, the state must take positive steps to ensure that the service is truly available to you through another system and that you know it is available.

FEDERAL REGULATIONS

In addition to the federal laws relating to religious institutions, there are federal regulations governing sterilizations for institutions that receive federal funds. Many hospitals are covered by these regulations. They include a mandatory waiting period, a specific informed consent form, a requirement for reaffirmation of consent, and other protections. They are a very important part of the law affecting sterilizations.

THE MENTALLY DISABLED

Involuntary Sterilization

Most of us are able to choose whether or not we want to undergo some form of sterilization, whether it is a vasectomy, a tubal ligation, or some other method. But not all people are able to make that type of decision. Some mentally disabled persons are not able to understand what it means to have sexual intercourse or to become pregnant. They are unable to use ordinary means of birth control or to make responsible decisions about intimate relationships. In these cases, guardians of mentally disabled persons may sometimes request to have the mentally disabled persons sterilized. This is known as involuntary sterilization.

The Guardian's Decision

This is a difficult decision for the guardian. The guardian— usually the mentally disabled person's parent—wants the mentally disabled woman to be sterilized because a pregnancy would be physically dangerous for her, as well as for the baby. In addition, the mentally disabled woman would most likely suffer psychological trauma by having a baby, only to have it taken away because she was incapable of taking care of it.

STATE LAWS

Involuntary Sterilization and Eugenics

Very few state legislatures currently have laws regarding involuntary sterilization. Part of the reason is that involuntary sterilization is often associated with the now discredited theory of **eugenics,** which is the science of improving the qualities of a breed or species.

 LEARNING THE LINGO

Eugenics: Improving the genetic qualities of the human race by allowing only approved people to have children.

The goal of eugenics is to create a better, more capable society by encouraging people who share the most desirable genetic traits to have children. The flip side is that eugenics discourages babies among people who are predicted to have defective children, including the mentally ill and the mentally and physically handicapped. Eugenics was promoted as a way to clean the gene pool and was often the tool of white supremacists.

In the early 1900s, many scientists believed that mental disabilities were inherited. Those disabilities were blamed for crime, poverty, and perversion. Involuntary sterilization was even mandatory for convicted criminals in some states. Sterilization was seen as necessary to protect the rest of society.

 BLAMING THE VICTIM

"The feebleminded are a parasitic, predatory class, never capable of self-support or of managing their own affairs. They cause unutterable sorrow at home and are a menace and danger to the community. Feebleminded women are almost invariably immoral, and if at large usually become carriers of venereal disease or give birth to children who are as defective as themselves. . . . Every feebleminded person, especially the high-grade imbecile, is a potential criminal, needing only the proper environment and opportunity for the development and expression of his criminal tendencies."

Albert Deutsch, The Mentally Ill in America: A History of Their Care and Treatment from Colonial Times *(Columbia University Press, 2d ed., 1949)*

Carrie Buck

The most famous case of involuntary sterilization is Carrie Buck, who tried to avoid being sterilized—and lost. Carrie was committed to the State Colony for Epileptics and Feebleminded in Virginia when she was 17 years old. She had left her husband and given birth to a daughter out of wedlock. She was committed for moral imbecility.

Her mother had been committed to the same institution four years earlier. Doctors pointed to Carrie and her mother as proof that mental illness and feeblemindedness were inherited and tried to have Carrie sterilized. Carrie's attorney fought all the way to the U.S. Supreme Court, arguing that involuntary sterilization violated Carrie's constitutional right of bodily integrity. Carrie lost. It was later reportedly discovered that she was not mentally ill.

In 1927, U.S. Supreme Court Justice Oliver Wendell Holmes wrote the historic opinion that allowed Carrie Buck to be involuntarily sterilized:

> We have seen more than once that the public welfare may call upon the best citizens for their lives. It would be strange if it could not call upon those who already sap the strength of the State for these lesser sacrifices, often not felt to be such by those concerned, in order to prevent our being swamped with incompetence. It is better for all the world, if instead of waiting to execute degenerate offspring for crime, or to let them starve for their imbecility, society can prevent those who are manifestly unfit from continuing their kind. The principle that sustains compulsory vaccination is broad enough to cover cutting the Fallopian tubes. Three generations of imbeciles are enough. (*Buck v. Bell,* 274 U.S. 200, 207 [1927])

This decision has never been explicitly overturned.

A Right to Privacy

Society began to turn away from eugenics and involuntary sterilization during World War II after learning that it was a favored technique of Adolf Hitler. During this time, the courts were beginning to develop a theory of law that gave us more privacy as to the choices we make in our intimate relationships, including whether to have children. Also during this time, society's perception of the mentally retarded began to change. The mentally disabled were no longer automatically confined to institutions.

By the 1960s, involuntary sterilization was considered an unjustified intrusion into our right to liberty and privacy. Today, involuntary sterilization is allowed only to protect the mentally disabled person. It cannot be used to protect society.

THE COURTS

The Judge's Role

The legislatures have chosen to not act, so the decision as to when a mentally disabled person should be sterilized is left up to judges. The judge's power to make such an important decision rests on a legal doctrine called *parens patriae* (the principle that the state is guardian of those under legal disability). This lets judges protect those people who are incapable of protecting themselves because of their disabilities.

The Best Interests Standard

Most states require judges to consider only the **best interests** of the mentally disabled person. Judges are not allowed to consider whether sterilization would be in the best interests of society or of the mentally disabled person's guardian or family.

The **best interests** standard requires the judge to consider several factors:

- Whether the disabled person is, in fact, able to become pregnant or to impregnate a woman.
- The likelihood that the person will have sexual intercourse, either voluntary or involuntary.
- Whether the disabled woman will experience psychological damage or trauma if she becomes pregnant or gives birth.
- Whether the disabled person will be traumatized by the sterilization procedure.
- Whether the person is unable to understand reproduction and birth control.
- The possibility that there are less drastic means of contraception, such as the pill or condoms, and whether those forms of birth control are medically advisable.
- The ability of the disabled person to care for a child.

- The possibility that scientific advances will occur in the foreseeable future that either will improve the person's condition or will be an alternative to sterilization.
- Whether the guardian's primary concern is for the disabled person, rather than for his or her own or the public's convenience.

A Real Patient

Let's apply these factors to an actual patient. One of the most recent cases involved a 24-year-old woman we will call Cathy, although that is not her real name. Cathy is mute, with the mental capabilities of a child about four years old. She suffers from moderately severe retardation, grand mal epilepsy, cerebral palsy, and scoliosis. Cathy's mother asked a judge to approve a laparoscopic tubal ligation for Cathy. The procedure would make Cathy sterile.

Cathy is physically capable of becoming pregnant. She also has a boyfriend at the assisted-living facility where she lives. There are times when Cathy is unsupervised and could have sex without the knowledge of her caretakers.

Cathy is extremely affectionate and craves physical closeness, to the point that she has hugged several members of a judge's staff. During an examination with a psychologist, Cathy exposed her stomach to him and attempted to tickle his. Cathy does not understand the consequences of sexual activity.

Getting pregnant would be traumatic for Cathy. The chances are good that a pregnancy would cause an increase in seizures. Also, Cathy relies on certain medications to stay alive. Those medications are known to cause birth defects in a fetus. It is doubtful Cathy would be able to carry a pregnancy to term. Even if she could, delivering the baby would jeopardize her life.

In contrast, the trauma from the proposed tubal ligation would be minimal. Her menstrual cycle would not change, and she is unable to understand how the tubal ligation relates to having a baby. A laparoscopic tubal ligation requires a small incision near the navel and is usually done on an out-patient basis. Cathy would probably have to stay in the hospital for a day or two to monitor her condition because of her other medical problems.

One of the most important factors is whether some other form of birth control would work instead. This requires the judge to consider and to compare all of the pros and cons of all the available contraceptives. Many contraceptives, though, have side effects that could be devastating to a person with other medical problems.

Cathy is required to take high levels of medication several times a day to control her seizures, which sometimes last for over an hour. Her doctors are concerned that birth control pills will interfere with her other medication, and sometimes Cathy refuses to take her medication altogether. Besides, her high levels of medication could have disastrous effects on a fetus. Cathy is not capable of using a contraceptive sponge or an IUD. Sex education was not a solution either. Cathy is very trusting, even of strangers, and seeks out physical contact with people she meets for the first time.

Cathy is totally incapable of caring for a child. She is, in fact, unable to take care of herself. Her caretakers usually check on her every 15 to 30 minutes because of her history of severe seizures. She is sometimes uncooperative and abuses herself by scratching and biting herself.

There do not appear to be any scientific advances on the horizon that would improve Cathy's condition. There is no cure for epilepsy and no way to repair her brain damage. There is no indication that a new contraceptive or sterilization technique will be developed soon that will provide an alternative to the tubal ligation.

Finally, Cathy's mother wants only what is best for Cathy. She requested the tubal ligation out of concern and affection for her daughter. She wants to protect her daughter's life and spare her any further trauma.

In this case, after weighing all the factors, the judge gave Cathy's mother the authority to consent to a laparoscopic tubal ligation.

As Applied to Men

While the main concern is the well-being of mentally disabled women, the same "best interests" standard applies when a guardian requests to have a mentally disabled man sterilized.

BANNING INVOLUNTARY STERILIZATION

There are some states that ban involuntary sterilization outright. Programs that allow mentally disabled persons to live and work in the community have changed the way we look at those with disabilities. They are no longer hidden away in institutions. They are now our neighbors and live relatively "normal" lives. Part of living a normal life is being independent and making your own choices as to sexual activity. Involuntary sterilization, according to some courts, is cruel and should not be tolerated.

THE WORLD AT YOUR FINGERTIPS

- Diane B. Paul offers a basic introduction to eugenics in *Controlling Human Heredity: 1865 to the Present* (Humanity Books, 1995). She discusses how it came to be prevalent in our history, whose interests it serves, and how it will affect our future.
- *Back to the Asylum: The Future of Mental Health Law and Policy in the United States* by John Q. La Fond and Mary L. Durham (Oxford University Press, 1992) offers a history of how the law has treated persons with mental disabilities, as well as some predictions for the future.
- *The Surgical Solution: A History of Involuntary Sterilization in the United States* by Philip R. Reilley (Johns Hopkins University Press, 1991) examines the role of eugenics in the United States, as well as the role it is currently taking among the mainstream population.

YOU MUST REMEMBER THIS

- Hospitals associated with religious organizations are not required to perform voluntary sterilizations.
- Involuntary sterilization is no longer considered a solution to crime, poverty, and degeneracy.
- In most states, a mentally disabled person's guardian can request that the person be sterilized.
- A judge will determine whether sterilization is in the best interests of the mentally disabled person.
- If there is some other way to protect the mentally disabled person, the judge will not authorize the sterilization.

CHAPTER 10

Midwifery and Birthing Choices

Traditional Alternatives Face Legal Challenges

Patty and Seth are planning for the birth of their first child. They do not want to be in a stark hospital when their baby is delivered. They would much rather have the baby delivered by a midwife at their home. As Patty and Seth begin their search for a midwife, they find that only specially trained nurses are allowed to be midwives in their state, and those nurses must be certified. Nurse-midwives must also be sponsored by a doctor in order to do home deliveries. The problem is that doctors' insurance companies do not allow doctors to sponsor midwives. Patty learned from a friend of a midwife named Betty with 17 years experience, but Betty is not certified. Betty recently moved to Patty's town from another state where midwives did not need to be certified. Betty is willing to deliver Patty and Seth's baby in their home, but Patty is worried that it would be illegal. Patty and Seth feel as though they can't choose to have their baby delivered as they wish.

CHILDBIRTH CHOICES

Childbirth is one of the most intense experiences you will ever face. At such an important time you want more control and more choices, not fewer. Yet the state has a powerful interest in your safety and security and in protecting you from harm.

The state legislature's difficult job is to pass laws that will protect your health while at the same respecting your individual rights to privacy and to choice in reproductive matters, such as having a baby. How childbirth should be handled is looked at from the standpoint of safety for you and the baby, the costs of childbirth options, your freedom of choice, and the quality of care available.

DRAWING LINES

Courts have ruled that our constitutional right to privacy protects our choice of whether to have a baby, what contraceptives to use, and whether a pregnancy can be terminated. However, a Colorado court ruled that a woman's right to privacy does not include the personal choice of whether to have a midwife deliver her baby.

Childbirth today is viewed much differently than it was even 20 years ago. Childbirth classes are now the norm, giving more information and allowing more choices during delivery. A number of communities offer parents the option of giving birth in a hospital, at home, or at a birthing center. The majority of births still take place in the hospital, but that experience has changed as well. Today women may accept or reject medication for pain, as well as enemas or other procedures. The woman's family and friends are allowed to remain with her throughout the labor and delivery. The new mother decides whether to keep the baby with her in her room or to have the baby cared for in the nursery.

What's Law Got to Do with It?

These changes were not, in large part, brought about by changes in the law (except for midwifery, which is discussed in a moment). Rather, hospitals changed their policies as a result of societal changes, such as women becoming stronger advocates in their health care. Also, as health care has become more competitive, hospitals have had to become more attuned to the needs and wants of pregnant women and change their policies accordingly.

This does not mean that parents haven't tried to use the legal system to change the status quo. Several couples who had taken Lamaze classes sued a hospital because the hospital prohibited fathers from being in the delivery room. The couples argued that they had a constitutional right to choose whether the fathers should be present at the birth. The court ruled that there is no constitutional right to choose birthing methods, and the couples lost their case.

Doctors and Home Births

The majority of doctors refuse to do home births because of the fear of malpractice lawsuits. Even a malpractice lawsuit that has no basis and is thrown out of court or won by the doctor is very costly and time-consuming. Nevertheless, some doctors are in favor of home births, believing them to be the better choice for expectant mothers at low risk of a difficult childbirth. One doctor in Chicago claims his group of physicians has delivered 14,000 babies in home births in the past 25 years.

MIDWIVES

In the United States, midwives were in charge of delivering babies until relatively recently. In Manhattan in 1916, only 19 percent of births took place in hospitals. In less populated areas, this percentage was even lower. For example, in Maryland, less than 3 percent of births outside Baltimore took place in hospitals in 1921. As training for medical doctors became more formalized, the practice of obstetrics gained prominence and a greater number of urban women began to seek doctors to oversee the birthing process. Midwives were still the predominant caretakers for pregnant women in rural areas, though, where fewer doctors were available. In 1930, the American Board of Obstetrics and Gynecology was established and obstetrics became a recognized specialty field of medical practice. Slowly, society began to view obstetricians as more educated and safer than midwives. Today, the vast majority of births occur in hospitals equipped with the technology and staff to handle any emergency that may arise in childbirth. Yet, midwifery still exists.

Midwifery Laws

Every state has a law regarding midwifery. These laws put restrictions on who may be a midwife, but they do not prohibit midwifery outright. Most of these laws do not regulate where and in what manner the birth takes place, only what type of medical professional is allowed to assist and attend to the expectant mother.

These laws do not ban parents from hiring midwives or from choosing to have the baby at home. Parents can choose to be attended by a midwife. The midwife, though, may not have hospital admitting privileges, so that might eliminate one option parents have for where their baby should be born.

MORE LINES DRAWN

Though we have certain constitutional protections regarding our reproductive rights, parents do not have a constitutionally protected interest in the manner and the circumstances surrounding the birth of their children.

Certified Nurse-Midwives

Today certified nurse-midwives are able to practice legally in all 50 states. Certified nurse-midwives are trained through programs approved by the American College of Nurse-Midwives (ACNM). An estimated 4,000 nurse-midwives are presently certified throughout the country, with most of them working in conjunction with doctors.

The certification requirements, like certification and licensing requirements for nurses and doctors, are an attempt to assure that qualified individuals in a specialty are recognized. They are a way of protecting the public.

How midwives are to be certified differs from state to state. One state allows that nurses can be certified as midwives, but the department that is to do the certification stopped certifying midwives years ago. So even though the law allows certified midwives to attend expectant mothers, in reality a soon-to-be mother would have a difficult time locating a midwife to be present at a home birth in that state.

Allowing for certified nurse-midwives is essentially a compromise between obstetricians and lay midwives. Certified nurse-midwives are registered nurses trained in obstetrics. How closely they are regulated varies from state to state. Some hospitals ban certified nurse-midwives from attending births in the hospital, preferring that only the hospital's doctors be present.

On the other hand, some states allow certified nurse-midwives to obtain hospital privileges, to prescribe medications to women, and to attend births in the home, hospital, or birth centers. They can provide family planning and women's health care, as well as prenatal and birthing care.

Licensed or Certified Midwives

Licensed or certified midwives (sometimes also called "direct-entry midwives") are not required to be nurses, although nurses are not excluded from being licensed or certified. These midwives are trained through a combination of apprenticeships, correspondence courses, self-study, and formal schooling. These midwives must meet or exceed the state's requirements for midwifery by documenting their experience and passing both skills and academic exams.

Direct-entry midwifery is legally recognized in some way in more than half the states. A handful of these states allow Medicaid reimbursement for licensed midwives, as do many insurance companies. Licensed midwives sign birth certificates and are generally required to have doctor backup and emergency procedures lined up in case something goes wrong during delivery.

TALKING TO A LAWYER
When a Midwife Lies about Being Licensed

Q. Our child was born at home with the assistance of a midwife. Our state requires that midwives be licensed. The midwife told us she was licensed, but after the birth we found out that she was not licensed. Do we have some legal recourse against the midwife for lying to us?

A. There are many potential avenues for redressing the intentional fabrication by the midwife about her licensure status. At the outset, a complaint could be lodged with the respective state professional licensing body. The midwife was practicing a licensed profession without the benefit of the applicable state license. Many states classify such an offense as a crime, and, thus, this could result in criminal liability for the midwife.

Additionally, the intentional misrepresentation of her credentials depending on the circumstances may rise to the level of false advertising, which could be criminally prosecuted by the state attorney general's office. The false advertising claim may also result in the court's awarding the parents the monetary costs of the midwife's service.

Finally, given the good result for the delivery, it is unlikely that a viable claim for malpractice or negligence exists. The necessary element of damages for such a cause of action appears missing. However, in this situation the parent's motivation for pursuing legal recourse must be somewhat altruistic, that is, protecting others and punishing a liar. Realistically there doesn't appear to be much of a financial incentive for action under these circumstances.

Answer by Salvatore J. Russo,
Executive Senior Counsel,
New York City Health & Hospitals
Corporation, New York, New York

Traditional or Lay Midwifery

States differ widely as to how they regulate lay midwifery. This means that the quantity and quality of available midwives varies greatly from one state to the next. Some states make traditional midwifery illegal, no matter what. Other states have laws regarding certified nurse-midwives, but these laws do not mention traditional midwives at all. In those states, lay midwives are generally considered acceptable as long as they follow the same rules as the rest of us in not engaging in the unlicensed practice of medicine. In some states this may mean that midwives are banned from asking for payment for their services.

 LEARNING THE LINGO

Traditional or lay midwifery: Midwives who are not licensed by a state and are not required to be trained as nurses.

Some midwives are part of a religious group and practice only within that specific community. There are currently an estimated 2,000 to 3,000 traditional midwives practicing in the United States. It is difficult to get an accurate count, however, because these midwives are not licensed.

Lay midwifery is considered in some states as the **unlicensed practice of medicine,** which is illegal. Midwifery is considered practicing medicine because courts have held that pregnancy is a physical condition that requires medical attention, the use of medical instruments, and possibly drugs. Those are the essential factors in practicing medicine, which only licensed doctors are allowed to do.

Midwives are rarely brought up on charges of practicing without a license, although it occasionally does happen. In California, several women acted as traditional (unlicensed) midwives for women in childbirth, even though a California law banned them from doing so. The women argued that the law deprived pregnant women of their right to privacy. The court said that the law against attending and assisting a pregnant woman in childbirth did not violate the expectant mother's right to privacy. The court said that the state has an interest in the life and the well-being of the unborn child. Thus, the state could require midwives to be licensed, even though that would significantly reduce the number of midwives available to expectant mothers.

At this point there is no incentive for midwives or expectant parents to go to the courts for an expensive and lengthy battle over birthing rights. The cost of the lawsuit would outweigh any financial gain for midwives. The lawsuit would likely take years—or at least longer than nine months. On the rare occasions when midwives have sued to try to be able to practice without being licensed, the midwives usually lose the court battle.

For the most part, traditional midwives regulate themselves within their states. Opinion is sharply divided over whether that self-regulation is enough to guarantee quality. Some observers point out that qualified midwives perform good work and provide an alternative for parents, but unqualified, unlicensed midwives can (and unfortunately sometimes do) cause real harm.

Some self-regulation programs appear to have real merit. In Oregon, the Oregon Midwifery Council puts forth its own certification standards for traditional midwives and requires intense training for its midwives. It offers advanced certification for midwives to specialize in higher-risk births, such as breech or multiple births. Some of the Oregon Midwifery Council's regulations were later enacted by the state legislature to license traditional midwives and to allow them to be reimbursed under the state Medicaid program.

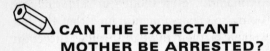 **CAN THE EXPECTANT
MOTHER BE ARRESTED?**

So what is your legal risk if you use a traditional midwife? Keep in mind that there is no law that says the expectant mother cannot hire a traditional midwife. The laws apply to the midwives. You cannot be arrested or charged with a crime for having a midwife deliver your baby, although an unlicensed midwife could be charged with the unlicensed practice of medicine for assisting you in childbirth.

THE WORLD AT YOUR FINGERTIPS

- For more information on your childbirth choices, read *Gentle Birth Choices: A Comprehensive Book and Video Guide to Making Informed Decisions About Birthing Centers, Etc.* by Barbara Harper (Inner Traditions Intl. Ltd., 1996).
- Read about the personal experiences of midwives in Penfield Chester's *Sisters on a Journey: Portraits of American Midwives* (Rutgers University Press, 1997). The book includes stories from midwives practicing both legally and illegally.
- One organization that lobbies for more birthing choices is the Center for Humane Options in Childbirth Experiences. For legislative updates on birthing options, visit their website at *http://www.birthchoice.org/*.

YOU MUST REMEMBER THIS

- Every state makes provisions for at least certified nurse-midwives.
- How midwives are regulated varies from state to state.
- State laws regulate who may practice as a midwife, not

whether an expectant mother may have a midwife present or have a home birth.

- Parents cannot be charged with a crime for using a midwife that is not licensed to practice.

CHAPTER 11

Abortion

*A Deeply Felt Issue Continues to
Spawn Litigation, Controversy*

*Jackie is 15 years old and unmarried. She wants to someday marry and have a
family—but not now. Jackie just found out she is three weeks pregnant. She is
considering having an abortion. Does she have to tell her parents? Does she
need their permission for an abortion? What about her boyfriend? Can he stop
her from having the abortion?*

HOW ABORTION BECAME LEGAL

Until the early 1970s, about two-thirds of the states banned abortion except where it was necessary to save a mother's life. The other states had similar laws but allowed for a few other instances where women could seek an abortion, such as incest or rape.

In the years leading up to the 1970s, the U.S. Supreme Court handed down a series of rulings that recognized a zone of personal privacy in reproductive matters. These rulings limited the authority of states. For example, the Court found that it was unconstitutional for the state to pass laws that limited your right to contraceptives. Another ruling struck down a law that prevented interracial couples from marrying or engaging in certain intimate relationships. The Court held that such laws invade the right to privacy. The Court ruled that the Constitution gives us the right to keep deeply personal concerns and choices to ourselves.

In 1973, the Supreme Court decided that women have a fundamental right to have an abortion in the landmark case *Roe v. Wade*. In that case a single pregnant woman (Roe) brought a lawsuit against the state of Texas. A Texas law made abortion illegal except in situations where the mother's life was at stake.

BEFORE LEGALIZATION

Before abortion became legal, an estimated 1.2 million women sought illegal abortions each year. Unlicensed persons who were not doctors performed many of these abortions. The conditions were often unsanitary, and women were at high risk of infection, hemorrhage, disfiguration, and death. Whiskey was sometimes used as an anesthetic.

At the same time, the fact that such laws were in place no doubt limited the number of abortions performed.

The Court decided that the Constitution guarantees you a right to privacy from state interference, which includes whether or not you decide to have an abortion. The practice remains highly controversial to this day.

In the words of the majority opinion of the Supreme Court in a case decided in 2000, "Millions of Americans believe that life begins at conception and consequently that an abortion is akin to causing the death of an innocent child; they recoil at the thought of a law that would permit it. Other millions fear that a law that forbids abortion could condemn many American women to lives that lack dignity, depriving them of equal liberty and leading those with least resources to undergo illegal abortions with the attendant risks of death and suffering. [These are] virtually irreconcilable points of view" (*Stenberg v. Carhart,* 530 US 914 [2000]).

The Court has put some limits on this right to an abortion. There is no absolute right to have an abortion at any time, in any place. A state can pass laws regulating abortion as long as certain boundaries are not crossed. The state cannot completely override a woman's right to terminate a pregnancy, but the state does have an interest in protecting the health of pregnant women and the potentiality of human life. A man's right to prevent an abortion—or to force his partner to have an abortion—is not protected because the pregnancy is not considered part of a man's "bodily integrity."

Until the end of the first trimester, only the pregnant woman and her doctor can decide whether a pregnancy should be terminated.

After the first trimester, the state can pass laws regulating abortion as long as the laws are reasonably related to the pregnant mother's health. Once the fetus becomes **viable,** meaning it can live outside the womb, the state can regulate and even outlaw abortion unless it is necessary to save the mother's life. At that point the state's interest in protecting the fetus becomes paramount over the mother's rights. There is no definite point, however, as to when a fetus becomes viable.

LEGAL ABORTION TODAY

Undue Burdens

The legal standard for abortion is largely the same today as it was after *Roe v. Wade* in 1973, with one major difference. Today, a court will look at a state law to see if it places an **undue burden** on a woman's right to have an abortion. If it does not place an undue burden on her access to an abortion, then the law is upheld. Again, after a fetus becomes viable, the state can pass laws making it more difficult for a woman to obtain an abortion.

LEARNING THE LINGO

Undue burden: The substantial hardship that a law would put in the path of a woman seeking an abortion.

Waiting Periods

Twelve states currently require a waiting period, usually 24 hours, before a woman can have an abortion. This waiting period requires women to make two visits to the clinic where the abortion will be performed. At the first visit, the woman will talk to the doctor or other medical professional about her choice to terminate the pregnancy. The doctor may be required to give the woman specific information, the effect of which may be to discourage her from having the abortion. The woman then has to wait 24 hours to think about whether or not she wants to terminate her pregnancy.

Such laws have been upheld as constitutional, although opponents of the waiting period argue that the woman already has time to think over her decision between the time she finds out she is pregnant and the time she schedules the abortion. Because the waiting period requires two visits to the clinic, some argue that it can be difficult and even traumatic for women considering abortion, especially if there are protesters outside the clinic.

Partial-Birth Abortions

The biggest debate today is over so-called "partial-birth abortions." State laws usually define partial-birth abortions as any abortion in which the doctor "partially vaginally delivers a living fetus before killing the fetus and completing the delivery." These bans generally apply to nonviable as well as viable fetuses.

In *Stenberg v. Carhart,* decided in 2000, the U.S. Supreme Court, divided 5 to 4, struck down a Nebraska statute banning partial-birth abortion unless it is necessary to save the mother's life. The Court held that the statute failed constitutional muster because it lacked an exception for the preservation of the health of the mother and because it unduly burdened the right to choose to have an abortion.

The Nebraska law also imposed third-party consent requirements on a woman's decision to terminate a pregnancy. The law created a private right of action, allowing the husbands of married women and the parents of minor women to sue the doctor unless they had consented to the partial-birth abortion. The Court held that this provision had the effect of requiring those family members' consent to the woman's abortion in violation of the Constitution.

Unconstitutional Undue Burden

This Supreme Court ruling was in keeping with judicial trends. In almost every state that has passed a law banning partial-birth abortions, courts have found the laws to be unconstitutional. These laws often impose an undue burden on a woman's right to terminate a pregnancy and place the health of women in danger. Most fail to include adequate exceptions for abortions when the woman's life or health require it.

Arizona

An Arizona court found that state's partial-birth abortion law unconstitutional because it was "susceptible to different interpretations" and therefore failed to give doctors fair warning of what conduct it prohibited. The court also held that the ban constituted an undue burden on the right to have an abortion because, in prohibiting the safest, most common methods of abortion after the first trimester, the ban would force women to undergo riskier procedures to terminate a pregnancy.

Illinois

An Illinois law banning partial-birth abortions was struck down on three grounds:

1. The law was unconstitutionally vague. Its terms, the court found, were "undefined and subject to more than one interpretation," leaving doctors uncertain "whether the legislature intended to ban a specific practice or entire abortion procedures."

2. The court found that the ban imposes an undue burden by banning the most common methods of abortion, including those used in both the first and second trimesters.

3. The law allowed parents to sue doctors who provided a partial-birth abortion to a minor without the parents'

consent. The Illinois court reasoned that this provision effectively imposes a parental consent requirement, without allowing a judicial bypass option.

Florida

In Florida, a court rejected the argument that the partial-birth abortion law targeted a single, discrete procedure. The law's definition contained "broad and amorphous language" that could cover virtually all abortions performed in the second trimester of pregnancy. Thus, the court held that the ban violated "a woman's right to choose to have an abortion prior to the viability of the fetus." The court also held the ban unconstitutional on the ground that it contained no exception that considered the mother's life and only a very narrow exception for when the mother's life was in danger.

On a National Level

Bills have been repeatedly introduced in Congress to make partial-birth abortions illegal on a national level. At this writing, none of the laws have passed.

MINORS AND ABORTIONS

Parental Consent Laws

The rights of parents to raise their children as they see fit collides with a woman's right to privacy and abortion when she is under the age of 18. When it comes to women under 18 years of age seeking abortions, state laws fall into three groups:

- Girls do not have to get their parents' permission or notify them of the abortion.
- Girls do not have to get their parents' permission, but they do have to notify their parents that they are planning on having an abortion.
- Girls have to get their parents' permission to have an abortion.

THE PEDIATRICIANS SPEAK

"Legislation mandating parental involvement does not achieve the in-tended benefit of promoting family communication, but it does increase the risk of harm to the adolescent by delaying access to appropriate medical care. . . . [M]inors should not be compelled or required to involve their parents in their decisions to obtain abortions, although they should be encouraged to discuss their pregnancies with their parents and other responsible adults."

American Academy of Pediatrics, Committee on Adolescence, "The Adolescent's Right to Confidential Care When Considering Abortion," Pediatrics 97, no. 5 (May 1996): 746

All parental consent laws are required to be very limited in their range, and they must include what is called a **judicial bypass option.** A judicial bypass option allows a woman under 18 to go to court for a judicial hearing when her parents refuse to consent to an abortion. This change allows minor women to request that a judge waive parental consent requirements, par-ticularly when the minor is mature or when the judge finds that an abortion would be in the best interests of the minor.

This can be a traumatic experience for young women. Court-

TOO YOUNG TO DECIDE?

"Depending upon what ruling I make I hold in my hands the power to kill an unborn child. In our society it's a lot easier to kill an unborn child than the most vicious murderer. . . . I don't believe that this particular juvenile has sufficient intellectual capacity to make a determination that she is willing to kill her own child."

A Missouri judge, denying permission for a young woman to have an abortion

rooms are intimidating even to adults, much less minors. Hearings are scheduled during school hours. The woman must discuss her most personal concerns with the judge, a total stranger.

The Argument on Parental Consent

Those in favor of parental consent laws say young women need the support of their families when making such significant decisions about abortions. Many believe that parental consent laws promote abstinence, arguing that if girls knew they couldn't have abortions without telling their parents, then they would not be so willing to have sex and risk pregnancy.

Those against parental consent laws point out that such laws may exacerbate already difficult situations in certain families and may even increase instances of abuse against the women involved.

A PRACTICAL EFFECT OF PARENTAL CONSENT?

A 1992 study by the American Medical Association showed that parental consent and notification laws "increase the gestational age at which the induced pregnancy termination occurs, thereby also increasing the risk associated with the procedure." A first- or second-trimester abortion is considered medically safer than childbirth. For each week that goes by after the first eight weeks, the risk of death or major complications significantly increases.

American Medical Association, "Induced Termination of Pregnancy Before and After Roe v. Wade, *Trends in the Mortality and Morbidity of Women," JAMA 268, no. 22 (December 1992): 3238*

After Massachusetts passed its parental consent law, one study found that one-third of the minors who had abortions traveled out of state to do so. Those minors tended to be affluent teenagers with access to the cash and transportation required to cross state lines.

HUSBANDS AND ABORTIONS

Wife versus Husband

In a perfect world, a husband and a wife would agree on whether the wife should have an abortion. In the present world, if a husband and a wife do not agree, then the wife's decision is final. There is no law that gives husbands the right to have input into whether their wives have abortions.

This is not because the husband's opinion does not matter. It is because the wife's right to control her body is paramount over any right of her husband. As long as women are the ones who become pregnant and the status of abortion law in this country remains unchanged, the women's right to abortion will outweigh the men's right to have any input into the decision.

A Husband's Consent

At one point some states required a husband's consent before a woman could have an abortion. This law was found to be unconstitutional because it placed the husband's interest above the wife's right to privacy. When the decision to have or not to have an abortion is not mutual, the husband cannot have veto power over his wife.

THE WORLD AT YOUR FINGERTIPS

- *Abortion: Rights, Options, and Choices (Issue and Debate)* by Tricia Andryszewski discusses the legal and philosophical aspects of the abortion debate, concluding with the political climate surrounding the issue today (Millbrook Press, 1996).
- *Abortion* by Rita James Simon (Praeger Publishing, 1998) compares American abortion laws with those in other countries. In addition, she discusses how a nation's policies on population control affect the countries' laws on abortion.

- *The Ethics of Abortion: Pro-Life Vs. Pro-Choice (Contemporary Issues)* by Robert M. Baird (Editor) and Stuart E. Rosenbaum (Editor) offers essays from both sides of the debate, as well as excerpts from three Supreme Court decisions regarding abortion (Prometheus Books, 1993).
- The American Civil Liberties Union's website offers a comprehensive look at women's rights to reproductive choices. Their online address is *www.aclu.org/issues/reproduct/hmrr. html*.

YOU MUST REMEMBER THIS

- States can pass laws regarding abortion as long as the laws do not place an undue burden on a woman's right to have an abortion.
- States can require a woman to wait 24 hours to have an abortion.
- Some states require minors to get parental consent before seeking an abortion. The laws are constitutional, but they must give minors the option of seeking a judicial bypass.
- Husbands do not have the right to stop their wives from having abortions.

PART FOUR

People with Disabilities

A Surprisingly Large Category,

Much Affected by the Law

Illness and injury can strike anyone at anytime. Such an illness or injury can affect every part of our lives, from the types of work we can do to moving about our own homes. The law provides some protection if you become disabled.

Initially we will go into depth on the Americans with Disabilities Act (ADA). We will explain what the law considers a disability and how your disability must affect your life before it falls under the act. We will also take a look at how the ADA applies to specific medical issues, such as menopause, pregnancy, and AIDS. Next we will explore your rights to confidentiality regarding your disability. In some cases your doctor is required to report your illness to the public health department. This is a major concern for those with HIV or AIDS, but it applies to other disabilities as well.

We will then discuss mandatory testing, particularly as it applies to vaccinations or people with HIV and AIDS. May your employer require that you be tested for tuberculosis or AIDS? We will answer that and other questions. Then we will explain the ins and outs of tort liability. We will define a tort and clarify what is needed to prove that someone committed one against you.

The final chapter in this section considers the legal implications and present status of quarantines. Quarantines do still exist, although the issue is controversial. When can the state keep you from leaving your own house? Find out in this chapter.

If you would like more information on these topics, please check at the end of the guide for additional resources and websites regarding these issues.

CHAPTER 12

People with Disabilities/AIDS

Read This Chapter to Learn About How the Law Protects You

Leroy is HIV positive. He is taking medication and so far he shows no symptoms of AIDS. Leroy's doctor does not want to provide medical treatment to him because he is afraid that Leroy will infect him, his staff, or his other patients. The doctor wants to refer Leroy to another doctor who specializes in HIV and AIDS. Leroy does not want to change doctors. Leroy claims that he is disabled due to his HIV status and that his doctor is discriminating against him in violation of the Americans with Disabilities Act. That is not Leroy's only problem. His employer switched to a different type of health plan, and his insurance coverage is being reduced from a $1,000,000 cap to a $5,000 cap on medical care costs. Without insurance, Leroy will lose his house and be forced to go on welfare, at which time Medicaid will cover his medical treatment.

THE AMERICANS WITH DISABILITIES ACT (ADA)

What Is It?

The ADA is a federal law enacted in 1990. It applies to all state and local government employers and private sector employers with at least fifteen employees. It also applies to unions with at least fifteen members and employment agencies. Its purpose is to protect you from discrimination if you have a disability. This includes discrimination in your employment, housing, public accommodations (such as hospitals or medical clinics), education, transportation, and communication. The ADA is somewhat controversial because it was meant to be flexible. That flexibility means that you and someone else, such as your employer, may understand the ADA as meaning two completely different things. The result is that a court in your state may find that you are not disabled under the ADA, whereas a court in another state could find that someone else with the same condition as you *is* disabled. These differences are still being ironed out.

A number of ADA cases reach the U.S. Supreme Court each year. The Supreme Court attempts to resolve many of these issues to make the ADA more uniform among the states. Sometimes the Supreme Court opinions clear up an issue that divides the states. Other times the opinions leave even more room for interpretation.

What Is a Disability?

The ADA defines a **disability** as a physical or mental impairment that substantially limits a major life activity. Keep in mind that impairment is not enough. It must limit a major life activity to a significant degree.

 LEARNING THE LINGO

Disability: A physical or mental impairment that substantially limits a major life activity.

Major life activity: An important part of a person's life, such as working, learning, caring for oneself, walking, hearing, speaking, breathing, performing manual tasks, and having children.

Is My Condition a Disability If It Can Be Treated?

Probably not. This is where the flexibility of the ADA comes into the picture. If your vision is bad but you can drive and carry on your life by wearing eyeglasses or contact lenses, you are not disabled under the ADA. If you have high blood pressure that cannot be treated with medication or lifestyle changes, you have a disability. If you have high blood pressure that is regulated with medication, you do not have a disability because your medical condition does not substantially limit any of your major life activities.

Who Enforces the ADA?

The Equal Employment Opportunity Commission (EEOC) investigates complaints and files lawsuits under the ADA. Individuals may also file lawsuits in either state or federal court alleging violations of the ADA after exhausting the administrative procedures set up by the EEOC. The EEOC has regional offices in major cities throughout the country. It offers brochures that explain how to register a complaint. To receive these brochures, call 1-202-663-4900.

The complaint process goes something like this: You must file a charge with the EEOC in writing, describing the conduct that you believe violates the ADA. You *must* follow this step. If you do not, the court will dismiss your lawsuit. After you file your charge, the EEOC investigates your claim. If your state has a law that covers the matter, you must first file a charge with the state agency responsible for enforcing the state law before you can file with the EEOC. The state agency must have at least 60 days to investigate the complaint. After 60 days you can file the charge with the EEOC. The deadline for filing the charge with the EEOC is 300 days from the date the discrimination occurred, or within 30 days after the state agency finished its proceedings, whichever occurs first. If your state does not have a law that covers the matter, you must file the charge with the EEOC within 180 days from the date of the discriminatory act.

After your charge is filed with the EEOC, the agency investigates the complaint to determine whether there is reasonable cause to believe the law was violated. If the EEOC decides there is reasonable cause, it enters into conciliation with your employer and tries to settle the case. If settlement is unsuccessful, the EEOC will send you a letter informing you that you have 90 days to file a lawsuit in court. This is called a **right-to-sue** letter.

Although the EEOC has the authority to file lawsuits in court, it does so only in a small percentage of cases. Most of the time you must pursue a lawsuit on your own. If, after the investigation, the EEOC decides there is no reasonable cause to believe the law was violated, it will still send you a right-to-sue letter. The law gives you the right to have a court determine the merits of the complaint, even when the EEOC decides there is no merit. The **statute of limitations** for filing the lawsuit is 90 days from the date of receiving the right-to-sue letter. Statutes of limitations are time deadlines set by law for filing lawsuits. If a suit is filed after the time limit set by the statute, the court will almost always dismiss it.

Does This Apply to Me If I Work for the Federal Government?

No. Federal employees use a different procedure. All federal government agencies have Equal Employment Opportunity (EEO) counselors whose job it is to try to resolve discrimination complaints. Thus, you must first file any charge with the EEO counselor within 45 days of the date of the discriminatory act. The counselor investigates the matter and attempts to resolve the complaint. If you are not satisfied with the counselor's proposed settlement, you must, within 15 days, either request a hearing on the complaint or request a decision by the head of the agency without a hearing.

If you request a hearing, it is conducted by an independent administrative law judge who issues a decision. The judge's decision is sent to the director of the agency in question, who may reject, accept, or modify it. After the agency head issues a decision, you have three options. You can (1) accept the decision of the agency head, (2) file an appeal with the EEOC within 30 days, or (3) file a lawsuit in court within 90 days. If you decide to appeal to the EEOC, the EEOC has 180 days to review the file and make a final decision. If you are not satisfied with the EEOC's final decision, you can file a lawsuit in court within strictive setting, without being a danger to themselves or to others, then the state should place those people in the less restrictive setting. The key factor is the individual's medical condition. A person who requires treatment that is best given in an institution will still be placed in an institution. The Court recognized that it would never be appropriate for some mentally disabled patients to be treated outside an institution.

DISABILITY BENEFIT PLANS

What Is a Disability Benefit Plan?

A disability benefit plan provides you with benefits that replace your income if you are unable to work because of an illness or accident. It is a form of insurance that may be sponsored by your employer or that you may purchase on your own. The purpose is to provide you with income if you suffer from a disability. The amount of disability income to which you are entitled depends on your income level rather than on the type of disability you suffer.

How Does This Differ from Medical Insurance?

Medical insurance pays for your medical services. Disability benefits are paid directly to you so that you can pay your bills, such as groceries, the mortgage, or a car payment.

When Can I Collect Disability Benefits?

The majority of disability plans only provide benefits when you become totally disabled and unable to work. The plan can be either short-term or long-term. A short-term plan provides benefits—usually a portion of your regular wages—for a specified time period while you are disabled. Long-term plans begin after short-term disability income ends. The purpose of a long-term plan is to replace part of your income when it is unlikely that you will ever return to work due to the permanency of your disability.

90 days of receiving the EEOC decision. For more on the types of remedies available to you, see Chapter 17 on tort liability.

MENTAL HEALTH AND THE ADA

A significant number of lawsuits are being brought under the ADA to challenge the institutionalization of the mentally disabled. The primary issue is the extent to which the ADA requires that the mentally disabled be integrated into the community. An example of this is the case of a woman in Pennsylvania. She was put in a nursing home even though she could have lived in her home with assistance through a home health care program, which would have cost less than the nursing home. The home health care program, funded by the state, did not have any more funds available for her. The nursing home fund, however, did have funds available, and the woman was placed in the nursing home, regardless of the greater cost to taxpayers. The woman sued, and the court held that the ADA required that she be treated in the setting most integrated into the community, which was her home.

Recently a similar case reached the Supreme Court. Two mentally retarded women with psychiatric disorders were on waiting lists to be placed into group homes within the community. In the meantime the women were in psychiatric institutions. The state of Georgia told the Court that there were not enough funds to provide the women with community placements at that time. The Court held that when mentally disabled people are kept in institutions, although they could live in some other form of housing within the community, illegal discrimination based on their disability exists. If it would not place an undue hardship on the state to provide a community placement for the mentally disabled person, the state must do so.

This does not mean that all mentally disabled people must be placed within the community. It only requires that when mentally disabled people could receive treatment in a less re-

Are Disability Benefit Plans Required
to Cover Mental Disability As Well?

No. If a disability benefit plan does cover mental disability, the odds are that this coverage is less than it would be for a physical disability. Typically an employer-sponsored disability plan will limit your eligibility to long-term benefits for mental disability to two years or less. If you were to suffer a physical disability, you are more than likely eligible for long-term benefits until you are 65 years old.

Why Is Mental Disability Treated Differently?

The goal of health plans and legislators is to keep your insurance premiums affordable while providing you with quality care. Mental disability is considered more difficult to diagnose and treat than physical disability. Whether this is true is open for debate. By not granting as much coverage for mental disability, health plans deter people from making false claims of disability and keep your premiums lower than they would be otherwise.

How Does This Relate to the ADA?

People are taking health plans into court to challenge this distinction between physical disabilities and mental disabilities. Their argument is that this distinction discriminates against them based on their disability. The courts' reactions to these lawsuits differ from jurisdiction to jurisdiction. The ADA states that employers shall not discriminate against a qualified individual with a disability with respect to "job application procedures, the hiring, advancement, or discharge of employees, employee compensation, job training, and other terms, conditions, and privileges of employment."

In one case the court found that differentiating between people with mental and physical disabilities did not violate the ADA. The court reasoned that the ADA only made it illegal to make distinctions between the disabled and the nondisabled. It did not make it illegal to make distinctions between the mentally disabled and the physically disabled. A court in another jurisdiction agreed with this reasoning and found that the ADA only required that all employees have equal access to the health plan. The ADA did not require that the health plan offer identical benefits for all disabling conditions. The majority of courts follow this line of reasoning.

There are some courts, though, that are ruling in favor of the mentally disabled plaintiffs. A Virginia court, for example, ruled that the ADA makes it illegal to discriminate between people based on their particular disabilities. Those in favor of this type of reasoning argue that discriminating between physical disabilities and mental disabilities encourages ongoing prejudice against Americans who suffer from mental illness.

THE REHABILITATION ACT

What Is It?

The Rehabilitation Act is similar to the ADA in that it prohibits employment discrimination against qualified individuals with disabilities. The difference is that the Rehabilitation Act applies to executive branch agencies of the federal government, the United States Postal Service, federal government contractors and subcontractors whose contracts are in excess of $2,500, and programs that receive federal funds.

Who Enforces It?

This depends on the employer. If the employer is the federal government or the U.S. Postal Service, then the EEOC has the authority to investigate complaints and file lawsuits. If the employer is a federal contractor or subcontractor, the responsibility lies with the Office of Federal Contract Compliance (OFCCP) of the Department of Labor. If the employer is a program that receives federal funding, private individuals can directly file a lawsuit in court because there is no government agency responsible for enforcement under these circumstances.

What Is the EEOC Process?

The EEOC process is exactly the same as the one for the ADA. That process and the remedies available to you are discussed in detail earlier in this chapter.

What Is the Process Against Federal Contractors?

An individual must file a written complaint with the OFCCP within 180 days of the date of the unlawful discrimination. The OFCCP investigates and determines what type of action to take. If the OFCCP decides that the law was violated, it enters into conciliation with the employer and tries to settle the case. If settlement is unsuccessful, a hearing is held before an administrative law judge. The decision of the judge is appealable to the Department of Labor. The final decision of the Department of Labor can be appealed to the federal district court.

If a violation is found, the government may terminate the contract, debar the contractor from further government business, or order the contractor to "make whole" the employee who was discriminated against. Individuals cannot file their own lawsuits alleging violations of the Rehabilitation Act. Only the OFCCP has the authority to enforce the law.

What Is the Process Against Programs That Receive Federal Funds?

There is no government agency that enforces the Rehabilitation Act against recipients of federal funds. Individuals may file a lawsuit directly in federal court. There is no uniform statute of limitations for filing a lawsuit. The deadline is based on the most closely analogous state statute of limitations, which can vary from one year in some states to as much as six years in others. Successful plaintiffs are entitled to injunctive relief, make-whole remedies, compensatory and punitive damages, and reasonable attorney's fees. For more on these remedies, see Chapter 17 on tort liability.

HIV AND AIDS

Is HIV Infection or AIDS a Disability?

Yes. Recently the Supreme Court declared that HIV infection is a disability because it is a physical impairment that substantially limits the major life activity of having children. This includes an HIV infection that so far shows no outward symptoms of infection or AIDS. This stage of the disease is known as the **asymptomatic** stage.

LEARNING THE LINGO

Asymptomatic: Showing no outward symptoms of a disease.

This Supreme Court decision was very controversial, even among the Court's justices. It would not be surprising if lawmakers amended the ADA to narrow this ruling. Rather than declaring asymptomatic HIV infection as always being a disability, an amended law would probably require the person to prove that the asymptomatic infection affected his or her ability to have children.

How Can HIV Infection Be a Disability If It Is Asymptomatic?

A physical or mental impairment includes body systems that suffer some sort of disorder or medical condition. The virus that causes AIDS travels from the circulatory system to the lymph nodes during the asymptomatic stage. This phase averages between 7 and 11 years. Even though there are no outward signs that a person is infected, the body's systems are constantly affected from the time she or he is infected.

The infection substantially limits a person's life because it affects decisions regarding sexual relations and children. Those activities are not impossible, but they are substantially limited.

So What Is the Controversy?

Until recently, courts would look at a person's individual facts and medical condition to decide whether that person—and only that person—suffered a disability under the ADA. In the Supreme Court case, the Court's definition of disability, required to determine if the woman who brought the lawsuit was discriminated against, may have been broad enough to encompass all asymptomatic HIV-infected women of childbearing years. This decision surprised many people in the legal and political fields. The debate continues to rage on how far-reaching the Court intended its decision to be. Look for Congress to consider amending the ADA to clarify how it affects asymptomatic HIV-infected people.

THE ADA AND THE REFUSAL TO TREAT HIV-POSITIVE PATIENTS

Can Doctors Refuse to Treat Me If I Am HIV Positive?

The Doctor-Patient Relationship

Traditionally, a doctor does not have a duty to treat you unless you have established a doctor-patient relationship, in which case the doctor would have agreed to treat you. If the doctor did not agree, there was no relationship, and the doctor does not have to treat you now.

If you do have a doctor-patient relationship, the doctor is obligated to continue providing you with medical care if you become HIV positive. This medical care, in some instances, may be nothing more than referring you to a doctor that specializes in treating HIV-positive or AIDS patients. After all, AIDS is a complicated disease that many doctors do not have the resources or education to treat. On the other hand, if the referral could be shown to be a pretext enabling the doctor to avoid giving care to the HIV-positive patient, then discrimination under the ADA might be established.

Where Does the ADA Come In?

Part of the ADA makes it illegal for public facilities to discriminate against a person because of a disability. To prove discrimination, you would need to show that your illness is a disability and that a public facility (such as a hospital, a medical clinic, or a doctor's office) discriminated against you because of your HIV or AIDS status.

What Does the ADA Consider to Be Discrimination?

If you are denied access to medical care by a hospital or a health care provider based solely on the fact that you are HIV-infected or suffer from AIDS, then that is discrimination. The exception to this rule is when you pose a **direct threat** to the health or safety of others.

LEARNING THE LINGO

Direct threat: A significant risk to the health and safety of others that cannot be eliminated through policies, practices, or procedures. The question is not whether a risk exists, but whether the risk is significant.

ADA AND INSURANCE

My Health Insurance Is Through My Employer. Do I Have a Legal Right to That Insurance?

Probably not. Most of us are "employees at will," which means that we work without a contract. Therefore, most of us don't have a personal employment contract and are not covered by a collective bargaining agreement. Without a contract, you do not have a legally enforceable right to health care benefits through your employer. Once you start paying premiums, you may have some legal recourse if your employer takes your health insurance away to retaliate or to discriminate against you.

Types of Health Insurance

There are two main types of health insurance. In a **group health plan,** the employer joins the plan, and the cost of medical care is spread over a large number of people from many companies. The premiums paid by that large group of people are enough to offset the cost of paying for treatment for the members who get sick. In a **self-insured plan,** the only members of the plan are those who work for one employer. The employer saves money on administrative costs but also carries the risk that the premiums paid by the employees will not be enough to cover the costs of medical treatment for the members.

Type Used by Most Employers

The majority of employers now use group health plans, but they can switch to a self-insured plan. This creates some problems. There are not as many people paying premiums, so employers would like to limit the amount of money that will be paid out for treatment. To do this they may be able to put "caps" on certain types of medical care. For example, the benefits might be changed at the end of a benefits year, if the employer had reserved the right to change them and if the change did not single out a particular individual. Caps may be necessary to provide adequate medical coverage at a reasonable cost, which in turn helps the companies stay in business.

So What Is the Big Deal?

Sometimes companies put caps on medical care that radically affect certain employees. Let's say that a company insurance policy pays for medical care until the costs reach $1,000,000. After that, employees are on their own. But HIV-positive individuals could be very seriously affected if the insurance policy is changed so that there is a $5,000 cap on medical treatment for a disease. After the insurance pays $5,000, employees must pay the rest out of their own pocket. In the best-case scenario, HIV-positive employees may have 15 to 20 years left to live. They could lose everything they have and end up on Medicaid. This happened to dozens of people in the first decade of the AIDS epidemic.

Is That Discrimination?

Under most state laws, yes. Several states have laws that require insurance policies to include coverage for AIDS. People with HIV or AIDS could do nothing about it, though, for many years. A federal law, the Employee Retirement Income Security Act of 1974 (ERISA), overrode the state laws. ERISA governs self-insured plans. ERISA does not state that employers can discriminate against people with AIDS. It does, however, allow employers to cap parts of their insurance plans. Unfortunately, ERISA was used as a weapon against people with HIV.

The ADA Changes the Picture

The ADA is a federal law and so not overridden by ERISA. Thanks to the ADA, now employers who cap certain benefits under ERISA must make sure that they have done so in a nondiscriminatory way.

CAPS CAN'T DISCRIMINATE

The ADA does not make it illegal to put caps on insurance. It makes it illegal to apply caps in a discriminatory manner.

Can Employers Still Put Caps on Benefits under the ADA?

Yes. But it's unclear whether they can single out one certain disease. There has been a tremendous volume of litigation on this and related issues in the past few years. Among the many issues: Is a disease a disability? Is a cap on benefits permissible if it affects nondisabled and disabled persons the same way?

A cap may apply to all catastrophic illnesses, but it is as yet unclear whether it can apply to only AIDS or heart transplants or dialysis. However, if statistical data shows that a particular disease requires medical care that is so costly that covering it could wipe out the insurance plan or drive the company into insolvency, the company may place a cap on that one disease. If the employer cannot prove that the cap is based on statistical data, the employer runs the risk of being fined.

Does the ADA Protect Against Preexisting Conditions?

No. Your insurance company may still deny coverage for any medical conditions you had before signing the insurance policy. The key to remember here is that the denial applies not only to people with HIV but to all persons with a preexisting condition.

Another federal law, the Health Insurance Portability and Accountability Act of 1996 (HIPAA) protects health insurance coverage for workers and their families when they change or lose their jobs. HIPAA often does affect preexisting conditions clauses in health insurance policies offered by employers.

THE WORLD AT YOUR FINGERTIPS

- The Department of Justice provides information on the Americans with Disabilities Act on its Internet site at *http://www.usdoj.gov/crt/ada/adahom1.htm*.
- The full text of the ADA is online at *http:www.robson.org/capfaq/ada.txt*.
- The Americans with Disabilities North Dakota Information Site, *http://tradecorridor.com/ada/*, provides an excellent overview and discussion on ADA topics.
- To visit the Centers for Disease Control's Internet site, go to *www.cdc.org*. This Web page includes a listing of topics from A to Z.
- There are several private organizations that focus on disability rights issues:

The Disability Rights Education and Defense Fund, Inc.
2212 Sixth St.
Berkeley, CA 94710

Mental Health Law Project
1101 15th St. NW
Suite 1212
Washington, DC 20005

Disability Rights Center
2500 Q Street NW
Suite 121
Washington, DC 20007

YOU MUST REMEMBER THIS

- A disability is a physical or mental impairment that substantially limits a major life activity.
- A major life activity is an important part of a person's life,

such as working, learning, caring for oneself, walking, hearing, speaking, breathing, or performing manual tasks.

- If your condition can be treated, such as with eyeglasses or blood pressure medication, you are not considered disabled under the ADA.
- HIV and AIDS are considered disabilities. Menopause is not.
- The ADA may provide you with legal recourse if your insurance policy is changed to put a cap on what will be paid to cover HIV and AIDS.

CHAPTER 13

Pregnancy

It's a Fact of Life, a Great Blessing— and a Big Legal Topic

Allison is applying for a retail sales job. She is six weeks pregnant with her second child. Her first pregnancy was difficult, and she was unable to stand for extended periods of time for the last six months of the pregnancy. The new job would require her to spend six hours of every day on her feet. If she is hired, is the employer required to make reasonable accommodations for her if she is unable to stand during her pregnancy?

PREGNANCY AS A DISABILITY

In the majority of jurisdictions, pregnancy itself is not considered a disability under the Americans with Disabilities Act (ADA). Some of the medical problems associated with pregnancy, however, are considered disabilities under the ADA. If the medical problem related to the pregnancy is a physical impairment that substantially limits a major life activity of the woman (such as working), it is considered a disability under the ADA. If the pregnancy-related condition does not limit a major life activity, it does not meet the ADA's definition of a disability.

There are two arguments that are most often made against considering pregnancy-related problems as a disability. First, pregnancy-related problems are always temporary. The disability can never last more than nine months. The argument goes that the ADA is only meant to cover those people with permanent disabilities. There is support for this in the guidelines set by the

Equal Employment Opportunity Commission (EEOC). Those guidelines state that "temporary, nonchronic impairments of short duration, with little or no long-term or permanent impact, are usually not disabilities." A few courts relied on this guideline in ruling that pregnancy and pregnancy-related medical problems are not disabilities under the ADA.

The other argument is that pregnant women are already protected from discrimination by the Pregnancy Discrimination Act (PDA). Under the PDA, employers are prohibited from discriminating against women who are pregnant or of childbearing age. However, these two laws are different in the burden they place on the employers and the pregnant women. The PDA gives women legal recourse if discrimination occurs, such as if she is fired for becoming pregnant. The woman would have to prove in court that she was discriminated against because she was pregnant. The ADA requires that the employer make a reasonable accommodation to a pregnant woman during the course of the pregnancy. The woman would have to prove in court that she was discriminated against because she had a disability that could have been accommodated by the employer. The legal standards are different.

When Pregnancy Becomes a Disability

No court has come up with a definitive answer as to exactly which pregnancy-related problems are disabilities. The ADA focuses on the individual with the disability, making it difficult to apply one standard across the board. Nevertheless, court cases do provide some guidance. Normal symptoms of pregnancy, such as swollen feet or morning sickness, are not pregnancy-related problems that rise to the level of disability. The test is whether the medical condition is part of a normal pregnancy or if it is part of an abnormal pregnancy. If it is part of a normal pregnancy then it is not a disability. There must be some unusual aspect to the pregnancy to qualify the condition as a disability.

THE FAMILY & MEDICAL LEAVE ACT (FMLA)

The FMLA gives certain benefits to employees, including those suffering from a serious health condition that makes it necessary for the person to leave his or her job for an extended period, but not permanently. To qualify for leave under the FMLA, an employee must have spent at least 1,250 hours in the past year working for her employer. Only employers who have 50 or more employees within a 75-mile radius are bound to comply with the FMLA. Qualified employees may take up to 12 weeks of leave for family or medical reasons. The law also makes it illegal for employers to discriminate against employees who do take leave.

A "serious health condition" under the FMLA is read more broadly by the courts than is "disability" under the ADA. The serious health condition must create an inability to work, attend school, or perform other regular daily activities. In other words, under the FMLA the person must show that he cannot work due to his medical condition. Under the ADA the disabled person is able to perform the duties of the job.

The FMLA treats pregnancy differently from other serious health conditions. Under the FMLA, any incapacity due to pregnancy is a serious health condition that entitles the employee to take a leave of absence. The FMLA even allows leave to pregnant women who suffer from severe morning sickness, regardless of whether the woman receives medical treatment.

Enforcing the FMLA

The Secretary of Labor has the authority to investigate complaints of violations and can institute a lawsuit to enforce the statute. You can file a complaint alleging a violation of the FMLA with your local office of the Wage and Hour Division of the Department of Labor. Individual employees also have the right to sue their employer for violations of the law. They may file suit directly in federal or state court. They are not required to file charges with the Department of Labor, although they may do so. The statute of limitations for filing a lawsuit is 2 years.

If You Win an FMLA Action

You may recover any lost wages, employment benefits, or other compensation you were denied because of the FMLA violation. You may also be reinstated to your job and granted employment benefits if the court deems it necessary. If you did not suffer any lost wages or salary because of the FMLA violation, you may not be able to recover anything from your employer. In one case a woman took 2 weeks leave after giving birth to a child that was stillborn. During her leave a supervisor telephoned her at home and warned her that if she did not return to work she would be fired. The woman returned to work at the same position and with the same salary. When the woman sued her employer claiming that the FMLA was violated, the court concluded that the woman had not suffered any loss that could be compensated under the FMLA. The woman would have had a better claim if she had refused to return to work and been fired, because then she would have suffered an economic loss.

THE WORLD AT YOUR FINGERTIPS

- *The FMLA Handbook: A Practical Guide to the Family & Medical Leave Act for Union Members & Stewards* by Robert M. Schwartz explains how unions and companies can better follow the law and meet the needs of employees. (Work Rights Press, 1996).
- For the full text of the Pregnancy Discrimination Act, visit the Department of Health and Human Services website at *http://www.dhhs.gov/progorg/ocr/sharass.htm*. The PDA is part of the prohibition against discrimination on the basis of sex.
- For more discussion on pregnancy leave or to see a sample of a pregnancy leave policy, visit the CCH site at *http://aol.toolkit.cch.com/text/P05_4402.asp*.

YOU MUST REMEMBER THIS

- Pregnancy is not a disability under the ADA. Pregnancy-related problems are a disability under the ADA.
- The Family and Medical Leave Act grants leave to pregnant women who work for employers that are covered by the law.

CHAPTER 14

Confidentiality and Disclosure

From Disabilities to HIV-Positive Status, the Law Provides Privacy— but with Exceptions

Craig is applying for a job at a manufacturing company. Craig suffers from depression, although he shows no outward signs of this disease. He is taking medication for his depression, and the depression would not affect his ability to do the job, as long as he is allowed to work flexible hours. Several other employees have requested to work flexible hours, but the company has declined to extend that benefit to any employee at this point. If Craig is offered the job, the other employees will be angry that he is given flexible hours. Can his new employer tell the other employees about Craig's illness so that there will be no appearance of preferential treatment?

CONFIDENTIALITY

Confidentiality and the ADA

Before the Americans with Disabilities Act (ADA) was enacted into law, your employer did not have an obligation to keep information about your medical condition confidential. Today, the ADA allows an employer to conduct a medical examination after it offers you a position or to ask you about your disability if it offers you a job only if the employer agrees to treat any information obtained about your medical condition or your medical history as confidential.

This does not mean that the person who hires you cannot tell anyone else at all in your company. Your employer is allowed to tell your supervisor or manager about your disability so that she can accommodate any special needs you may have as a result of your disability. Your employer cannot, however, tell the other employees with whom you work. This can cause some conflict between you and the other employees because they may think that you are getting preferential treatment for no apparent reason. Not disclosing your disability could lead to some resentment toward you. This is especially true if your disability is one that is not visible to others, such as depression, alcoholism, or a bowel disorder.

The ADA does not allow your potential employer to require a medical examination before making you an offer or to ask you whether you are disabled. Your employer can ask you whether you would be able to perform any functions that are job-related. If you are qualified for the job and can perform the essential functions of the position with or without reasonable accommodation by the employer, you must be considered for the position in the same manner as any other qualified applicant.

The Exceptions

The ADA allows three exceptions to the confidentiality requirement. First, your employer may provide your supervisor with any medical information that is necessary to accommodate you so that you may do your job in spite of your disability. Second, your employer may also, if needed, inform any first aid and safety personnel of your medical history. Third, your employer is required to give the government enough of your medical information so that the government can make sure the company is complying with the ADA.

Unions and the ADA

The ADA has created an unforeseen problem between employers and unions. The ADA focuses on the individual's needs, whereas unions focus on the needs of a group of employees. Under the National Labor Relations Act (NLRA), an employer must abide by the terms of a collective bargaining agreement.

If the employer provides accommodations for a disabled employee, such as more frequent bathroom breaks or special equipment, the employer violates the NLRA, which forbids the employer from making material changes in working conditions for employees without the agreement of the union. The employer cannot inform the union of the need for the special treatment because of the ADA's confidentiality requirement. If the employer tells the union that the employee requires special accommodations, the union may request the employee's medical records so that the union can be sure the bargaining agreement is being followed. This puts the employee's confidentiality rights squarely at odds with the union's needs, with the employer caught in the middle. Although this particular scenario has not yet hit the courts, in similar cases the courts have refused to force employers to reveal medical information. The reasoning is that your confidentiality right outweighs the union's need for access to your information.

PRIVACY AND HIV

Your Privacy Interest

You have a privacy interest in your blood as well as any medical information that can be obtained from testing a blood sample you provide. If someone performs a test on your blood sample without your consent, your privacy is violated. For example, if you give a blood sample that is to be tested for iron deficiency, it violates your privacy to test your sample for HIV without telling you and getting your permission to do so.

INVADING A STUDENT'S PRIVACY

A medical assistant student at Cambridge College in Cambridge, Massachusetts, told his college instructor that he was HIV positive. Later the instructor had the class submit blood samples to be tested for rubella. The instructor asked the laboratory to test only the one student's blood for HIV. The test results were reported to the college. A jury found that the college invaded the student's right to privacy. The case is *Doe v. High-Tech Institute, Inc., d/b/a Cambridge College,* 1998 WL 379926 (Colo CT App July 9, 1998).

Why Test Results Are Kept Confidential

Results of HIV and AIDS testing are kept confidential to encourage people to be tested. If the results are kept confidential, then people will not be afraid of being shunned by family, friends, and society if they find out they are positive. Unlike other diseases, such as cancer, AIDS carries with it a social stigma that is frightening to many people. Some states have laws that make it illegal for health care professionals to give out medical information without your consent. The laws usually include an exception for notifying health departments and others of HIV or other sexually transmitted diseases.

"Their" Privacy

Although you have a right to privacy, your family and friends and the community have an interest in protecting themselves from disease, regardless of whether it is AIDS, venereal disease, smallpox, or tuberculosis.

Your Sexual Partners

Your sexual partners cannot accept the risk of being with you if they do not know the risks. If your sexual partner knows that you are infected, that person can choose whether or not to accept the risk and can decide what precautions to take. It allows your

THE "AIDS BABY" LAW

In New York, one of the most interesting HIV laws requires that every newborn child be tested for HIV. The law, enacted in 1996, provided that the test results could only be used for statistical purposes. Neither the baby's doctor nor the baby's parents were told the outcome of the test. A later law allows for disclosure to the baby's mother if she requests it. This law has been criticized by some for not being enforced enough and by others for being enforced in a discriminatory manner.

The reasoning behind the nondisclosure requirement was that the mother had a right to privacy. (If the baby is HIV positive, then the mother is infected.) The state did not want mothers to be afraid to seek prenatal treatment.

---

sexual partner to be tested for HIV and to be given medical care to slow the onslaught of the disease if it turns out your partner is infected. All of these precautions will help to slow the spread of the disease to others.

Public Health Departments

The public health authorities need health information to track the disease to protect the health and safety of both you and society. If the disease is not tracked, there would be less urgency in providing funding for research and medical care because the health authorities would not know that it is an epidemic.

Tracing the sexual partners of persons with sexually transmitted diseases is nothing new. Originating in Europe in the mid-1800s, partner tracing came to the United States in the 1930s to fight an epidemic of syphilis. The epidemic was largely cured by the development of penicillin. So far there is no known cure for AIDS. When the public health authority notifies your sexual partners that you are HIV positive, it is called **partner notification.**

Partner Notification

Partner notification usually works like this: The public health department talks to the person infected with HIV. The person tells the health department the names of the person's sexual partners. These people are then located by the health department and told that one of their previous sexual partners is infected. The specific person is not usually named in order to maintain that person's confidentiality. The sexual partners are then offered testing, medical care, and personal counseling. If the sexual partners learn they are HIV positive, the process starts over again with them. The goal is to let people know that they may be infected so that they will not unwittingly pass the infection on to others.

 ## HOW NOTIFICATION WORKS

Partner notification is the responsibility of state health departments, although federal funding is provided to those departments through the Centers for Disease Control and Prevention. The specific methods for notifying partners vary from state to state.

States That Currently Require Partner Notification

At this writing, the forty states in which the public health department is required to notify sexual partners of the HIV-infected person are: Alabama, Arizona, Arkansas, California, Colorado, Connecticut, Florida, Georgia, Hawaii, Idaho, Illinois, Indiana, Iowa, Kansas, Louisiana, Maryland, Michigan, Minnesota, Mississippi, Missouri, Montana, Nebraska, New Hampshire, New Jersey, New York, North Carolina, Ohio, Oklahoma, Oregon, Pennsylvania, Rhode Island, South Carolina, South Dakota, Tennessee, Texas, Utah, Vermont, Washington, Virginia, West Virginia, Wisconsin, and the District of Columbia.

The Federal Government

Notifying partners of persons infected with HIV is left to the states and local communities. There is no federal program for partner notification. The federal government does, however, provide federal funding to the states for partner notification programs with strings attached. To receive these funds, the states must agree to some conditions, such as making a good-faith effort to notify the spouse of the person infected and to offer the spouse testing.

DISCLOSURE

The Duty to Disclose

What Is It?

Many states have *duty-to-disclose* laws that apply to people with infectious diseases such as HIV. These laws put a legal duty on HIV-infected persons to tell their sexual partners that they (the partners) were, or will be, exposed to the HIV virus.

 THE DUTY TO WARN

In the early 1900s, patient confidentiality took a back seat to the duty to disclose as more and more married women contracted syphilis from their husbands, who had frequented prostitutes. The duty to warn became an ethical duty that was later made into law in several states.

Who Has to Disclose?

Unlike partner notification, which is done by the public health department, the duty to disclose is on the person who is infected. This does not mean you have a choice. If you are infected and you fail to tell your sexual partner, your partner may be able to sue you in civil court for assault or battery, or the state may prosecute you on criminal charges.

When Does This Duty Begin?

HIV is unique from other contagious diseases in that a person may be infected for years and not know it. You must have some reasonable basis for knowing that you might be infected for the duty to begin. A reasonable basis would be testing positive for HIV or finding out that a previous partner is HIV positive.

The Duty to Warn

What Is It?

Many states impose a duty to warn as well as a duty to disclose. The *duty to warn* puts a legal duty on health care workers to warn your partners that they were exposed to infection. If you are HIV positive, this means your doctor may have a duty to warn your spouse. This duty is not meant to frighten your loved ones but to give them the chance to receive medical treatment and to make decisions that protect the health and safety of themselves and others.

What If I Don't Want My Doctor to Tell My Partner?

This duty applies regardless of whether you consent and may not include assurances of maintaining your confidentiality. It would be difficult to warn your partner and not tell him or her that it is you who is infected.

What About the Doctor-Patient Relationship?

Technically, telling your partner that you are infected violates the confidential relationship that exists between a doctor and a patient. When it comes to HIV infection, courts and legislatures often decide that the health and safety of your partner is more important than keeping your status confidential. It is a difficult line to walk and a decision that did not come about easily. This balancing act continues to be debated. Until AIDS is curable, though, the health of others will continue to take priority over your right to confidentiality.

What If I Don't Have a Spouse or a Partner?

The duty to warn includes warning you of the possibility that you might infect others. If your health care professional does not tell you that you could infect others, and you do in fact go on to infect someone, that third person may be able to sue your health care provider for **negligence.**

LEARNING THE LINGO

Negligence: The failure to protect others from an unreasonable risk of harm.

When Do They Decide There Is a Duty to Warn My Partner?

The duty-to-warn laws vary by state but carry a basic format:

- **You have refused to tell your partner.**
- **There is a significant risk that you will pass on the infection to your partner.**
- **Your doctor has told you that your partner will be notified of your infection.**

What If My State Doesn't Have a Legal Duty to Warn and My Doctor Tells My Partner Anyway?

Even in states where there is no law that requires your doctor to warn your partners, you have little recourse if your doctor tells your partner anyway. Most courts will respect your doctor's decision to warn your partner when your doctor feels that that person's life is in danger. Because AIDS is currently incurable, possibly transmitting the infection is considered life threatening.

States with a Legal Duty to Warn

The following thirty-two states have laws that impose a legal duty to warn on doctors and other health care professionals: Alabama, Arizona, California, Connecticut, Florida, Georgia, Hawaii, Idaho, Illinois, Indiana, Iowa, Kansas, Kentucky, Louisiana, Maryland, Massachusetts, Michigan, Missouri, Montana, Nevada, New Jersey, New York, Ohio, Pennsylvania, Rhode Island, South Carolina, Tennessee, Texas, Virginia, Washington, West Virginia, Wisconsin.

WHEN A DOCTOR IS HIV POSITIVE

Do I Have to Tell My Patients That I Am HIV Positive?

Most health care providers who are HIV positive voluntarily refrain from certain types of surgical procedures that pose a higher risk of transmission. Though there is no absolute legal requirement that doctors tell patients of their HIV status, courts have struggled with this question for years. The risk of you passing the infection on to your patients is very small. Nevertheless, the disease is still fatal. So the trend seems to be that, yes, you must tell your patients that you are HIV positive or have AIDS.

A HIGHER STANDARD

In essence, doctors and health care workers are granted fewer privacy rights than the rest of us. Most of the workforce is not required to tell their clients their HIV status. In general, though, doctors are required to tell their patients if they are HIV positive.

For one thing, your HIV status has been held to be part of the patient's right to informed consent. Only the patient has the right to decide whether to accept the risk of being infected through doctor-patient contact, even if that risk is very small and remote. An accidental needle stick or scalpel scratch may not pass the infection along to the patient, but it will subject the patient to months of testing for the virus and would probably cause the patient emotional distress.

 AN UNDERSTANDABLE RELUCTANCE

Why doctors may not want to disclose their HIV status:

- They want to protect themselves and their families from social stigma.
- They fear that they will lose their patients and their practice.

Can I Continue to Practice?

Yes, although both the American Medical Association and the American Dental Association recommend that HIV-positive health care providers do not perform invasive procedures. These guidelines are not laws, but they do set the standard of care for doctors and dentists. It is this standard of care that will be used when deciding whether a doctor acted negligently.

Can the Hospital I Work for Require Me to Be Tested for HIV Infection?

No, but it can encourage voluntary testing. Some states have laws that require that doctors or other health care workers be tested for HIV. Few of these laws are found to be constitutional.

If you are tested for HIV, the ADA requires that this information be kept confidential. Hospitals have the right to require surgeons to notify their patients beforehand that they, the surgeons, are HIV positive or have AIDS. Hospitals also have the right to choose to not let an HIV-positive surgeon perform invasive procedures, thereby ending the doctor's career as a surgeon.

How Much of a Risk Is There That I'll Contract HIV from a Patient?

Health care professionals are required to report needle sticks to the Centers for Disease Control and Prevention (CDC). The CDC receives about 800,000 reports of needle sticks each year. Of these 800,000, about 56 health care professionals become infected with HIV. Granted that is a very small percentage of health care professionals that become infected. Still, for those 56 that become infected, it is way too high.

Do I Have Any Legal Recourse If I Become HIV Positive from a Needle Stick?

That depends on the situation. One doctor was serving an internship at the Yale-New Haven Hospital when she became infected with HIV from a needle stick. The doctor claimed that Yale University did not provide her with proper supervision and safety instructions. The jury awarded her $12.2 million dollars in damages. Keep in mind that it took nearly 10 years for her to get that damages award.

If you decide to bring such a claim, the jury will consider the amount of training you were given, your experience, and whether your employer or hospital provided you with safety devices that could have given you some protection from infection.

THE WORLD AT YOUR FINGERTIPS

- For legal advice and links to federal laws regarding employment law, visit the website of Advice Council at *http://free advice.com/law/531us.htm*.

YOU MUST REMEMBER THIS

- Your employer cannot disclose the fact that you have a disability to your co-workers.
- You have a privacy interest in any blood samples taken from you.
- You must consent to having an HIV test performed on your blood sample.
- If your state has a "duty to disclose" law that applies to people with infectious diseases such as HIV, you have a legal duty to tell your sexual partners that they were, or will be, exposed to the disease.
- In states with a "duty to warn," health care workers are legally obligated to warn your partners that they were exposed to infection. If you are HIV positive, this means your doctor may have a duty to warn your spouse.

CHAPTER 15

Vaccinations

*They're a Public Health Boon, but Not
Free from Defects—the Law Provides
Some Guidance*

*Patricia is the mother of a two-year-old girl. Her doctor tells her that state law
requires that her daughter be vaccinated. Patricia believes that the vaccinations
are unnecessary. Can she refuse to have her daughter vaccinated?*

MANDATED VACCINES

There are several vaccines that children are required by law to receive before they may attend school. These include the vaccines for diphtheria, measles, mumps, rubella, polio, and hepatitis B. A vaccine for chickenpox was approved and recommended for use in 1995. The chickenpox vaccine is voluntary in the majority of states.

The law requires vaccines because vaccinations are believed to be necessary to protect society. Vaccines are considered the best way to prevent an epidemic of these diseases. In other words, the benefits of protecting the vast majority of the population from diphtheria outweigh the risk that one person may suffer the side effects of a vaccination.

Some people object to mandatory vaccinations. This is nothing new. At the turn of the twentieth century, there was an outbreak of smallpox. One man had been given a smallpox vaccine as a child and had suffered a severe reaction. His son had also suffered a reaction. He did not want to be vaccinated again as an adult, even though the law required vaccinations for adults. The man had two choices: he could give in and be vaccinated, or he could pay a five-dollar fine. The man refused to be vaccinated or pay the fine. The case went all the way to the U.S. Supreme Court, which held that the need to protect the public from the smallpox epidemic overrode the man's personal interest in avoiding an allergic reaction or monetary fine. It is unknown whether the man paid the fine or received the vaccination.

Although all states require vaccinations, the states also allow for some people to be exempted from this requirement. All fifty states allow that people who would suffer severe medical reactions to vaccines are not required to submit to the vaccinations. Virtually all states also allow exemptions for people who object on religious grounds. Seventeen states allow exemptions for people who have other personal beliefs against vaccinations. The personal-belief exemption does not guarantee, however, that you can refuse to vaccinate your children. In 1995 the California Department of Social Services charged a woman with medical neglect for refusing to vaccinate her two children. The woman's children were taken away until she agreed to have them vaccinated. This occurred even though California has a personal-belief exemption and the mother claimed that vaccinating her children violated her personal beliefs.

TALKING TO AN EXPERT
Paying for Vaccinations

Q. My state requires that children be vaccinated, but my health plan does not pay for these vaccinations. I cannot afford the vaccines. What can I do?

A. Most pharmaceutical companies in the United States that make vaccines have programs that will pay for them or provide them free to people who cannot afford them.

Answer by Charles Inlander, President, Peoples' Medical Society, Allentown, Pennsylvania

INFORMED CONSENT

Just as you must agree to other forms of medical treatment, you must be given enough information so you can make an informed choice as to whether to immunize your child. Of course, in the majority of states you must give your consent unless you claim a medical or religious exemption, so your choice is limited. For the most part this information will come from your doctor. Your doctor will tell you about the benefits and the risks associated with giving your child a vaccination. A reaction to a hepatitis vaccination, for instance, may include a rash, hair loss, joint pain, chronic fatigue, and even rheumatoid arthritis. Your doctor should also tell you about the dangers of contracting the disease if your child is not given the vaccination, as well as the risk of getting the disease despite the vaccination. If you agree to the vaccination (and in some states you have no choice), then the doctor must document what vaccination was given to your child, the expiration date of the vaccination, and the lot number of the vaccine that was administered.

Your doctor may give you a vaccination information sheet published by the Centers for Disease Control and Prevention (CDC). Your doctor may also give you the package insert that is published by the vaccine manufacturers, although this may be written in a more technical manner. Read these information sheets so that you will know the risk of giving your child a vaccine and what you should do if your child suffers a serious reaction, such as a seizure.

THE NATIONAL VACCINE SAFETY ACT AND THE NATIONAL CHILDHOOD VACCINE INJURY ACT

The United States Congress responded to concerns about the safety of vaccines and the rising costs of litigation against vaccine manufacturers by enacting two laws in 1986: the National

Vaccine Safety Act and the National Childhood Vaccine Injury Act. These laws created two important programs regarding vaccinations: the Vaccine Adverse Event Reporting System (VAERS) and the National Vaccine Injury Compensation Program (NVICP).

The VAERS is a database that tracks medical reactions to vaccinations. Since the VAERS was created in 1990, approximately 12,000 to 14,000 adverse reactions to vaccinations have been reported each year. Of these, 17 percent resulted in life-threatening illness, hospitalization, permanent disability, or death.

The NVICP was established to act as a no-fault system to compensate those who are injured by vaccinations. It is, in essence, an indemnity plan so that the federal government bears the costs of vaccine reactions rather than vaccine manufacturers. The program was considered necessary because vaccine manufacturers were unable to get insurance and many manufacturers refused to develop new vaccines or to continue to supply those vaccines already in existence and required by law. The NVICP creates a more stable market for vaccine manufacturers and provides relief to those who are injured regardless of whether negligence is present. The result is fewer court cases and lower legal costs. Vaccine manufacturers are able to get insurance. Vaccines are priced more reasonably, and the extra costs are not passed on to you.

The goals of the NVICP are to:

1. improve the coordination of vaccine research, development, use, and evaluation;
2. assure an adequate supply of vaccines;
3. assess the benefits and the risks of vaccines and ensure that the public and doctors are aware of the benefits and risks;
4. ensure adequate regulatory capacity to evaluate vaccines;
5. improve tracking of adverse reactions;
6. establish research priorities;
7. promote rapid development and introduction of improved vaccines;

8. ensure optimal immunization levels in all high-risk and target groups.

To qualify for compensation due to a vaccine-related injury, you must prove that the vaccine caused the injury and that the injury is one that is covered under the NVICP. If the injury is not one specifically covered by the NVICP, it will be evaluated on a case-by-case basis. First, you must file a petition with the U.S. Claims Court. The petition must be accompanied by affidavits or supporting documentation showing that you suffered an injury as a result of your vaccination.

If the court finds that you have shown by a preponderance of the evidence that your injury was the result of a vaccine that you were required by law to receive, you will be compensated. Compensation is divided into four categories: (1) medical and rehabilitative care, (2) a death benefit of $250,000, (3) lost earnings, and (4) pain and suffering. There is no recovery under the NVICP for punitive or exemplary damages. If you accept this compensation, you must agree to waive any rights you have to bring a lawsuit against the manufacturer of the vaccine. The benefit of the NVICP is that you will be more quickly compensated than if you opt for a lengthy court battle against the manufacturer.

If you do not receive compensation under the NVICP or if you believe that you deserve more compensation, you can turn down the offer from the NVICP and sue the vaccine manufacturer. If you turn down the compensation and later lose your lawsuit against the vaccine manufacturer, you cannot go back and try to reclaim compensation under the NVICP. Between the time the NVICP began through September 1999, there have been 5,698 claims filed for vaccine injury. Of those, 1,447 resulted in compensation for the person bringing the claim. More than $1.048 billion has been paid out to date. The program is funded by a tax on each dose of vaccine that is sold.

There is one instance in which you might consider a lawsuit against the vaccine manufacturer: when the manufacturer is negligent. If your injury is the result of the manufacturer's negligence, the manufacturer bears all of the costs of its actions. The goal is to provide an incentive to manufacturers to produce safe, high-quality vaccines. If the manufacturer knowingly produces and sells a bad batch of vaccines, the government does not want to be held financially responsible. In that case you might also be eligible to receive more compensation (such as punitive damages) than you would under the NVICP system.

CALIFORNIA AIDS VACCINE VICTIMS COMPENSATION FUND

California has a law similar to the NVICP. It was enacted in 1986 to encourage vaccine manufacturers to develop and produce a vaccine for the AIDS virus. It also establishes a fund to compensate patients who are injured by an approved vaccine. It was modeled after the NVICP, although there are some notable differences.

The California law applies specifically to AIDS vaccines. The law limits litigation costs to vaccine manufacturers by having the state compensate anyone who is injured by the vaccine. The patient who is injured may be compensated up to $550,000 for medical injuries, lost income, and pain and suffering. The most important difference between the California law and the federal law is that California allows you to seek compensation from the state fund and to bring a lawsuit against the manufacturer at the same time. This benefits you because you will be more quickly compensated under the state fund than you will be in a court case. You will be able to receive medical treatment and to pay your bills, and you will not be quite so hard pressed to accept a settlement. The law also allows the state to go after a manufacturer for indemnity if it finds that your injury was the result of negligence.

THE WORLD AT YOUR FINGERTIPS

- The National Vaccine Injury Compensation website may be accessed at *http://www.hrsa.dhhs.gov/bhpr/vicp/*. Visit this site for information on how to see a current listing of the vaccine injury table, to file a claim, and to get answers to frequently asked questions.
- The Food and Drug Administration oversees the VAERS program. Visit the VAERS website at *http://www.fda.gov/cber/vaers/vaers.htm* to find out how to submit data to VAERS or to get more information on the program.
- There is an organization called Parents Requesting Open Vaccination Education (PROVE) that works to provide information and education regarding the benefits, risks, and legal rights surrounding vaccinations. They can be reached on the Internet at *http://home.swbell.net/prove/*.
- If you are planning a trip abroad, you will need to comply with the vaccination laws of that country. For a country-by-country list of vaccinations that may be required, compiled by the U.S. Department of State Bureau of Consular Affairs, see *http://travel.state.gov/foreignentryreqs.html*.

YOU MUST REMEMBER THIS

- Every state requires that your children be vaccinated with a range of vaccines. Possible exemptions from these laws include medical reasons, religious objections, and personal beliefs.
- There is a federal fund that will provide compensation for you if you are injured because of a vaccination.

CHAPTER 16

Mandatory Testing

A Quick Look at a
Very Controversial Question

*Allen is a firefighter in excellent physical shape. He knows that he
is HIV positive, but his employer, the fire department, does not
know. Allen believes that the risk of his infecting someone else on
the job is very small. Nevertheless, the department announced that
all firefighters will be tested for HIV during their annual physical
examinations. Allen believes this is an invasion of his privacy and
consults an attorney to find out if his department can legally
require him to be tested for HIV.*

MANDATORY TESTING VERSUS VOLUNTARY TESTING

Voluntary Testing

The Benefits

In a perfect world the people most at risk for a particular disease
or illness would voluntarily seek medical testing right away. If it
were found that they had the disease, they would receive medical
care and prevent further spread of the disease. If they did not
have the disease, they would learn how to modify their behavior so
that they would be less at risk. We do not live in a perfect world.

The benefits of voluntary testing are:

- It helps to stop the spread of the disease.
- People can be educated about protecting themselves regardless of their test results.
- It assists public health departments in studying the effects and the spread of the disease.

- **It provides medical care to diseased people as soon as possible.**

The Disadvantages

There are many reasons why a person would not want to be tested voluntarily. Even if your test is negative, the simple fact that you requested the test might lead some unenlightened people to make assumptions about your lifestyle. They might assume you are gay or a drug user or promiscuous. You might worry that your employer would find out because your insurance through work paid for the test. Then there are your family and friends. Being a carrier of hepatitis or HIV or tuberculosis carries with it a social stigma that can be frightening.

 WHEN YOU TRAVEL

China now requires that all foreigners be tested for the HIV virus. Those who test positive are barred from establishing long-term residency. Taiwan requires that foreigners be tested for the HIV virus before entering the country. It may evict those persons who either test positive or refuse to be tested.

If you test positive for a communicable disease, your doctor or the laboratory that does the testing is required to report your case to the public health department. Every state requires this, although the exact diseases that must be reported vary by state.

Some states go further. In some states pharmacists are required to report the names and addresses of people who purchase certain medications, such as those used to treat HIV or AIDS. As long as the state has safeguards to keep that information confidential, this reporting by pharmacists is not considered an invasion of your privacy.

VOTING WITH THEIR FEET

For two years the state of Illinois required mandatory testing for HIV for any people applying for marriage licenses. During those two years an estimated 40,000 people left Illinois to marry in other states.

Mandatory Testing

Mandatory testing means that you are required by law or by your employer to submit to a medical examination. Mandatory testing at your workplace is generally permitted with certain legal safeguards. Other persons who may face mandatory testing include blood donors, pregnant women (and, later, their newborns), prisoners, and people charged with sex crimes.

Testing of Blood Donors

Mandatory testing for blood donors for HIV began in the 1980s after several people were infected from blood transfusions. To protect the blood supply from the virus, many people called for mandatory testing for all blood donors. Today, blood donations are tested for the virus as a matter of routine.

 TESTING PUBLIC WORKERS

In some states, public employees such as firefighters, paramedics, and police officers may be tested for HIV as part of their annual physical examinations. The rationale is that the privacy of the public employees is outweighed by the need to protect the health and safety of the citizens. In other jurisdictions, such as the District of Columbia, a firefighter may not be denied a position with the fire department because of HIV status.

Testing of Pregnant Women

Another instance of mandatory testing is testing pregnant women for drug use and reporting the results to law enforcement. Some public hospitals test all pregnant women as a result of public concern over the number of crack babies being born. The policy is considered necessary to protect the health of the unborn children. Pregnant women addicted to cocaine could be charged with distributing a controlled substance to a minor and required to attend treatment for substance abuse. The practice is controversial and is expected to spark court challenges.

Mandatory HIV Testing

Because your HIV or AIDS status is considered very personal and sensitive, mandatory testing carries with it much debate. If you are not HIV positive, you have a vested interest in staying that way. If you are HIV positive, you have the right and the need to keep that information private. The state must balance one person's right to stay healthy with another person's right to privacy.

Mandatory HIV testing of current employees, not job applicants, is generally allowed as long as the testing is job related and necessary to the business. That means that all employees must be tested, not just those the employer believes are, for example, homosexuals. If an employee starts taking a lot of sick leave, the employer cannot mandate testing for HIV for only that person.

The mandatory-testing issue usually arises in the case of health care workers, prisoners, public employees, pregnant

---

 TESTING PUGILISTS

Fifteen state boxing commissions require that professional boxers be tested for HIV before stepping into the ring. No other major sport currently has mandatory HIV testing for its athletes.

---

women, and newborns. Another situation where mandatory HIV testing comes up: when victims of sex crimes want to know if their attacker is HIV positive.

How mandatory HIV testing plays into the public health/ personal privacy balance is open for discussion. For instance, Nebraska wanted all employees of a county health agency to be tested for HIV. These employees worked with the mentally disabled who sometimes bit or scratched the employees. The state believed that mandatory testing was the only way to prevent transferring HIV from the employees to the disabled. A court disagreed and ruled that the risk of transmission was so small that it did not warrant invading the employees' privacy.

In Alabama the law requires that all prison inmates be tested for HIV. Those that are HIV positive are segregated from the rest of the inmates. A court ruled that the state had a compelling interest in preventing the spread of HIV within the prison system. Alabama was allowed to continue its mandatory HIV testing of inmates. The debate on how to balance these competing interests will continue for years to come.

The City of Miami Beach, Florida, required that all its police officers be tested for tuberculosis. In order to accurately test for tuberculosis, the officers had to disclose their HIV status. One officer sued the city for making him disclose his HIV-positive status. A court ruled that the city's right to test for tuberculosis outweighed the officer's right to keep his HIV status private.

MANDATORY TESTING AND AIDS BABIES

The Controversy

When your child goes to the doctor, you, the parent, are required to sign consent forms that allow the doctor to treat your child. The same goes for you. If you do not want the doctor to test you or your child for the HIV infection, you can refuse to sign the consent form—except when your child is first born. When newborns are tested for HIV infection, their mothers are, in a way, also being tested for the virus—without their consent. Normally this would violate your constitutional guarantee that the state will not subject you to unreasonable searches. When it comes to HIV-infected newborns, though, the state has the right to take certain precautions to protect their health and welfare. The debate is how to balance your constitutional rights with the rights of the state to make sure that its infants are getting the medical care they need.

The Benefits of Testing Newborns

An HIV-positive adult can live with the infection for several years before any symptoms of AIDS appear. Babies do not have that luxury. AIDS symptoms usually show up within the first year after birth, and 10 percent of untreated infants die before they reach the age of one. These children suffer and die from AIDS-related illnesses such as pneumonia.

If newborns are found to be HIV-infected, they can be given medication to prevent the onset of these symptoms. This medication slows down the infection so that AIDS does not develop as quickly. It also protects against AIDS-related infections such as pneumonia. Early medical care enables children to gain weight by treating metabolic and digestive problems, which in turn helps them fight the disease.

The Downside to Testing Babies

Not all states that test newborns are equipped to deal with the information once they receive it. These laws are highly criticized because the mothers are not necessarily provided with the information or the treatment they need to deal with the disease. There is a fear that the hospital will inform the parents in a way that will violate their confidentiality, such as leaving letters notifying them of the positive result with family members or telling them in a hospital nursery in front of other people. Sometimes the test results are not released for months after the birth, by which time the baby is already showing symptoms of AIDS.

The other criticism is that many of the women who are HIV positive are the most vulnerable. These women are teenagers. Some are homeless or are victims of abuse. These women, it is argued, need the most counseling and assistance. If they do not receive it, their babies become victims once again because the mothers do not know where to find the special medical care their children need.

MANDATORY TESTING ON THE JOB— THE AMERICANS WITH DISABILITIES ACT (ADA)

To comply with the law, your employer may require you to submit to a medical examination or to release information about your medical condition only if that information is related to your job or is a business necessity. The law that governs medical examinations in this manner is the ADA, although the medical examination may not reveal that you have a disability.

The medical exam or inquiry is allowed when:

1. You are having difficulty performing your job effectively. A medical examination may be necessary to determine whether you can perform the essential job functions with or without an accommodation.

2. You believe that you have become disabled. A medical examination may be necessary to determine if your condition meets the ADA's definition of "disability."

3. You request an accommodation on the basis of disability. A medical examination may be necessary to determine if you have a disability covered by the ADA and to help find an appropriate accommodation.

4. Federal, state, or local laws require medical examinations.

Your employer may require a medical examination under these laws without violating the ADA.

5. You choose to take part in medical examinations as part of a "wellness" program, such as blood pressure testing and cholesterol screening.

An employer may require you to pass a medical examination after extending to you an offer of employment and before you begin work for that employer. The employer may require that you pass the medical examination before you can begin work if all new employees are subjected to a medical examination regardless of disability. The information on your medical condition and history must be treated as a confidential medical record, with a few exceptions as discussed in Chapter 14, Confidentiality and Disclosure.

An employer may not base its decision to hire (or not hire) you on whether you suffer a disability. It may only base its decision on whether you could do your job, regardless of any disability you might suffer. Your employer may not ask whether you have a disability or, if your employer knows you have a disability, about the nature or severity of your disability *unless* those questions are related to whether you could do the job.

THE WORLD AT YOUR FINGERTIPS

- *Reducing the Odds: Preventing Perinatal Transmission of HIV in the United States* by Michael A. Stoto, Donna A. Almario, and Marie C. McCormick argues that HIV testing should become an ordinary part of prenatal care in order to stop the transmission of HIV from mother to baby (National Academy Press, 1999).
- *More Harm Than Help: The Ramifications for Rape Survivors of Mandatory HIV Testing of Rapists* by Lisa Bowleg argues that mandatory testing for those charged with sex crimes

may not be the answer to providing victims with peace of mind (Center for Women Policy Studies, 1991).

YOU MUST REMEMBER THIS

- Your employer may require you to submit to a medical examination or to release information about your medical condition only if that information is related to your job or is a business necessity.
- Some states allow mandatory HIV testing for public employees such as firefighters, paramedics, and police officers.
- Almost every state requires that newborns be tested for HIV status.
- A court will balance the health and safety of citizens with the privacy interests of the individual when deciding whether mandatory HIV testing should be allowed.

CHAPTER 17

Tort Liability

Your Guide to ADA Discrimination, "AIDSphobia," and Other Civil Wrongs

Patricia decides to comply with state law and allow her two-year-old daughter to be vaccinated. Her daughter suffers a terrible reaction to the vaccination and winds up staying in the hospital for two weeks, during which time Patricia and her husband must take unpaid leave from work. Patricia wants to sue the manufacturer of the vaccine for negligence. Can she recover damages?

While taking his son to an urgent care center, Patrick goes into the public restroom, washes his hands, and dries them with paper towels. When he throws the paper towels into the garbage, Patrick feels a sharp prick on his hand. Patrick pushes aside the towels and finds a syringe in the garbage can. Patrick leaves the syringe in the garbage can and returns to the waiting room. When he gets home, Patrick tells his wife about the syringe in the trash can. His wife is afraid that the syringe might carry the HIV virus. Patrick gets afraid, too. What if he gets AIDS now? Patrick goes into a deep depression for months until it is finally determined that, no, he is not HIV positive. Can Patrick recover damages from the urgent care center for the emotional trauma he went through?

TORTS IN GENERAL

What Is a Tort?

A **tort** is a legal wrong or injury committed by one person against another. It is not a crime. This is a civil action. In a civil action the state prosecutor is not involved. Instead, a private party or a government agency brings a lawsuit against another private party. In other words, a person hires a lawyer and sues, for example, a doctor or insurance company or medical manufacturer.

The person or corporation being sued then also hires a lawyer to handle the legal action.

A recent example of an action for tort liability is *Equal Employment Opportunity Commission v. Wal-Mart Stores, Inc.* In that case a hearing-impaired Wal-Mart employee was told to attend an employee training session even though there would be no sign language interpreter at the session. The employee refused to attend the training session, and his manager fired him. The employee sued the parent company under the ADA and won $3,500 in back pay and $75,000 in punitive damages. (Punitive damages aren't available in every proceeding for damages, and in fact are rare.)

What makes the case unusual is that it is one of the first times that a parent company was held liable for the actions of a midlevel manager under the ADA. Wal-Mart argued on appeal that it should not be held responsible for the manager's actions because the parent company had a written training and education policy to help its managers comply with the ADA. The employee argued, though, that the policy was rarely used. The court ruled that it is not enough for employers to have policies against discrimination. The company must make a good faith effort to educate its employees about the ADA.

What Is Liability?

Liability is a general legal term for responsibility. If you injure another person, you are responsible to that person for the injury you caused. In legal terms, you are "liable" to that person. Exactly what the responsibility will mean to you depends on your situation. **Damages** usually mean a monetary award. Tort liability is used to discourage people from hurting others by requiring them to compensate victims for their injury. The person responsible for hurting you must pay you in order to make you "whole" again.

The tort remedies available include both **injunctive relief** and a **make-whole remedy.** You may also be eligible to receive compensatory damages and **punitive** damages. Under the ADA, compensatory and punitive damages amounts are capped based on the size of the employer. For example, small employers with fewer than 101 employees are liable for no more than $50,000 total in compensatory and punitive damages. Employers with more than 500 employees are liable for no more than $300,000 total in damages. The court, at its discretion, may award attorney's fees to the prevailing party.

POSSIBLE REMEDIES

Compensatory damages: These may include compensation for any indirect injuries you suffer as a natural consequence of negligence or discrimination (such as pain and suffering) as well as compensation for your direct injuries (such as back pay).

Punitive damages: These damages are intended to punish the wrongdoer and to deter others from engaging in similar conduct. Courts award these damages when the wrongdoer acts with malice or reckless indifference to your rights.

Injunctive relief: This is a court order directed at wrongdoers, requiring them to engage in certain types of action. The order might tell them to stop violating the law and not do it again in the future. Or an order might require them to take certain affirmative steps to restore things to the position they would have been in had the law not been violated, such as hiring you if you were wrongfully denied a job.

Make-whole remedy: This puts you in the position you would have been in had there been no wrongdoing. For example, if you are illegally fired from your job, the make-whole remedy would include reinstating you, paying you the wages (with interest) you would have earned had you remained employed, providing the seniority and pensions benefits you would have been credited if you had remained employed, and reimbursing you for any medical expenses you incurred that would have been covered under the employer's health plan.

Under the ADA and the Rehabilitation Act, you are required to file a complaint with the Equal Employment Opportunity Commission before you can bring a tort action. For an explanation of this process, see Chapter 12.

What You Must Prove

To win on a tort claim under the ADA or the Rehabilitation Act, you must prove three things:

1. you have a disability;
2. you were qualified for the job in question; *and*
3. you were fired or disciplined because of your disability.

To qualify as disabled, you must suffer from a physical or mental impairment that substantially limits one or more of your major life activities. Exactly what constitutes "substantially limits" is an issue that comes up again and again in the courts. You must prove your disability by offering evidence that the extent of the limitation on a major life activity in your own experience is substantial. For example, let's imagine that you are a truck driver, recently diagnosed with amblyopia (poor vision caused by abnormal visual development secondary to abnormal visual stimulation). You are no longer able to drive a car, much less a truck. Are you disabled? Yes, because seeing is a major life activity. If your vision problem can be corrected with glasses, however, you are no longer disabled as defined by the ADA.

To show that you were *qualified for the job in question,* the court will look at whether you can perform the essential functions of the job with or without reasonable accommodation. Do you have the appropriate licensing, experience, or educational requirement? If not, then you are not a qualified individual and you will not be able to prove your claim. To determine whether a function is essential to the job, the court will look at written job descriptions and the work experience of those in similar jobs and consider whether the function is fundamental to that position. One job function that is always considered essential is the ability to show up for work on time. If alcoholism or substance abuse causes a person to be absent or late excessively, then that person cannot perform an essential function of the job and is not qualified within the meaning of the ADA.

In most jurisdictions you must prove that you were *fired or disciplined based solely on your disability.* In other jurisdictions you only have to prove that your disability played some part in your termination or discipline. It is helpful if you can show that you were replaced by a nondisabled person or that you were treated less favorably than nondisabled employees. This does not mean that every decision your employer makes gives you an ADA claim if you are disabled. It only means that you cannot be discriminated against because of your disability.

Example

In one case, a man's job required that he have a valid driver's license. When the man was convicted four times of driving under the influence of alcohol, he was demoted to a position that required no driving. The man sued his company, claiming that his alcoholism was a disability and that his demotion was based on this disability in violation of the ADA. The man lost his case because he could not prove that his alcoholism, rather than his poor driving record, was the cause of his demotion. Furthermore, the court found that to make the company liable under the ADA or the Rehabilitation Act in this situation would undermine laws that protect society from the dangerous behavior of others, such as drunken driving.

The Next Step

Once you give your evidence, the burden shifts to the defendant (the person or the company you are suing). The defendant must give some nondiscriminatory reason for firing or disciplining you. After that you may offer evidence that the employer's real reason was discriminatory. The main burden of persuasion lies with you to show that your employer fired or disciplined you because of your disability. If you suffer from alcoholism or substance abuse, you are required to prove, among other things, that you successfully completed a supervised drug rehabilitation program and that you no longer use illegal drugs. Alcoholism and substance abuse are not, in themselves, included in the ADA's definition of a disability.

TORT LIABILITY FOR VACCINES

Burden of Proof

Traditionally the tort system is based on the assumption that by making parties responsible for the consequences of their actions, the parties will act in the most appropriate manner possible. In any action for tort liability, you, the patient, have the burden of proving that the other party's action caused your injury. For example, some people believe that childhood vaccinations cause autism. To sue for tort liability on this issue, you would have the burden of proving that the vaccine your child received caused your child to become autistic. This can be difficult to do.

Another hurdle is that some jurisdictions recognize that all vaccines, by their nature, carry some risks, even if the vaccines are properly manufactured. This is known as being **unavoidably unsafe.** Other products that are unavoidably unsafe include knives, firearms, and explosives. To win a tort liability lawsuit against a vaccine manufacturer, you would have to prove not only that the vaccine caused the injury, but also that the manufacturer was negligent in making the vaccine or in failing to warn of the risk associated with vaccines.

In general, the manufacturer is not required to warn you directly of the risks of a vaccine. Rather, the manufacturer must inform your doctor of the risks. Your doctor then has the duty to explain these risks to you. If your doctor does not explain these risks to you and you are injured, then you may have a medical malpractice claim against your doctor for violating your right to informed consent.

The Federal Tort Claims Act
(FTCA) and the Swine Flu

In 1976 Congress believed the country was facing an epidemic of a form of influenza known as swine flu. A similar strain of influenza had caused 20 million deaths worldwide. Health officials wanted every person in the country to be vaccinated. Drug manufacturers, however, refused to release the vaccination because their insurance companies refused to cover any liability for adverse reactions. Congress enacted the Federal Tort Claims Act, which gave swine flu vaccine manufacturers immunity from liability for injuries caused by any adverse reactions to the vaccine. The FTCA allowed those who were injured by the vaccine to seek damages directly from the federal government. More than 40 million people received the swine flu vaccination. By 1985 at least 4,165 people filed claims under the FTCA for adverse reactions to the vaccine. Approximately 1,600 lawsuits were filed after the government denied claims for vaccine-related injuries. These were usually settled before reaching the courtroom. Today you may bring a vaccine-related claim under the National Vaccine Safety Act, which is discussed in Chapter 15.

TORT LIABILITY FOR HIV AND AIDS
The Health Care Setting

The issue of liability for infecting others—or the potential to infect others—almost always comes up in the health care setting. That does not mean that it always involves patients and doctors. Some cases include security officers, drivers, or cleaning personnel. Some involve HIV-positive doctors who operated on patients without telling them about their (the doctors') HIV status. Others involve patients who underwent surgery knowing they were HIV positive but who failed to inform their doctors. The most common scenario, though, is a health care worker who is accidentally stuck by a needle while treating a patient. Regardless of how the scenario comes about, it is time-consuming and difficult to prove that the person who exposed you to HIV should be held liable to you under the law.

ARTIFICIAL—AND POSSIBLY DEADLY

A very unusual form of HIV transmission occurs when women are artificially inseminated with sperm from men who are HIV positive. The only known instance in the United States happened to two women in Wisconsin, both of whom received sperm from a man who was HIV positive. Neither woman became infected. In Australia, eight women were artificially inseminated with sperm from an HIV-positive man. Four of the women became infected. Whether these women could recover damages in the courts from sperm banks or donors for becoming infected is not yet known.

AIDSphobia

Tort cases that involve the fear that one may be infected with HIV or AIDS are called AIDSphobia cases, fear of AIDS or fear of future disease. This is not the first time that fear of getting a disease sometime in the future brought about court cases. "Fear of cancer" was a common theme among people exposed to asbestos. Manufacturers of asbestos were sued repeatedly by people who had been exposed and were worried that, somewhere down the line, they would develop cancer because of the asbestos. The first fear of AIDS cases were decided along the same lines as the fear of cancer cases. As the years wore on, a few courts began to follow a different path, which will be discussed in greater detail in a moment.

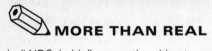 **MORE THAN REAL**

In "AIDSphobia" cases, the ultimate question is not whether the fear is real, but whether the fear is reasonable. People claiming fear of AIDS have a legal responsibility to educate themselves about whether the risk of developing AIDS is realistic.

HOW STATES DIFFER ON FEAR OF AIDS CASES

Actual Exposure

There are two lines of reasoning when it comes to tort liability and HIV. The majority of states follow a line of reasoning that requires "actual exposure" to HIV or AIDS. **Actual exposure** means that you were actually exposed to the virus. For example, it is not enough to say that you were stuck with a needle. You must prove that the needle that stuck you carried the virus at the time you were stuck. If you cannot prove actual exposure, you do not have a case of tort liability.

Fear on the Part of a "Reasonable" Person

The other line of reasoning does not require that you show that you were exposed to the virus. You simply must show that you are a reasonable person and that you feared that you would be infected from the incident (such as a needle stick). In states that do not require you to prove actual exposure, fear of AIDS cases are much easier to prove.

Why "Fear of AIDS" Cases Are Controversial

The person bringing the lawsuit claims that she suffered emotional distress at the thought that she might get HIV or AIDS. How does she prove that she suffered emotional distress?

Distress is a difficult thing to prove and an easy thing to fake. Some people believe that fear of AIDS is no more reasonable than fear of lung cancer from second-hand smoke or fear of herpes— neither of which are claims that are allowed in a court of law. Of course you will be upset if you are stuck by a needle. The question is whether you should be allowed to sue for emotional distress before you even know whether the needle carried the virus.

A SAMPLE OF STATES WITH FEAR OF AIDS CASES

California—Requires Actual Exposure

A woman underwent surgery to have a tumor removed from her uterus. Unbeknownst to the woman, the doctor who performed the surgery was HIV positive. There was no indication that the doctor's blood ever came into contact with the patient's blood. The woman later found out that the doctor was HIV positive. Her HIV test turned up negative. Still, she sued the doctor for emotional distress due to her fear of getting AIDS. In California, you must prove not only that you were actually exposed to the virus, but also that it is more likely than not that you will be infected. The woman could show no actual exposure to the virus. Hence, she lost the case.

West Virginia—Requires Actual Exposure

A hospital patient bit a security guard. The patient had AIDS, and the patient's blood came into direct contact with the guard's blood. The security guard tested negative for the virus; but because he was in fact exposed to the virus, he was allowed to claim emotional distress for his fear of getting AIDS.

Maryland—Actual Exposure Not Required

A surgeon who knew he was HIV positive performed surgery on two patients. The patients were not informed that the surgeon was HIV positive. A year after the surgeries, the patients read about the doctor's HIV status in the local newspaper. The patients were tested for the virus. Both patients were HIV negative. The patients sued the doctor's estate and the hospital where the operations were performed. Both patients argued that the surgeon should have told them about his HIV status so they could choose another surgeon if they wanted to. The doctor's estate and the hospital argued that the patients were never exposed to the virus. The patients won the case, however, because the court ruled that a reasonable person would suffer emotional distress after learning that the surgeon was HIV positive at the time of the surgery. The patients did not need to prove that they were actually exposed to the virus at all.

New Jersey—Actual Exposure Not Required

New Jersey does not require you to show that you were actually exposed to the virus. This state differs from the other states that do not require actual exposure to claim emotional distress by adding a **"window of anxiety"**—a time period. You can claim emotional distress only for the time in which an average person would have suffered emotional trauma. This is the "window of anxiety."

How long would an average person suffer emotional distress? That depends on the medical data regarding HIV and AIDS that is available at the time. The current "window of anxiety" in New Jersey is 3 to 6 months. The court figures that after 6 months an average person should know for sure whether or not he is infected. Therefore, you can only claim emotional distress for 3 to 6 months, not a year or 2 years or 10 years. As more becomes known about AIDS and as testing methods become more reliable, look for that "window of anxiety" to narrow to a few weeks.

THE WORLD AT YOUR FINGERTIPS

- *Bendectin on Trial: A Study of Mass Tort Litigation* by Joseph Sanders (University of Michigan Press, 1998) looks at the lawsuits surrounding Bendectin, which was given to pregnant mothers to control morning sickness. The book discusses how lawyers developed the tort liability claims, how scientific evidence was used during trial, and the part judges played in managing and resolving the cases.
- To find cases that deal with tort liability in the health care setting, visit the Internet Law Library at *http://www.priweb. com/internetlawlib/110.htm.* The subject matter of the cases is in parentheses after the case name.
- The National Vaccine Information Center is a nonprofit educational organization founded in 1982. It provides information on vaccinations and links to immunization tracking organizations and victim compensation programs. You can visit their website at *http://www.909shot.com/.*

YOU MUST REMEMBER THIS

- A tort is a legal wrong or injury commited by one person against another.
- Liability is a general legal term for responsibility to another person for an injury.
- You must prove that the other party's actions caused your injury.
- To recover damages, it isn't enough to show liability—you have to show that your injury caused deprivations/hardships that could be compensated by money.
- A parent company may be held liable for the actions of its managers or supervisors.
- In fear of AIDS cases, you may be required to prove that you were actually exposed to the virus in order to win your claim.

CHAPTER 18

Quarantine

An Old Public Health Measure Raises New Legal Issues

Jerome is a state legislator. He and his fellow representatives are concerned about the rising number of tuberculosis residents in his state. They want to protect their residents from the disease for many reasons, including keeping the cost of health care reasonable. Jerome sees no other way to effect this protection than to isolate all tuberculosis carriers from the rest of the population. He proposes quarantine for any person who is a tuberculosis carrier.

QUARANTINE

What Is Quarantine?

Quarantine is the isolation of a person or group of persons (or animals) from the rest of society to prevent them from spreading a disease. Before antibiotics were invented, a quarantine was the most important tool in preventing the spread of a disease. The disease could not be treated, so the source of the disease—the person who was suffering from it—had to be kept away from other people to avoid spreading it. One of the first known quarantines is referenced in the Bible. The Bible makes references to lepers who were cast out to avoid the spread of leprosy. Quarantines were later used to combat the spread of cholera.

 LEARNING THE LINGO

Quarantine: To isolate people so as to prevent the spread of disease.

Can the Government Quarantine People?

Yes. The state is responsible for protecting the health and safety of its citizens. This includes the right to quarantine people with contagious diseases. In most states the health department is responsible for quarantining contagious people.

Whatever the disease, certain procedures must be followed before you can be quarantined. Federal law requires some of these procedures; others depend on the state in which you live. The United States Constitution says that you cannot be deprived of life, liberty, or property without due process. That means that the state must provide safeguards so that your liberty to go about your life as you wish will not be taken away on the whim of the government. One of the ways that your state may do this is by holding a hearing before you are quarantined.

Most of the state laws were enacted in the early or middle 1900s. These laws do not take into account new methods of treatment or court cases that expanded the safeguards against involuntary confinement. In fact, only ten states have overhauled their tuberculosis-related laws at the time of this writing.

At the present time thirty-three states allow public health authorities to isolate people with contagious diseases in their homes. Forty-two states allow public health authorities to commit people with tuberculosis to treatment facilities, although only thirty-six of these states require a court order to do so. A court order will generally lead to a hearing to determine whether the person should be committed. Only thirteen states, however, expressly grant a person the right to be represented by an attorney at the hearing. Indigent people who cannot afford an attorney have a right to a court-appointed attorney in only eleven states.

A person is released from quarantine when that person is no longer infectious or a threat to the public health. A person in quarantine often has the right to petition the court for release, which the court may either grant or deny.

Civil Commitment

Civil commitment refers to the state's power to confine you to your home or to a hospital, even though you have not committed a crime. Civil commitment requires a balance of society's right to be protected from people who are harmful and your constitutional right to liberty and due process. In order to deprive you of your liberty, the state must present convincing evidence that you are a danger to others.

In 1980, a renewed interest in civil commitment for quarantine cases began in West Virginia. Under the West Virginia Tuberculosis Control Act, the health authorities filed a petition in state circuit court, claiming that a man had active communicable tuberculosis. The court scheduled a hearing, and the man was served with notice of the hearing. He was not advised of his right to an attorney. He was appointed an attorney when he arrived for the hearing but was not given time to discuss his case. After the hearing the court ordered that the man be committed to the hospital for treatment. In other words, the man was involuntarily quarantined.

The man filed a petition for habeas corpus, arguing that his due process rights were violated. He argued that his right to counsel was violated, that he was not given the right to confront witnesses or to present his own, and that the court did not require that the evidence be clear and convincing. The West Virginia Supreme Court agreed with him and ordered him released and a new hearing held.

The West Virginia Supreme Court ruled that people could not be quarantined unless:

1. the person was given adequate written notice detailing the grounds and underlying facts on which the commitment is sought;

2. the person had a chance to obtain and consult with an attorney;

3. the person was present and had the chance to cross-examine, confront, and present witnesses;

4. the court required the evidence to be clear and convincing;
5. the person was allowed to obtain a verbatim transcript of the hearing for appeal purposes.

These procedural safeguards are now available in a few other states, including New York and Washington. The Centers for Disease Control and Prevention (CDC) also released its guidelines for quarantine. The CDC recommendations of the Advisory Council for the Elimination of Tuberculosis (ACET) state that:

> [a]s in commitment proceedings under state mental health laws, any law under which a person may be examined, isolated, detained, committed, and/or treated for TB must meet due process and equal protection requirements under state and federal statutes and constitutions. Also, all patients who are subject to these legal proceedings should be represented by legal counsel.

HOW QUARANTINE WORKS

When Will a State Quarantine People?

Each state keeps a list of communicable diseases that threaten the health of the public. You cannot be quarantined unless you have one of the diseases on that list. If you suffer a disease on the list and the state considers you a threat to the health of the community, you can be quarantined. Whether your state puts AIDS on its list of communicable diseases that may require quarantine is up to the state. At the present time, no state includes AIDS on its list.

Where Would I Be Put If I Were Quarantined?

You would usually be confined to your home. Signs would be posted outside your house warning people against coming into your home. If you needed medical care, you could be confined to

A NATIONAL AIDS QUARANTINE

In 1987 Cuba became the first country to quarantine all people with HIV or AIDS. Every person in the country is required to be tested. Those infected are put in a former sanitarium near Havana for an indefinite length of time. Patients are allowed to leave the sanitarium for family visits or other activities but must be accompanied by a chaperone.

one small part of a hospital. In some cases you might simply be restricted from doing certain things, such as attending school or preparing food for others.

Can I Ignore the Quarantine?

The state has the power to enforce the quarantine by watching your house to make sure you do not leave. If you do not follow the quarantine order, the state may put you in a locked facility, such as a prison.

Should There Be a Quarantine for People with HIV or AIDS?

Many people in the late 1980s thought that people with HIV and AIDS should be kept separate from the rest of the population. AIDS was considered a plague to be contained at all costs. Today, support for total isolation for people with HIV and AIDS is far less common in the United States. As the public becomes more educated about how the disease is spread, the widespread panic of a few years ago is subsiding.

Historically, quarantine was used only when the rapid spread of a disease could not be controlled in any other way. HIV and AIDS are different from many of the contagious diseases of yesterday. Unlike those diseases, casual contact does not spread AIDS.

In addition, historically, quarantine was only required while the person was contagious. The person either soon died or became better and was no longer contagious. Right now there is no certain cure for HIV or AIDS. The infected person may live with the disease for more than a dozen years before death. To quarantine a person for that long, it is argued, would place an immense burden on the person and the person's family.

 A SELECTIVE AIDS QUARANTINE

In the 1980s Sweden began to quarantine some people with HIV or AIDS who would not agree to medical supervision. The people were sent to a care center on an island 25 miles west of Sweden.

Civil rights groups also fear that because AIDS is associated with groups such as drug users and gay men, quarantines will become a tool for discrimination against those groups.

States have taken more modest quarantine measures. New York used its quarantine authority to close down gay bathhouses. Virginia and Colorado put procedures in place to deal with people with AIDS who refused to change their behavior and stop putting others at risk for getting the disease. Some states also divide prison inmates into two groups—those with HIV or AIDS and those without—in order to stop the spread of the disease.

QUARANTINE AND IMMIGRANTS
United States Policy

In June 1987, the United States adopted a policy that refuses to allow HIV-positive foreigners into the United States. The policy is meant to protect Americans from infection of contagious diseases. Other diseases on the list have included gonorrhea, leprosy, infectious syphilis, and active tuberculosis. The U.S. government began testing immigrants for the HIV virus on December 1, 1987.

Haitians

When Haiti's democracy fell to a military coup, some Haitians were forced to flee their country. Many were granted political asylum within the United States. About 270 Haitian men, women, and children were not granted refugee status but were detained in a compound surrounded by armed guards on the U.S. Naval Base at Guantanamo Bay, Cuba. This group of Haitians was HIV positive. Their disease set them apart from the other refugees.

Some of the HIV-positive refugees were sent back to Haiti. The others lived in the camp, surrounded by barbed wire. The military doctors did not have the facilities to treat the Haitians who developed AIDS, but their requests to transfer the immigrants to adequate medical facilities were denied by the U.S. Immigration and Naturalization Service (INS).

After a class action lawsuit on behalf of the refugees, the Haitians were sent to the United States for medical care and INS processing in 1993. That does not mean that the refugees were allowed to remain in the United States indefinitely—only that they could no longer be detained in the camp without medical care or a determination of their INS status.

Current U.S. Policy

Under the National Institutes of Health Revitalization Bill, HIV infection is considered a communicable disease of such significance to the public health that non-Americans with the infection may be denied entry into the United States.

The law is not an absolute bar to HIV-positive aliens, however. The decision on whether to forbid someone from entering the country is based on:

1. the stage of the person's disease,
2. the length of the person's visit,
3. whether the person has insurance to cover medical expenses, and

QUARANTINE OF GUIDE DOGS

In 1920 Hawaii enacted a law to prevent the spread of rabies. The law requires that all animals must be quarantined for 120 days before being allowed into the general area of that state. The law specifically includes guide dogs used by the visually impaired and other disabled people. The state of Hawaii is subject to the federal Americans with Disabilities Act (ADA) and Rehabilitation Act laws, which seek to provide the same treatment to disabled people as to nondisabled people. There are no court cases so far that have gotten far enough to challenge the quarantine law under the ADA or the Rehabilitation Act.

---

4. whether the INS has reason to believe the person will pose a danger to the public health in the United States.

THE WORLD AT YOUR FINGERTIPS

- To learn more about tuberculosis, go to the website for the U.S. Department of Agriculture at *http://www.fsis.usda.gov/OPHS/tbbroch.htm.*

- *Quarantine!: East European Jewish Immigrants and the New York City Epidemics of 1892* by Howard Markel (Johns Hopkins University Press, 1999) chronicles how America's fear of immigrants and disease led them to blame Jews for the typhus and cholera epidemics. The actions parallel those taken to deal with immigrants with HIV and AIDS.

- *Typhoid Mary: Captive to the Public's Health* by Judith Walzer Leavitt (Beacon Press, 1997) is the story of 13-year-old Mary Mallon, the Irish immigrant who later became known as Typhoid Mary, and how she was isolated on an island in the East River after an outbreak of disease among wealthy New Yorkers for whom she was a servant.

- *Fevered Lives: Tuberculosis in American Culture Since 1870* by Katherine Ott (Harvard University Press, 1999) discusses how science and prejudice combined to blame the spread of tuberculosis on the poor and the immigrants.

YOU MUST REMEMBER THIS

- You cannot be deprived of your liberty without due process of law. In the case of quarantine, this may mean you are entitled to a prequarantine hearing.
- The state has the authority to quarantine you if you are a danger to the health and safety of others in your community.
- The quarantine may last only as long as you are contagious.
- The majority of states allow you to be quarantined for tuberculosis.
- U.S. law gives the INS the right to bar HIV-positive immigrants from entering the United States.

PART FIVE

Nursing Homes

Information to Help You

Make the Right Choices

As we age, or as we watch our parents age, we begin to wonder about our options for health care when we can no longer manage by ourselves. Will we be forced into a nursing home? How will we pay the costs? Are there any alternatives? If we do decide to go to a nursing home, what rights do we have as patients? The chapters in this section will answer these questions and many others.

Chapter 19 spells out your rights as a nursing home patient. We will give you some suggestions for things to look for when choosing a nursing home and fill you in on how the law tries to protect you from poor nursing home care. We will also tell you what to do and where to go when you need to make a complaint or to take action against a nursing home.

Chapter 20 discusses your best options for paying for your nursing home care. As the costs of health care and nursing homes rise, you will need to be aware of the steps you need to take NOW to protect yourself—and your money—in the future. Will the Medicare or Medicaid programs pay for your nursing home care? We will answer that question in Chapter 21. We will delve into why Medicaid may not be right for you, as well as what you will need to do to protect your assets and still qualify for government programs.

Finally, we explore some of your alternatives to nursing home care in Chapter 22. There are many options out there, but it can be confusing when you factor in quality and costs of care. This chapter will explain some of the alternatives available to you right now and advise you on some of the ways you can pay for care while protecting your family and your home.

If you would like more information on these and other topics, please check at the end of the guide for additional resources and websites regarding these issues.

CHAPTER 19

Choosing a Nursing Home

Tips on Making Sure That Your Loved Ones Will Be Well Treated

MaryLou and Kathy are worried about their mother, Helen. She is in good physical health, but she is becoming more and more forgetful. Last week Helen put a kettle on the stove to heat water for a cup of tea. She forgot about the kettle until the smoke detector went off. There was some minor smoke damage to the house. Helen was shaken but unhurt. Now either MaryLou or Kathy goes to Helen's house every day to check on her. Each day they become a little more afraid of what they will find when they get there. But what choice do they have? Are there home care services that could help? Should they put her in a nursing home? How would they go about choosing one? How will they know if she is getting good care there? What options do they have if their mother is not given the care she needs?

NURSING HOMES IN GENERAL

Unlike hospitals, which developed largely as charitable institutions, nursing homes developed as small "mom and pop" businesses. Today, large chains dominate the industry. While many hospitals are nonprofit, most nursing homes are run for profit. There are more than 20,000 nursing homes in the nation. The leader in the industry runs more than 700 nursing homes across the country, with annual revenues of nearly $3 billion. Nursing home care can cost as much as $7,000 per month. In 1999 alone, $90 billion was spent on nursing home care. The federal government paid about $35.6 billion for nursing home care, primarily through Medicare and Medicaid.

Is a for-profit home likely to provide worse care than a not-for-profit provider? No. There are good homes and bad homes in both categories. And some observers think that the profit motive drives more efficient, consumer-responsive products and service to attract paying customers. The only way to select a good nursing home is to do your homework—evaluate one or more homes carefully, asking the right questions until your concerns are satisfied.

We're Not Getting Any Younger

The baby boom generation is facing retirement age. The number of Americans who reach age 65 is expected to double between the years 2010 and 2030. People who celebrate their 65th birthday can expect to live almost 20 more years. In other words, the number of Americans aged 85 and older is expected to triple during that same period. These baby boomers currently sit on juries and take care of their parents. As they look to their futures, they are becoming more and more willing to award large sums of money when nursing homes are sued and found liable for malpractice or negligence. We will take a look at what is happening in the courtroom in a moment.

Who Lives in Nursing Homes?

More than 1.5 million people now live in nursing homes. Most of these people are 85 years old or older, and most do not have family members nearby. At one time, too many people were put into nursing homes and forgotten. Now our society has come to realize that even a very elderly person's life is meaningful and valuable. Think of how much you would value your life if you were told you probably had only two years left to live.

LEARNING THE LINGO

Nursing homes: Places that provide nursing care to people who are not able to live at home but who are not sick enough to be hospitalized. In general, people in a nursing home require 24-hour care.

What Makes Nursing Homes Good?

Good nursing homes exist. These nursing homes protect and watch over our loved ones for us. They provide, at the very least, the basic care: food, fluids, mobility, and hygiene. These are the most basic elements of keeping our dignity, our health, and perhaps even our lives. Nursing homes are highly regulated by state and federal governments to protect the residents, who are among those members of society most vulnerable to abuse and neglect.

A GOOD NURSING HOME

In general, a good nursing home actively supports residents' freedom, privacy, choice, independence, and control. This includes letting residents:

- organize and participate in resident groups;
- participate in social, religious, and community activities;
- examine the results of the most recent inspection of the home conducted by authorities;
- manage their own financial affairs or delegate the responsibility;
- refuse medication or treatment and be told of the result of that decision;
- have privacy when caring for their personal needs;
- be treated courteously and fairly and with dignity;
- use personal clothing and other items (space permitting);
- know before being assigned to a different room.

What Makes Them Bad?

Unfortunately, some nursing homes do not provide decent care to their residents. Unlike hospitals, where the person who cares for you is usually a nurse, the primary caregivers in nursing homes are nursing assistants or aides. In a good economy, with low unemployment, it's hard to find and retain good people to do these important jobs. Too many nursing assistants are poorly trained, overworked, underpaid, and insufficiently supervised. The result? You or your loved one may not get even your most basic needs met: you may not get help eating your meal, going to the toilet, or moving from your bed to your chair. This lack of care could mean you would end up getting bedsores and infections or perhaps suffering even worse consequences. Complaints against nursing homes include everything from malnutrition and dehydration to beatings and sexual assaults.

CONSUMER ALERT

An investigation by *Consumer Reports* found that thousands of nursing homes nationwide give care that is poor or questionable at best.

SIGNS OF A BAD NURSING HOME

- A large number of residents assigned to each nursing assistant.
- Constant turnover among the staff. Some nursing homes replace their entire staff every year because so many of their employees quit.
- Patient records that are not specific regarding the resident's treatment. These records should include a detailed plan of care (a copy of which should be given to you), doctor's orders, nurses' notes, and charts of the resident's progress.
- Failure to follow the nursing home's internal policies.

KEEPING NURSING HOMES SAFE

The Law

State and federal laws specify how nursing homes are to take care of their residents. For example, after a 1980 Dade County (Florida) grand jury investigation reported that 60 percent of the nursing homes in the state provided very poor care, the Florida legislature enacted a resident bill of rights to protect residents from neglect. In 1979, Illinois passed a nursing home care reform act that permits residents to sue homes for neglect or abuse. Medicaid includes a patient bill of rights, too. The problem is that these laws are not always enforced. When these laws are not enforced, the care of people living in the homes can suffer.

Medicaid Protection

Nursing homes that accept Medicaid are required to follow certain procedures that apply to *all* their residents:

- Basic care and services must be the same for Medicaid residents as for private-pay residents.
- The nursing home must provide information on how to apply for Medicaid.
- The facility must explain the Medicaid "bed-hold" policy (how many days Medicaid will hold the resident's bed or give priority readmission after a hospitalization or other absence).
- The nursing home may not require, request, or encourage residents to waive their rights to Medicaid.
- The facility may not require a family member to guarantee payment or be held financially liable.
- The nursing home may not charge, solicit, accept, or receive gifts, money, donations, or other items of monetary value as a precondition for admission or continued stay under Medicaid.
- Residents must receive at least 30 days advance notice of a transfer or a discharge, along with information on how to appeal or how to contact the state long-term-care ombudsman program.
- The facility must provide adequate discharge planning to prepare and orient residents for a safe and orderly transfer from the facility.

The Nursing Home Reform Act (NHRA)—Resident Bill of Rights

Congress passed the NHRA in 1987. It applies to all nursing homes that participate in Medicare and Medicaid (almost all do). It sets forth a national nursing home bill of rights. NHRA requires that nursing homes give their residents care that will maintain or improve the quality of their lives.

Residents' rights are enforced largely by state health care regulatory agencies, such as a state's department of health. For serious violations of the law, a home could lose its license or be denied participation in Medicare and Medicaid. Another potentially effective sanction is a fine. Having to pay a fine takes away the financial benefit of providing substandard care—unless the fine costs less than the monetary gain from giving substandard care.

Fines and the other sanctions only punish the nursing home, however. A fine or the loss of license does not compensate the patient for the lack of care. For the patient to be compensated, the patient may need to bring a civil action against the nursing home, which is discussed later in the chapter.

 RESIDENT RIGHTS UNDER NHRA

- the right to information, including written information about your rights, written information about fees, advance notice of changes in room assignments or roommate, and information about eligibility for Medicare and Medicaid;

- the right to voice complaints without fear of reprisal, and to receive a prompt response;

- the right to be free from physical or chemical restraints that are not required to treat the resident's medical symptoms;

- the right to be free from verbal, sexual, physical, and mental abuse; corporal punishment; and involuntary seclusion; *and*

- the right to access all records pertaining to the resident within 24 hours.

State Laws

New York is considered to have one of the best legal recourse systems for nursing home residents. When a resident is treated in a way that is considered abusive or neglectful, the resident may sue for money damages for each day the resident is injured. If the nursing home acts with willful disregard of the resident's rights, the resident can ask for punitive damages against the nursing home.

In Wisconsin, a woman was admitted to a nursing home after she suffered a stroke. In a later lawsuit, evidence showed that the nursing home staff did not put her into her shoulder brace. They let her lay in her own feces for more than an hour. The staff placed her food on her left side even though they were repeatedly told that she could not feed herself unless the food was placed on her right side. Because of this, she often went without food and became malnourished. Within two months she died. A jury awarded the woman's family $125,000 based on the nursing home's mistreatment of the resident.

Family members are not always allowed to sue the nursing home on behalf of the resident. Generally only the resident's guardian is able to sue on behalf of the resident. If you do not have a guardian, your family members may be able to sue on your behalf, depending on the state in which you live.

The method for becoming guardian varies by state. In general, you may appoint someone as your future guardian by putting your intentions in writing in a durable power of attorney or health care advance directive and signing it in front of two people acting as the witnesses. (A model health care advance directive is included in this book as appendix C.) Some states may require that this document be notarized. This document should include the name of the person you wish to be appointed as your guardian, but that person cannot be one of the witnesses.

You do not need to file this document with the court. If the time comes when you need a guardian, the person you have named will need to bring the document to the court to be named your legal guardian. Keep this document in a safe place and be sure that your future guardian knows about it and its location. You may want to include one or two other people in your document who could act as guardian if the first person is unable to fulfill that role. You can change your mind at any time by writing a new document and appointing a different person as your guardian.

Evaluating the Resident

You must be evaluated within 14 days of being admitted to a nursing home. This evaluation should be revised periodically to make sure it continues to cover your needs. The evaluation is meant to help the staff develop a care plan for you. This care plan should cover your medical and emotional needs while you are in the nursing home.

It should be shared with the resident and the resident's health care representative and family at a care planning conference involving interdisciplinary staff of the nursing home. There should be a quarterly review of the plan at least, as well as a review whenever there is a major change in the resident's physical or mental condition.

Your care plan should be used to guarantee that if you enter the nursing home:

- without bedsores, you will not develop bedsores;
- with bedsores, you will get treatment to heal the sores, to prevent infection, and to stop new sores from developing;
- without an internal catheter, you are not catheterized unless your condition shows that it is necessary;
- without a limited range of motion, your range of motion will not be reduced unless your medical condition shows that it was unavoidable;
- with a limited range of motion, you will get treatment to increase your range of motion.

Health Care Financing Administration (HCFA)

HCFA is part of the federal government. It is responsible for putting regulations in place that control the more than 80 percent of nursing homes that take part in the Medicaid and Medicare programs. HCFA contracts with an agency within each state. The state agency is supposed to make sure that the nursing homes are complying with the federal regulations. If a nursing home is not, it is cited as deficient. The nursing home is then supposed to correct the deficiency. In theory, the nursing home could be fined, closed, or kicked out of the Medicare and Medicaid programs, which would result in a big financial loss for the nursing home. In reality, this rarely happens.

 A SLAP ON THE WRIST

Regulation of nursing homes is not always strict. A Texas nursing home was fined and kicked out of the Medicaid program after two of its residents died from neglect. Seven months later, the nursing home was reinstated in the Medicaid program and negotiated to have its fines reduced to $7,500.

The United States General Accounting Office reported in July 1998 that several California nursing homes were not providing the residents with proper food, fluids, or medication. Yet when the California agency found that a nursing home was not providing proper care, the nursing home was rarely cited as deficient.

The Courtroom

Many states allow residents or their guardians to sue the owners of nursing homes when residents suffer unnecessary injury or death. These lawsuits are usually called **negligence** or **wrongful death** cases.

Old Age as a Cause of Death

Can you simply die of old age? No. Your heart may give out or your kidneys may fail, but you would be hard-pressed to find "old age" listed on a death certificate. Yet when a nursing home resident dies, nursing homes often claim that of course the person died, he was old. "Dead of old age" is a common argument used by nursing homes when they are sued for malpractice or wrongful death.

Lost Wages and Life Expectancy

In many states, you must prove that you lost your ability to earn money in order to win a lawsuit. The amount of money you are awarded by the jury is based on how much money you could have earned if you had not been injured. The problem is that nursing home residents no longer earn money. There is nothing on which to base an award. Few of us could afford to spend years and thousands of dollars to fight a nursing home in court, only to win and receive nothing for our injuries.

Another problem is the resident's life expectancy. Many nursing home residents suffer medical illnesses or injuries before they go into the nursing home. It can be difficult for a jury to figure out the fault of the nursing home when a resident has preexisting medical conditions. For these reasons, nursing homes won almost every lawsuit brought against them through the mid-1980s.

 POSSIBLE DAMAGES

In Florida, nursing home residents can be awarded money for:

- any bodily injury they sustain that is the fault of the nursing home;
- any pain and suffering, disability, disfigurement, or mental anguish as a result of the injury;
- the loss of capacity for the enjoyment of life experienced in the past or to be experienced in the future;
- medical expenses; and
- lost earnings.

Pain and Suffering/Wrongful Death

In the mid-1980s, juries began granting verdicts for nursing home residents and awarding large sums of money. Even though nursing home residents are no longer wage earners, the juries could still award them money for pain and suffering or **wrongful death.**

LEARNING THE LINGO

Wrongful death: The death of a person that is caused by the wrongful act of another person.

In 1986, the family of a resident who wandered away from a nursing home in the early hours of the morning was awarded $25,000. Ten years later, a company that owned a chain of nursing homes in the Philadelphia area paid $575,000 to settle claims after the federal government found that at least three nursing home residents were malnourished.

Problems in the Courtroom

Although some state laws allow—or even encourage—you to sue for neglect or abuse, these lawsuits are not without their problems. Some states put a limit on the amount that you can win. This is sometimes a very small amount and provides little incentive for a resident, a guardian, or an attorney to risk a lawsuit. Remember, you could lose, in which case you would end up with less than when you began.

COMPLAINTS ABOUT NURSING HOME CARE

What to Do

Here are some steps to take when problems arise in nursing home care. The step you choose to take first will depend on the type of problem you are experiencing.

1. Keep a written log of the relevant details of the problem, such as when, where, who, what, and why.

2. Try to resolve the problem informally by talking to the supervising nurse, social worker, or administrator.

3. If the resident's needs have changed or if the care plan is inadequate, you have a right to a new assessment and care planning conference. This should result in an individually tailored plan of care.

4. Bring the problem to the attention of the resident council or family council. Better facilities have active councils of this sort.

5. Contact your long-term-care ombudsman.

6. Contact the state agency that licenses nursing homes. In most states, this is the department of health.

7. Contact a community legal assistance program or other advocacy organization. For problems involving serious physical, mental, or emotional harm, consult an attorney experienced in long-term-care issues.

The Long-Term-Care Ombudsman

The federal Older Americans Act requires every state to operate a long-term-care ombudsman program. The ombudsman is responsible for advocating on behalf of nursing home residents and residents of other long-term-care facilities. The ombudsman can provide information about options and rights and can resolve complaints.

Most states have local or regional programs. Ombudsman staff can be effective partners in resolving problems. Federal law requires nursing homes to allow the ombudsman access to residents and facilities. In addition, the ombudsman usually has special authority under state law to inspect records and to take other steps necessary to respond to complaints. However, the ombudsman does not have authority to impose penalties on the nursing home that violates care standards. Those kinds of problems are referred to the state agency responsible for licensing and certification.

Any nursing home or agency on aging will be able to tell you how to contact the ombudsman program in your area.

THE FUTURE OF RESIDENTS' RIGHTS

As the population continues to age, more and more baby boomers will become concerned about the type of care they will receive if and when they enter nursing homes. Look for more states to enact laws that will specifically allow nursing home residents to sue if they are abused or neglected. On the other hand, most nursing home residents suffer physical or mental disabilities, making it difficult for them to stand up for themselves. Any future laws will need to allow residents' family members to stand up for the residents. Otherwise, the laws have little bite, and nursing home owners have little reason to fear that they will be held accountable for their actions.

THE WORLD AT YOUR FINGERTIPS

- *The Inside Guide to America's Nursing Homes: Rankings and Ratings for Every Nursing Home in the U.S., 1998–1999,* by Robert N. Bua (Warner Books, 1997) will help you to find dependable, quality nursing care. It explains alternatives to nursing homes and ranks nearly every nursing home in the country.
- *The Nursing Home Choice: How to Choose the Ideal Nursing Home* by Marian R. Kranz (Branden Publishing Co., 1998) includes questions to use when interviewing the staff at your potential nursing home, as well as the type of answers you should expect. The book is intended to be a quick read to help you make an informed choice about nursing home care.
- *Life Worth Living: How Someone You Love Can Still Enjoy Life in a Nursing Home—The Eden Alternative in Action* by

William H. Thomas (VanderWyk and Burnham, 1996), a nursing home medical director in New York, shows how to make life worth living for nursing home residents by improving their quality of life through plants, pets, gardens, and children.

- For newsletters and articles on finding and paying for care for an older person, go to *http://www.eldercare.com/*.
- To find other Internet sites on nursing home care, go to your favorite search engine and enter "aging parents."

YOU MUST REMEMBER THIS

- Nursing home care is expensive. It can cost up to $7,000 per month.
- Most nursing homes are businesses run for profit.
- Good nursing homes do exist, but several investigations have turned up nursing homes that do not provide appropriate care.
- Federal law gives every nursing home resident the right to have their needs cared for and to live with dignity.
- If you believe that you or some other nursing home resident is not being adequately cared for, first call the ombudsman program. If that doesn't work, then call your state department of health or human services. This department should be able to tell you how to lodge a complaint against the nursing home.
- You may be able to sue the nursing home for abusing or neglecting a nursing home resident. In most states, though, you may not be able to recover much money.

CHAPTER 20

Paying for Long-Term Care

Planning Ahead for
When You're No Longer Able
to Care for Yourself

*Luke and Emma are in their sixties. Their insurance agent wants
them to buy something called long-term-care insurance. They do not
think they need it. They both have Medicare and Medicare supplemental insurance. They believe that they are covered for all their
care in the future. Are they?*

PAYING FOR LONG-TERM CARE

What Is Long-Term Care?

Long-term care does not refer to your medical treatment. Long-
term care is the help you will need in living your life, such as
making meals or feeding yourself, going to the bathroom, taking
a shower, brushing your teeth, or getting out of bed.

Why You Need to Worry About It

Many of us think that we are already covered for nursing home
care or home health care. Medicare will pay for it, or our health
insurance, or we will sell the house and use that money. That
should be enough, right? Wrong. Consider this: If you are under
the age of 75, there is a 50 percent chance that you will need
either home health care or a nursing home. If you are over 75,
the odds are 60 percent. The average stay in a nursing home is
2.5 years, with the average cost being $47,000 per year.

LIVING ON A FIXED INCOME

Many older people are on fixed incomes. They receive no pay increases. Most pensions do not contain cost-of-living adjustments (though Social Security does). At the same time that incomes are largely fixed, the cost of long-term care goes up, making it out of reach for many people.

You should be especially concerned if your family is middle income. People with few assets will end up on Medicaid. Wealthier people are more apt to be able to use investment income to pay for their care. Which income level are you in?

Won't Medicare Cover It?

Only a portion at best. Medicare does not usually cover nursing home costs unless you are hospitalized first. Even then, Medicare will only pay the whole nursing home bill for the first 20 days. For the next 80 days, you will have to make a daily copayment of up to $99 (for the year 2001), which your Medicare supplemental insurance will usually cover. After that first 100 days, you are on your own. Remember that Medicare does not pay for unskilled or long-term home care, which is what many elderly patients, such as those with Alzheimer's, need.

What *Will* Medicare Cover?

Medicare will pay for nursing home care only if you are in the hospital for at least 3 days before being brought to the nursing home. It will only pay for 100 days in the nursing home, and you must meet certain conditions:

- Your condition must require, on a daily basis, skilled nursing or skilled rehabilitation services that, as a practical matter, can be provided only in a skilled nursing facility.
- You must be admitted within a short time after you leave the hospital.

- The skilled care you receive must be based on a doctor's order.

This Medicare coverage is only meant for short-term stays in the nursing home. In fact, most nursing home residents do not require the level of nursing services considered "skilled" by Medicare, so Medicare pays for relatively little nursing home care.

Although Congress continues to struggle to meet the demands of an aging population, look for Medicare coverage for nursing home care to hold steady or to decrease. There simply will not be enough taxpayers in the workforce to pay for the long-term care of the baby boomers.

 LIMITED COVERAGE

Medicare does not pay for custodial care, such as help in getting dressed, preparing meals, or bathing. But if you meet the criteria for skilled care, these are included.

What About My Medicare Supplement Insurance?

This type of insurance usually covers only the difference between the medical bill and the Medicare payment. If it is not covered by Medicare, odds are it is not covered by your Medicare supplement insurance. These plans rarely cover nursing home care or home health care, unless Medicare covers them.

What About My Health Insurance Through Work?

Most individual and group health insurance policies specifically state that long-term care such as nursing homes or home health care are only covered under limited circumstances. These policies are very much like Medicare. This insurance covers only medical treatment, not assistance in your daily activities.

COSTS RISING

The cost of long-term care goes up every year. In 1997, nursing homes in the Boston area cost about $200 per day. In Texas, the average cost was about $94 a day. A nursing home in New York City costs just under $300 a day, while those in the rest of New York State cost approximately $200 per day.

Will Medicaid Cover It?

Medicaid may cover your long-term care, but only after you sink below the poverty line. Medicaid is a public welfare program. Few elderly people relish the thought of going on welfare in their twilight years. Nevertheless, Medicaid ends up paying for more than half of nursing home care in the country. It pays little or nothing for home health custodial care. Most of the people who go into nursing homes are not poor enough to qualify for Medicaid. They must first sell or otherwise liquidate most of their personal assets to pay for care. When that is gone, they may qualify for Medicaid.

ILL HEALTH, THEN IMPOVERISHMENT

People who use their personal assets to pay for nursing homes will usually exhaust their assets within 11 months. In other words, within a year they are broke and forced to go on Medicaid.

At Least I Can Count on Medicaid, Can't I?

As the baby boomers age, the number of people in the tax base decreases. That means that the government might decrease Medicare and Medicaid payments in the future because there simply will not be enough money to go around. Meanwhile, the cost of long-term care is going up. If you rely on Medicaid, the care you get in your old age is in the hands of the government.

USING YOUR HOME TO PAY
FOR LONG-TERM CARE

Under Medicaid rules (see Chapter 21), your home is an exempt asset in most cases—you can't be forced to sell or otherwise liquidate it to pay for your long-term care. Nonetheless, if you want to avoid Medicaid, there are several ways you can use the equity in your home to pay for your care. There are pros and cons to all of these options.

Reverse Mortgages

A reverse mortgage allows you to borrow against the equity in your home, without having to repay the loan right away. You can get the money in a lump sum, in monthly cash payments for life, by drawing on a line of credit, or in a combination of these options.

How Much Can I Borrow?
The amount you can borrow and the size of the loan installments are based on several factors, including:

- your age;
- the value of your home;
- the equity you hold;
- the interest rate;
- the kind of loan you select.

These loans can be costly, but the relative costs lessen over time and you will never owe more than the value of your home.

When Do I Have to Pay It Back?
Most reverse mortgages have no restrictions on how you use the money. The loan usually does not have to be repaid until you sell your home, move from it, or die. Some loans, however, must be repaid at the end of a specified number of years. Some lenders

combine a reverse mortgage with an annuity that allows you to receive loan payments under the annuity even after you sell your home and move.

When you sell your home or move, or at the end of the term, you must repay the money you have borrowed plus the accrued interest and fees. The house can be sold to repay the loan, or the funds can be collected some other way. The lender is not allowed to collect more than the appraised value of the house at the time the loan is repaid, even if the loan exceeds that amount.

Where Can I Get a Reverse Mortgage?

The most widely available product is the federally insured Home Equity Conversion Mortgage (HECM). Under this program the Federal Housing Authority (FHA) provides insurance for reverse mortgages placed through private financial institutions. Another reverse mortgage program available nationally through private lenders is Home Keeper Mortgage, backed by the Federal National Mortgage Association (Fannie Mae). A few private companies also offer their own reverse mortgage products. These tend to be more costly because the lender must charge customers more in order to self-insure against potential losses. Federal law requires all reverse mortgage lenders to inform you, before making the loan, of the total amount you will owe through the course of the loan. This enables you to compare costs.

Who Is Eligible for a Reverse Mortgage?

Eligibility depends on the individual product, but most lenders have rules similar to the FHA and Fannie Mae programs. The borrower and every other person whose name is on the deed must be at least 62 years old and own the property free and clear, except for liens or mortgages that can be paid off with proceeds from the loan.

The property must be the borrower's primary residence (as opposed to a vacation home) and a single-family residence. Condominiums are acceptable under some programs, but mobile homes and cooperatives are not.

Will a Reverse Mortgage Affect My Social Security?

No. Income from a reverse mortgage will not affect your eligibility for Social Security, Medicare, or other retirement benefits or for pensions that are not based on need.

What about Other Government Benefits?

Unless you plan carefully, reverse mortgage payments may affect your eligibility for Supplemental Security Income (SSI), Medicaid, food stamps, and some state benefit programs. These benefits are designed to meet basic needs, and recipients must meet strict financial guidelines.

The general rule is that reverse mortgage payments will not affect your eligibility for benefits if you spend the money during the month in which it is received. But if you do not spend that money during that month, it will be counted as a resource. If your resources are greater than the allowable limit, your benefits could be reduced or eliminated. Some state benefit programs follow the federal rules on this issue, but it is important to check the rules in your own state.

Is This True for Reverse Annuity Mortgages, Too?

Federal eligibility rules for reverse annuity mortgages, under which you receive payments even after you move from your home, raise tax and benefits issues different from regular reverse mortgages. Reverse annuity mortgage payments are counted as income for purposes of SSI, Medicaid, and similar need-based benefits, even if they are spent in the month in which they are received. They will reduce benefits and may affect your eligibility altogether. Annuities also receive less favorable tax treatment than do loan advances.

What Are the Tax Consequences of Reverse Mortgages?

So far the IRS has not taxed reverse mortgage payments on the grounds that the money is a loan. However, a portion of reverse annuity payments will be taxed. The interest on a reverse mortgage cannot be deducted until it is actually paid. Because you do not pay the interest on a reverse mortgage until the loan comes due, it most likely will not be deductible until that time.

Reverse mortgages may also affect estate taxes. Consult a tax adviser to assist you with these issues.

Will a Reverse Mortgage Affect My Estate Plan?

Reverse mortgages allow you to spend your home equity while you are alive. You may end up using all of your equity and not have any left to pass down to your heirs. Some plans allow you to set aside some of the equity so that it is not used.

Sale-Leasebacks

In a sale-leaseback you sell your home but keep the right to live there, and you pay rent. The buyer usually makes a substantial down payment to you. You act as a lender by giving the buyer a mortgage. You get the buyer's mortgage payments, and the buyer gets your rent payments. You stay in the home and use the down payment and the mortgage payments as income. The buyer can deduct the mortgage interest payment from his or her income and will benefit if the value of the property increases.

The IRS requires that both the sale price and the rental payments be at a fair market rate. At one time, sale-leasebacks were good investments, especially for adult children. Today, there are fewer tax advantages, so finding an investor may prove difficult.

Life Estates

In a life estate, you sell your home but keep the right to live there during your lifetime. The buyer pays you a lump sum, or monthly payments, or both. You are usually responsible for taxes and repairs while you live in the house. At your death, full ownership passes automatically to the buyers. This arrangement is used most commonly within families as part of an estate plan.

Charitable Remainder Trusts

In a charitable remainder trust, you donate your home to a charitable institution in return for a lifetime annuity and possibly a tax deduction. You retain a life estate, and you remain responsible for taxes and maintenance. When you die, your home becomes the property of the charitable institution.

Regular Home Equity Loans

A traditional home equity loan is very different from a reverse mortgage and can be risky for an older person on a fixed income. As with a reverse mortgage, you borrow against the equity you have built up in your home. But in a home equity loan you must make regular monthly payments or you may lose your home.

Home equity loans do have tax advantages. With home equity loans you can borrow up to $100,000 on the equity in your first and second homes, use the money for any purpose, and deduct the interest you pay on the loan. You can deduct the interest on a home equity loan that exceeds $100,000 if you use the money for home improvements.

LONG-TERM CARE INSURANCE

Long-term-care insurance gives you an alternative to using up your personal savings, home equity, and other assets, or going on Medicaid.

What Is It?

Long-term care (LTC) is given to you when you have a long-term illness or condition from which you are not likely to recover, such as Alzheimer's or a stroke. LTC does not cover hospital or doctor visits or medical treatment. LTC pays for the help you will need as you go through your daily life, such as with bathing, eating, dressing, or using the toilet. The purpose of LTC is to help you when you are so chronically ill or impaired that you can no longer live independently. An LTC policy may cover only nursing homes, only home health care services, or both. Some also cover additional services, such as assisted living, respite care, and care coordination.

TOO LITTLE INCOME, TOO MUCH COST

The average income of people over the age of 65 was $16,684 in 1996. The cost to have a home health care aide come to your home for 8 hours every day would be about $40,000 a year.

Is It Important?

Yes! Long-term-care insurance is absolutely crucial for most of us who are not rich or poor. LTC insurance will fill in the gaps left by Medicare while letting you, your spouse, or your family keep your financial security. Who wants to be 92 and broke? It would be better to live to be 92 and have money to buy gifts for our children or grandchildren, to live in our own home, or to go to a restaurant or the hairdresser on occasion. Getting older is scary enough without losing control of your life and bank account.

GOVERNMENT MAY NOT HELP

Many elderly people would prefer to remain at home and could do so with some help. In general, though, the rules are complex and there are exceptions. Medicare or Medicaid covers only a small portion of this type of care. You will either have to pay for it yourself or purchase an LTC policy.

Who Should Buy LTC Insurance?

Oddly, many of the buyers of LTC insurance tend to be somewhat affluent and under 65. These are the people that could most likely afford to pay for long-term care out of their income. It is quickly becoming one of the hottest insurance products around, though. As a general rule, you should not spend more than 7 percent of your income on LTC insurance.

Middle-income people are most likely to have too many assets to qualify for Medicaid but not enough to pay for long-term care out of their own pockets. LTC insurance gives middle-income people the opportunity to protect their financial assets.

When Should I Buy LTC Insurance?

That depends in part on your health and your financial situation. Keep in mind that many people under 65 require long-term care. You should also remember that the younger you are when you buy the LTC policy, the lower your premiums will be and the less likely you are to suffer from one of the preexisting conditions in an LTC policy. On the other hand, the current average age of someone buying an LTC policy is 68. While LTC insurance is still a good idea at that age, the ideal time to buy is probably when you are in your forties or fifties.

Some financial planners suggest that if you are in your thirties or forties, you should purchase LTC insurance for your parents so that you will not deplete your own assets caring for them. Then, when you are in your fifties, purchase LTC insurance for yourself.

When Will My LTC Policy
Begin Paying for My Care?

There are dozens of companies that sell LTC insurance, and their policies can differ. Generally, your LTC policy kicks in when you can no longer perform one or more activities of daily living, such as feeding yourself, getting out of bed, going to the toilet, or bathing. Compare at least three different LTC policies. There is no need to buy more than one LTC policy.

CHOOSING LONG-TERM CARE INSURANCE

Is the Benefit Monthly or Daily?

Your policy will typically either pay you a flat amount per day or per month. For example, your policy may specify that it will pay $250 per day for your care. Or it may state that it will pay $6,000 per month. The benefit to a monthly payment is that your costs may change from day to day. One day you may use only $175 worth of care, while another day your bill will be $300. A monthly benefit will absorb that daily fluctuation much more easily.

 COST-BENEFIT ANALYSIS

When choosing an LTC policy, compare the cost of the insurance with what your care will probably cost if you pay it out of pocket. Although these policies may seem expensive, the cost of insurance is usually much less than the cost of your future care.

Is Your Policy Based on a Reimbursement Basis or an Indemnity Basis?

A reimbursement basis means that the insurance company will pay you the exact cost of the care (up to your policy limit). It will not pay more than what you are actually charged. With an indemnity basis, you get the flat daily or monthly amount of the benefit, regardless of the cost for the care. If your benefit is more than the bill for your care, you can use that extra money to pay for other things, such as to a laundry service or to someone to rake the leaves outside your house. Premiums on a policy with a reimbursement basis are usually less expensive than a policy with an indemnity basis.

What Type of Care Is Covered?

You will want an LTC policy that covers all levels of care, such as skilled care in a nursing home and custodial care in your home. Make sure that the amount paid for home care is at least as much as the amount paid for nursing home care. For instance, if your benefit is $5,000 per month for nursing home care, it should be at least $5,000 per month for home health care. You will want to be covered in an adult day care center or assisted-living facility as well.

 CONDITIONS NOT COVERED BY LTC POLICIES

LTC policies do not usually cover schizophrenia, manic-depression, or alcoholism. Practically all LTC policies now cover Alzheimer's disease and stroke.

With regard to nursing homes, your policy should cover all room, board, and care costs. Home health care costs that should be covered include washing your hair, fixing your meals, helping you with bathing, and helping you take your medicine.

Must You Be Hospitalized First?

Medicare requires that you be hospitalized for three days before it will cover nursing home costs. You do not want this requirement in your LTC policy. Many times people need their LTC benefits to assist them in day-to-day living, perhaps in their own home. There is no hospitalization. Make sure that your policy does not require you to be hospitalized before you can receive your insurance benefits. If you purchased an LTC policy in the early 1990s, you may want to double-check this clause. Many of the older LTC policies required hospitalization before coverage.

Does Your Policy Protect Against Inflation?

Let's assume for a moment that you are in your sixties. You purchase LTC insurance today that covers your care at a rate of $5,000 per month. By the time you are in your eighties, $5,000 per month may not be enough to pay for a room in a nursing home. Even today there are nursing homes that cost as much as $7,000 per month. *If you do not expect to need long-term care within the next 10 to 15 years,* your LTC policy should offer inflation protection, which is sometimes called the future-purchase option. This option gives you the right either to buy more LTC coverage or to purchase a rider that will increase your benefits. How does this help you? Because you are already covered, and in 10 to 15 years you may have a preexisting condition that would prevent you from getting an LTC policy then.

 SOME GOOD NEWS

LTC insurance is becoming less expensive every year because of more competition. More companies are offering these policies now that the population is aging.

Do You Have a Preexisting Condition?

Just as with life insurance, you will be expected to go through some sort of medical examination to get an LTC policy. The extent of this examination will depend in part on your medical history and your age. The older you are, the more in-depth the examination. Some preexisting conditions that may be excluded are Alzheimer's, AIDS, multiple sclerosis, diabetes, and alcoholism.

Is There a Waiting Period Before
the Policy Pays Benefits?

How long will it take for you to be eligible to receive benefits? You may choose a policy that states that you are not eligible for benefits until you have received help in your day-to-day living for, say, 90 or 180 days. The longer the waiting period, the lower your premiums. You may decide you have enough assets to pay for 6 months of care before you need LTC benefits. Some states require that the waiting period be limited to a maximum of a certain number of days, such as 180 days.

Is Your Policy Guaranteed Renewable?

This clause states that your policy cannot be canceled unless you stop paying the premiums. In addition, it limits any increases in your premium. The company may still increase your premium, but it may need to get the approval of your state insurance commissioner first, and it must increase the premiums of a group of people, not just you. *If your policy does not have this clause—and many of the first policies did not—your insurance company can cancel your policy at any time.*

What Is the Benefit Period?
The Lifetime Maximum?

The benefit period is the length of time for which the insurance company is required to pay for your care. In some states, LTC insurance must cover at least two years. In other states, the benefits period may be anywhere from one year to your lifetime, with an average being three to six years. *A five-year benefits period is your best bet, especially if you are a woman.* Only a small percentage of people stay in a nursing home for more than five years. Find out if there is a dollar limit to your policy. Depending on the cost of care in the area in which you live, a million dollar policy may not be enough.

LIFETIME COVERAGE PROBABLY NOT NECESSARY

Lifetime coverage is very expensive, and the odds are that you will not need long-term care for more than a few years. If you do not have family nearby to help you, lifetime coverage is something you may want to consider. People with family or friends to help care for them enter nursing homes at a much later stage than people who do not.

Do You Stop Paying Premiums When You Start Collecting Benefits?

You do not want to have to keep paying premiums once you start needing long-term care. Make sure your policy has a clause known as a **waiver of premium.** This clause should state that once you start collecting under your policy, you no longer pay premiums. Read this closely. It may state that your premiums

QUESTIONS TO ASK ABOUT LTC INSURANCE:

1. Are the benefits daily or monthly? Reimbursement or indemnity?
2. What level and type of care is covered?
3. Is there a hospitalization requirement?
4. Does the policy protect against inflation?
5. What preexisting medical conditions are not covered?
6. When will the policy begin paying benefits?
7. Does the policy have a guaranteed renewability clause?
8. How long is the insurance company obligated to pay benefits for your care?
9. Is there a premium waiver?

are waived starting on the day you enter a nursing home or after a certain number of days of living there. Many policies do not waive premiums until you have been in a nursing home for 90 days.

Will the Policy Return a Percentage of Your Premiums to Your Estate?

Some policies will offer to return a percentage of your premiums to your estate if you do not use benefits exceeding the amount of premiums you have paid. This option will drive up the cost of your premiums. You will almost always end up losing money with this option. You are better off without it in your policy.

OTHER THINGS TO CONSIDER

What Is Excluded Under Your Policy?

Your policy may include restrictions on where you receive care. For example, your policy may not cover your care if you choose a nursing home that is owned by the government or located outside of the United States. It may not cover long-term care that is provided by your family members or that is related to mental illness. Whatever exclusions might be included, be sure you know what they are.

How Do the Various Policies Differ?

As more insurance companies offer LTC policies, the companies try to set their insurance apart from the others. One company may offer a policy that covers both disability and LTC. Another company may offer a policy that lets you use the LTC benefits on your spouse's policy. Some companies will even offer you the use of an LTC coordinator. The coordinator takes care of finding the best nursing home or home health care, making sure your care is paid for by your policy, and answering your questions. This is helpful if you do not have family nearby to fill that need.

Whether you need any of these features depends on you, your family, and your situation.

What Are Tax-Qualified LTC Policies?

This is a tricky area because the tax laws are new and there are few regulations explaining them. In short, benefits from a tax-qualified LTC policy are not considered income. Some policyholders may be able to deduct the cost of their premiums. At this point the law seems to benefit employees because it encourages companies to offer LTC insurance. These laws are too new to predict how they will affect you. Your accountant or attorney is the best person to keep you up-to-date on how the IRS is treating LTC insurance.

How Do I Figure Out the Plan Best for Me?

Your accountant, estate planner, financial planner, or attorney should bring up the subject when you are doing long-term planning. If not, ask that person for information and advice on long-term-care insurance. If that person is not familiar with it, find someone who is. This is your future, and you need someone who is able to advise you.

Even if you decide to not buy long-term-care insurance, you need to know what will happen to you, your house, your children, and your spouse if you end up in a nursing home. What if your spouse enters a nursing home at the age of 65? How will that affect you if you live to 80? Will you lose your house? Will you be forced to go back to work?

GUIDANCE ON PAYING FOR LONG-TERM CARE

Your state's insurance department should have information on the consumer protection guidelines and standards that insurance companies in your state must follow. The insurance department may also be able to provide you with information on how to evaluate the policies that are available.

There are also state programs called Insurance Counseling and Assistance (ICA) that provide free help with questions on paying for long-term care. If you have questions about Medicare coverage of nursing home services, Medicaid eligibility requirements, private long-term-care insurance, or any other health insurance questions, contact your state ICA for help. The complete list of numbers is in Appendix A.

THE WORLD AT YOUR FINGERTIPS

- The National Association of Insurance Commissioners offers a free booklet with advice on purchasing long-term-care insurance. To request a copy, call 816-374-7259.
- HCFA offers a free book, *Your Medicare Handbook,* which discusses the conditions under which Medicare will help pay for nursing home costs in a Medicare-certified nursing home. To receive a copy, call 1-800-638-6833.
- *And Now What Do We Do? A Guide for the Selection of the Right Long-Term-Care Facility for You or a Loved One* by Robin and Loranelle Schroeder (EMMPS Publishing, 1997) is the story of one family's struggle to find 24-hour care for Robin's mother, who suffered from Alzheimer's.
- *Believe It or Not Mama Likes the Nursing Home!* by Kathryn Martin (Beacon Hill Press, 1996) offers inspirational reading for those facing life in nursing homes, as well as their families.
- For articles and rate comparisons on long-term-care insurance, visit these websites:
  - *http://www.longtermcareinsurance.org/main.html*
  - *http://www.insuremarket.com/basics/ltc/*
  - *http://angelfire.com/tn/NursingHome/finance.html*

YOU MUST REMEMBER THIS

- You and your family will be expected to pay for the bulk of your long-term care, especially as government programs such as Medicare and Medicaid become less able to provide funding for everyone.
- You may be able to use the equity in your home to pay for your care, though these options may affect your estate plan.
- A good LTC policy will protect you and your family while allowing you to get the long-term care you need and want.
- Changes in the tax laws are making it more attractive for employers to offer LTC insurance as an employee benefit.

CHAPTER 21

Medicaid Planning

Some Suggestions on
Qualifying for Medicaid

Kelly lives a comfortable life. As she gets older, she sees more and more of her friends entering nursing homes and losing everything they worked so hard for all those years. A friend told her that if she gave away all of her assets to her children, she could go on Medicaid. Then she would not have to pay for a nursing home. Kelly thinks this is a good idea. Is it?

MEDICAID

What Is It?

Congress created the Medicaid program in 1965. It is part of Social Security. The purpose of Medicaid is to pay for medical care for people who are very poor. It is, plain and simple, a welfare program. Congress makes the general rules for Medicaid, but each state is given some flexibility to adjust the program. The nursing home benefit is especially valuable because Medicaid is the only program that covers significant amounts of nursing home care.

Why a Medicaid-Paid Nursing Home
May Not Be Right for You

If you pay for your nursing home care yourself (or through long-term-care insurance), you will have much more control over the location of your nursing home and the type of care you receive. Remember that Medicaid is a government program, and, like all government programs, your benefits may be limited and could be cut back. There is also the belief of many people that the care you will receive in a Medicaid facility is not as good as the care you would receive in a more expensive, private nursing home.

Many persons qualify for Medicaid; others can qualify by taking certain steps. These steps—known generally as Medicaid Planning—must be taken in advance. This chapter will try to provide some guidance, but be aware that almost every generalization in this complex area has several exceptions. You'd be well advised to get the advice of a lawyer who knows this area and is familiar with the facts of your particular case.

How Does Medicaid Work?

Medicaid is a program run jointly by the federal government and the states. Medicaid providers send their bills directly to Medicaid, rather than to you. The state Medicaid program reimburses providers. An increasing number of states are contracting with managed care organizations to serve all their Medicaid beneficiaries. Providers cannot charge you additional amounts for covered services. Medicaid will not reimburse you for the charges you paid. If a person qualifies for it, Medicaid will pay the full cost of most services. The cost of prescription drugs is an exception; for those, there may be a nominal copay. When it comes to nursing home care, Medicaid will pay the part of the bill that the poor person cannot pay.

To find out if you are "poor enough" for Medicaid, the state will look at your monthly income and the fair market value of your resources. A *resource* is the term for the property that you own. To qualify for Medicaid in most states, your resources—certain property but not all of the property that you own—must not be valued at more than $2,000. Some states have a slightly higher minimum. Even a person who is one dollar over the income gap is ineligible, no matter how high the medical bills. Fortunately, certain assets are not counted, such as the home you own, which makes the program available to more people than you would otherwise think.

Will Medicaid Pay for the Full Cost of Medical Care?

As noted earlier, Medicaid pays very nearly the full cost of *medical* care, but the story is different for nursing homes, where you will be expected to use the money you have coming in, such as Social Security, to help pay for the bill. Medicaid covers the portion of the bill that your income will not pay. You may receive both Medicare and Medicaid. In that case, Medicaid usually pays the portion of the expenses under Medicare for which you would normally be responsible.

If you do not qualify for Medicaid, but your income is low and meets special income and resource tests discussed later, you may qualify for help from Medicaid in paying your share of Medicare costs as a **Qualified Medicare Beneficiary (QMB)** or a **Specified Low-Income Medicare Beneficiary (SLMB)**.

QUALIFYING FOR MEDICAID

Medicaid programs in each state have different eligibility standards. All states require that adults without dependent children must be at least 65, blind, or disabled *and* that they meet income and asset tests.

Income Test

The **income tests** are linked to the federal Supplementary Security Income (SSI) program or, for younger applicants, to Temporary Assistance to Needy Families (TANF). In most states, persons eligible for SSI or TANF are automatically covered. These are **categorically eligible** individuals.

Income-Cap States

In nineteen states, there is a gross-income cap for certain benefits—specifically, nursing home care—set at three times the maximum SSI benefit for a single individual. These states are Alabama, Alaska, Arizona, Arkansas, Colorado, Delaware, Florida, Idaho, Iowa, Louisiana, Mississippi, Nevada, New Mexico, Oklahoma, Oregon, South Carolina, South Dakota, Texas, and Wyoming. This cap changes yearly, because the SSI maximum benefit is adjusted yearly for inflation. See the sidebar for how this works in a representative state.

 HOW THE INCOME CAP WORKS

In Florida (one of the income-cap states), the income cap for a nonmarried person was $1,590 per month. To be eligible for Medicaid, therefore, a nonmarried person's income had to be $1,590 per month or less. Income from all sources, before deductions, is counted.

If the person has $1,590 or less in income and lives in a nursing home, he or she can keep a certain amount for items such as clothing, toiletries, and books. Other income must be paid to the nursing home.

"Medical Neediness"

In some states, **medical neediness** is an exception to the Medicaid income criteria. If your medical expenses (after you subtract payments made by other insurance) are more than your monthly income, you may be considered medically needy and you might qualify for Medicaid. To qualify for medical neediness, in most states you cannot have resources worth more than $2,000, though once again remember that your home, car, and other specified assets aren't counted in this figure.

 HOW MEDICAL NEEDINESS WORKS

An example of medical neediness would be a nursing home resident who receives an income of $2,000 per month, which is not enough to cover the nursing home fee of, say, $4,000 per month.

Resource Test

As noted earlier, in addition to these provisions regarding *income,* you must meet certain standards regarding *resources.*

Is Everything I Own a "Resource"?

No. As noted earlier in Chapter 5, there are certain things that are *not considered countable* resources for Medicaid purposes:

1. your home, if you can show that you intend to return there to live or that your spouse or a dependent child lives there (some states have a time limit; for example, Virginia has a six-month return window);
2. basic items in your day-to-day living, such as clothing, furniture, and household appliances;
3. one motor vehicle, although some states limit how much the car can be worth;
4. one wedding ring and one engagement ring;
5. prepaid funeral expenses totaling $3,000 or less (including burial plots, gravesites, caskets, headstones, and maintenance of the gravesite);
6. property that is essential to earning a living;
7. property that cannot be sold without creating an undue hardship;
8. reparation payments, such as those made to victims of Agent Orange or the Holocaust,
9. cash value of life insurance, if the face value is less than $1,500 (if the face value is higher, the cash value is counted as an asset).

When Does Medicaid Consider the Fair Market Value of My Resources?

Medicaid will use the fair market value from the day you were admitted to the nursing home. If you are married, in some states the value of your resources will be split in half, with half going to the community spouse and the other half to the spouse in the nursing home. In about a dozen states, the community spouse will be allocated an amount equal to the federal maximum (currently $84,120); so if a couple had assets of $80,000, the community spouse would be credited with all of this property, the nursing home spouse with none.

What Is a "Community Spouse"?

When your spouse enters a nursing home, you are called a "community spouse" because you still live in the community. Until the late 1980s, the community spouse's income was taken into account when qualifying for Medicaid. The community spouse would be left almost penniless because all of the family's income and resources were required to go to pay for nursing home expenses. The effect of this is that both spouses would end up on welfare, rather than just one. Today the community spouse is allowed to keep a certain level of income and resources.

WHO OWNS THE ASSETS?

The community spouse can keep all income, no matter how much, that belongs exclusively to the community spouse. When deciding who owns which income between spouses, Medicaid looks at whose name is on the check. If a pension check is written only to your spouse, that income is considered to belong only to your spouse and not to you. If your spouse enters a nursing home, this could leave you without a significant portion of your income.

Medicaid will, however, allow you a minimum living allowance and enough income to pay your mortgage, insurance, and taxes. Under the **minimum monthly maintenance needs allowance** program, part of the nursing home spouse's income may be used by the community spouse if the community spouse's income is below an amount set by the state. (For more detail, see a companion book in this series, the *ABA Legal Guide for Older Americans*, pages 85–86.)

Are My Children Financially Responsible for My Care?

In most states, children do not have a legal obligation to pay for their parents' care. Children, though, often feel a moral or personal obligation to help pay for a parent's nursing home. A shortage of Medicaid-eligible nursing home beds puts this to the test. Some nursing homes admit private-pay patients before Medicaid patients because private-pay rates are higher than what Medicaid pays. Giving priority to private-pay patients is allowed in many states but is illegal in others.

In all states, federal law prohibits nursing homes from requiring private payments from families of a resident or from requiring a period of private payment prior to applying for Medicaid coverage. That includes asking for deposits from beneficiaries who are approved for Medicaid but who are not yet receiving it at the time of admission. Nursing homes cannot obligate an adult child or other third party to guarantee to pay the nursing home's charges. The child's obligation extends only as far as his or her authority over the parent's assets. For example, the child who is an agent under the durable power of attorney of a parent may be obligated, as the agent, to pay the nursing home bill out of the parent's assets (but not out of his or her own personal assets). Federal law also prohibits nursing homes from requiring patients to waive or even delay their right to apply to Medicare and/or Medicaid.

MEDICAID PLANNING

Your Countable Assets

Most Medicaid planning begins with dealing with countable assets. These are those resources that are considered by the state when you apply for Medicaid. In most states, you are only allowed to have $2,000 in countable assets if you want to qualify for Medicaid.

Can't I Just Give My Resources
to My Family?

No. One of Medicaid's strictest rules is on transfer of assets. This rule states that you cannot give property away for less than its fair market value *if you are giving away the property just to qualify for Medicaid.* (Transfers between spouses are permitted, however.) If you are giving your property away for some other reason, you are not violating the transfer of assets rule. However, it's not easy to verify that you were indeed giving the property away for some other reason; and in any event you have to show that you have enough left to meet expected needs.

You always want to be careful to abide by this rule. If the state decides that you gave away your property just to qualify for Medicaid, it can refuse to give you Medicaid coverage for a period of time, as explained in the next section.

As you can imagine, it can be very difficult to determine why someone is transferring assets, especially because a transfer might have several equally compelling reasons—to "spend-down" for Medicaid eligibility and to help a child. That is why Medicaid has set up certain rules, as explained next.

The "Look-Back" Period

The state will assume that you gave away your resources in order to qualify for Medicaid if you transferred your assets within *three years* of applying for Medicaid or entering the nursing home, whichever is later. This is known as the "look-back" period, which can result in a period of ineligibility for Medicaid. The length of the ineligibility period is found by dividing the value of the assets given away by the average monthly cost of a nursing home in your area. For example, let's say you live in an area where the average monthly cost of nursing home care is $3,000 per month, and you gave away $90,000 on January 1, 2001. The ineligibility period is $90,000 divided by $3,000, or 30 months. You are disqualified from Medicaid until July 1,

2003. Thus you must wait at least 30 months to apply for Medicaid in order to avoid a penalty.

The purpose of the rule is to prevent people from making such transfers when in a nursing home or when moving to a home seems imminent. If you plan far enough ahead, there is less of a problem. For example, let's say you give all your assets to your children on January 1, 2000, and enter a nursing home on January 1, 2004. On January 2, 2004, you apply for Medicaid. The state will look-back three years to January 2, 2001, to see what resources you had then and any transfers you may have made. The resources you gave away in 2000 will not pose a problem because you gave them away before the look-back period.

Exceptions to the Look-Back Problem

You can transfer some assets within the look-back period that will not affect your eligibility for Medicaid. These include:

1. a transfer to your spouse or to someone else for the sole benefit of your spouse;
2. the transfer of a noncountable resource other than the home;
3. the transfer of a home to your spouse; to your minor disabled or blind child; or to certain other relatives;
4. any transfer for the fair market value of the asset (what the asset is worth on the open market);
5. any transfer that you can show was done for a reason other than to qualify for Medicaid.

The Undue Hardship Exception

Like all good rules, the look-back rule has an exception. If you transferred your assets within the look-back period and do not qualify for Medicaid, you may still be able to get Medicaid if you can show *undue hardship*—that without Medicaid you would not be able to get medical care and your health or life would be at risk. You can also show undue hardship by showing that you would not be able to get food, clothing, or shelter if Medicaid is withheld, regardless of when you transferred your assets. This exception is seldom used successfully.

QUALIFYING FOR MEDICAID

Spending Down Your Assets

When you get rid of your resources now in order to qualify for Medicaid later (at least 36 months later, under the look-back rule), you are *spending down* your assets. If you want to spend down your assets now to qualify for Medicaid later, you should consider:

- **investing in exempt assets;**
- **transferring assets directly to your children;**
- **changing title to your property; or**
- **writing a durable power of attorney that permits another individual whom you designate to continue the spend-down program should you become incapacitated.**

Because the states all have their own rules, you may find in your state that other techniques could be effective.

 QUALIFYING FOR MEDICAID

Medicaid is a medical assistance program for low-income older or disabled persons. People automatically qualify in most states if they meet the income test of the federal **Supplemental Security Income (SSI)** program. The program also covers certain younger persons receiving welfare payments under **Temporary Assistance to Needy Families (TANF).**

AN EXAMPLE OF SPENDING DOWN
AFTER YOU'RE IN A NURSING HOME

If you don't plan ahead and divest yourself of assets before the look-back period, you will have to spend down your assets while in the nursing home to eventually become eligible for Medicaid. Here's how this works. Ms. Smith enters a nursing home, having an income of $1,200 per month and $50,000 in savings. The nursing home private-pay rate is $3,000 per month, and Ms. Smith's additional incidental expenses amount to $100 per month. She must spend down her savings at a rate of $1,900 per month (i.e., $1,200 in income + $1,900 in savings are needed to meet the monthly total expense of $3,100). At this rate, Ms. Smith's savings are depleted down to the Medicaid asset level ($2,000) in just over two years if she only spends her money on nursing home expenses, sooner if she can spend it to cover certain other expenses.

Many persons who are not eligible for Medicaid become eligible, like Ms. Smith, after a period of time in a nursing home. The rules in this situation vary considerably from state to state.

Investing in Exempt Assets

- *Your Home.* The entire value of your house is excluded from Medicaid. You can sell some of your countable resources and buy a more expensive home, pay off the mortgage on the home you already own, or renovate your home. If you need money later, you can take out a mortgage or a home equity loan. All rural land that is adjoining your homestead is excluded as well, even if it is rented or leased to someone else.
- *Burial Plots.* You can purchase burial plots for your family members and set aside up to $1,500 in a burial expense fund. These arrangements will take the burden off your family and help you qualify for Medicaid.

Transferring Assets Directly to Your Family

Remember that you should not give your countable resources to your children as gifts if you think you will be entering a nursing home or applying for Medicaid within the next three years. There are some exceptions to this rule, though.

You can *transfer your home* to:

- your spouse;
- any child who is under age 21 or who is blind or disabled;
- your brother or sister, if he or she has an ownership interest in the house and lived there for at least one year immediately before you entered the nursing home; or
- any child who lived in your home for at least two years immediately prior to your admission to the nursing home and who cared for you so that you could stay in your own home.

 LIMITATIONS ON HOME TRANSFER

Except for minor children or those who are blind or disabled, only a child who cared for you in your home for at least two years can receive that asset within the look-back period without causing problems. The rule does not apply to grandchildren, in-laws, or other relatives. This can be a shock when a son and a daughter-in-law care for an ailing mother and then the son dies first. The house cannot be transferred to the daughter-in-law because the mother would become ineligible for Medicaid.

Change Your Will and the Title to Your Property

It is very important that you change your will when your spouse enters a nursing home. You probably plan to leave most of your assets to your spouse. Let's suppose that your spouse enters a nursing home and qualifies for Medicaid. You die while your spouse is still living in the nursing home. Your spouse just inherited your house and all of your assets and no longer qualifies for Medicaid. Your spouse will be forced to spend everything you left behind in order to qualify for Medicaid again and the rest of your family will receive nothing.

The same goes for property that has both of your names on the title. If your spouse enters a nursing home, the title to your property should be transferred to you (the community spouse) alone. That way it won't pass automatically to the nursing home spouse on your death, and it will be out of the nursing home spouse's estate, so that the state can't attempt to take it to recover the cost of the nursing home care.

Durable Power of Attorney

When you own property jointly with your spouse, both of you must sign the documents to transfer the property to the other. If you become incompetent, you will not be allowed to sign the transfer, and the property will stay in both your names. This is where a durable power of attorney comes in. With a durable power of attorney, you or your spouse will be able to transfer assets into one name.

Durable powers of attorney are also very useful for disability planning in general. And, given the number of younger people who become unable to manage their affairs because of accident or illness, they are recommended for people of every age.

What Does My Spouse Get to Keep?

When you or your spouse apply for Medicaid, the state puts all of your assets into one pool. In many states, the community spouse gets to keep half of that, up to a set amount. In other states, the community spouse is allowed to keep the full amount. The amount is set by the state, which can go as high as $84,120. The amount is adjusted each year for inflation. The half or more that you get to keep is called the "community spouse resource allowance." If the amount you get to keep is not enough to live on, you can appeal this allowance and try to get it increased, or you can try to get a court order.

Using Irrevocable Trusts to Your Advantage

A regular trust may be revoked by the person who created it and is considered an asset by Medicaid. On the other hand, an irrevocable trust, if it is created at least 60 months (five years) prior to applying for Medicaid, may slow down the depletion of your estate while helping you become eligible for Medicaid. The key is that the trustee's discretion to distribute income and principal must be sharply limited.

An irrevocable Miller trust (named for a legal case) may be useful if you live in an income-cap state. In an income-cap state, you cannot get Medicaid coverage of nursing home care if your monthly income is even a dollar over the cap. A Miller trust provides a legally-recognized way to lower your income below the cap. In an income-cap state, your income may be just over the Medicaid income cap but less than the amount needed to pay for a nursing home bed. Federal law requires that income-cap states exempt trusts created for your benefit if the trust is composed only of your pension, Social Security, or other income and, if at your death, the state is reimbursed by the trust for all Medicaid assistance paid on behalf of you. These trusts work by paying out a monthly income just under the Medicaid cap and retaining the rest. The result is that most of your income, supplemented by Medicaid, goes toward payment of the nursing home. The remainder of your income remains in the trust until your death. The accumulated residue is then paid to Medicaid.

OTHER MEDICAID OPTIONS

Medicaid in your state may cover a variety of home or community-based services. Many states have instituted Medicaid "waiver" programs that allow the state to use Medicaid dollars for home- and community-based services that normally would not be covered by Medicaid. These programs usually target persons who might otherwise have to live in a nursing home. Services may include personal care, adult day care, housekeeping, care management, chores and companionship, and respite care that enables caregivers to take a break from their responsibilities. Check with your local office on aging or department of human services about the options available in your state.

HOW TO APPLY FOR MEDICAID

Where to Go

Each county has a social services office. This office processes applications for Medicaid. You can fill out the application yourself; or your family, your agent under a durable power of attorney, or another guardian may fill it out for you. Before you will be given Medicaid, you are required to provide enough information to verify that you are unable to pay for your care.

What You Will Need for the Application

Each state requires some basic information for a Medicaid application:

- **birth certificate;**
- **Social Security card (or some other way to verify your Social Security number);**
- **documents to show your income;**
- **documents to show the value of all your countable assets;**
- **documents to show the amount of your medical bills that you cannot pay.**

Your state may require more information than what is listed here.

Appraising Your Property/Assets

The type of appraisal you will need for your property will depend on the type of property you own. Medicaid does not require that you get certified appraisal on all property, but you will not be able to rely on your own value estimates either.

- *Bank accounts* can be verified by providing your most recent bank statement.
- *Stocks and bonds* may be appraised by a stockbroker or an accountant.
- *Automobiles, boats, and motor homes* can be valued by using a published valuation guide, such as the *National Auto Dealers Association's "Blue Book."*
- *Other personal property,* such as jewelry, can be appraised by a dealer or a buyer of that type of property.
- *Residential property* may be valued by the amount on your tax records, which you can get through your county auditor; you can also get an appraisal.
- *Agricultural land* must be valued by an appraiser, a real estate agent, a loan officer in the local agricultural lending institution, or some other person knowledgeable of land sales in your area. Your tax records will not be accepted for agricultural land.

When Will I Find Out If I Qualify?

Once you have provided all the necessary information, the state has 45 days to make a decision on your application. When a decision is made, the state will notify you.

MEDICAID ESTATE RECOVERY

States are required by federal law to try to recover the cost of nursing home care, home- and community-based services, and related services provided to individuals and paid by Medicaid. No recovery can occur from the person's estate until after the death of the Medicaid beneficiary and the beneficiary's spouse and only if there is no child who is under the age of 21 or who is blind or disabled. Every state must have a procedure to give information about estate recovery to all Medicaid applicants. One way a state can assume recovery against an estate is to place a **lien** on the property of the Medicaid beneficiary. A lien is a legal document filed in the court clerk's office that gives notice that there is a charge against the property. The usual target of the lien is your home. Liens may be used only to recover for the cost of care of persons permanently residing in a nursing home. The state cannot impose the lien if you have a spouse or a child who is under age 21 or who is blind or disabled living in the home. In certain cases the same will apply if your sibling co-owns the house and lives there.

The rules change somewhat upon your death. During probate the state's claim for recovery of Medicaid benefits may be converted to a lien against your property even when one of the above-mentioned persons still lives there. However, the state may not seek to enforce the lien while the surviving spouse is alive or while a child who is under age 21 or who is blind or disabled is living, even if they are not living in the house. In addition, the state cannot enforce the lien under limited circumstances if your brother or sister lives there or if your adult (nondisabled) child lives there if that child was your caregiver under certain conditions defined by Medicaid.

IMMIGRANTS AND MEDICAID

Two 1996 laws restrict the eligibility of noncitizens for federal benefits such as Medicaid. These laws ban eligibility for these benefits for most legal immigrants who are not citizens. People who are in this country illegally are not eligible for benefits. The following groups, however, are still eligible:

- refugees;
- people granted asylum;
- people whose deportation has been withheld by the Immigration and Naturalization Service;

- U.S. veterans with honorable discharges and spouses or unmarried dependents of those veterans;
- people who have worked in the United States for a certain period of time or those who get credit for the work of parents, children, or a spouse.

WHEN YOU DISAGREE WITH MEDICAID

You have the right to appeal all decisions that affect your Medicaid eligibility or services. You should receive prompt written notice of any decision about your Medicaid coverage. This will include an explanation of how you can appeal. The appeal process differs slightly from state to state, but it always includes a right to a fair hearing before a hearing officer.

THE WORLD AT YOUR FINGERTIPS

- For a list of frequently asked questions (and answers) about Medicaid, go to *www.seniorlaw.com* and click on the link for Medicaid.
- The Health Care Financing Administration (HCFA) is the branch of the federal government that is in charge of Medicaid. To get information on Medicaid from the source, go to *http://www.hcfa.gov/*.
- A good resource for other websites that deal with Medicaid is Murphy's Unofficial Medicaid Page at *http://www.geocities.com/CapitolHill/5974/*. This site will lead you to the Medicaid website for your state.

YOU MUST REMEMBER THIS

- Medicaid is a welfare program. It can be changed by your state or federal government at any time.

- You will be expected to apply most of your income to your medical care, even if you are on Medicaid.
- Some of your assets will not be counted when you apply for Medicaid.
- You should change your will if your spouse enters a nursing home before you do.
- Do not transfer assets for less than fair market value if you expect to apply for Medicaid or enter a nursing home within the next three years.
- Seek legal advice on the estate implications of Medicaid benefits before seeking Medicaid nursing home coverage.

CHAPTER 22

Alternative Care and Living

*It's Not Just Your Home or the
Nursing Home Anymore*

*Dillon is 82 years old and lives in the home he's owned for 50 years. He is able
to take care of himself for the most part, but he can no longer drive and he
relies on neighbors and family members to bring him groceries. It is getting
more difficult for Dillon to prepare meals for himself, so now he sticks to
breakfast cereal and other things he does not need to cook. His house could use
some repairs. Dillon and his family agree that he is unable to keep up his house,
but they do not think he needs the daily care in a nursing home. Is a nursing
home Dillon's only option?*

CHOOSING AN ALTERNATIVE
TO A NURSING HOME

Why You Should Consider an Alternative

The range of choices for many older people is enormous. Some
include living with family, life-care-at-home programs, living in
congregate housing, assisted living, and living in a continuing-
care facility. Moreover, none of these alternatives is permanent.
People often move from one to another as their need for a level
of care changes.

Most—if not all—of the alternatives cost much less than living in a nursing home. All of the alternatives discussed in this
chapter will give you much more privacy and independence than
you will find in a nursing home. Another big advantage to these
alternatives is that you would get to have your own personal living space. In a nursing home you would likely share a room with
another person.

Things to Keep in Mind When Considering Alternatives

There is no uniform definition for these alternatives. In this chapter we will use the most popular terms. Keep in mind that these alternatives may be called something different in your community. Some of these alternatives have become popular only within the past few years. In many states these alternatives are not regulated by either the state or the federal government. This is sure to change as our population gets older and these alternatives become even more commonplace. Until then, you must gather as much information on your own as you can in order to make an informed choice.

Questions to Ask Yourself

- How much independence do I want?
- How much privacy do I want?
- How much help do I need?
- What kind of medical services do I need?
- What kind of housekeeping services do I need?

Questions to Ask the Management When Deciding on an Alternative

- Exactly what services are included in my fee?
- What kind of training does the staff receive?
- Are background checks done on the staff?
- How are records kept confidential?
- How do I file a complaint if I don't like something?
- Can I be kicked out of the facility or program for any reason?
- How can I end the arrangement if I choose another alternative?

- Under what circumstances would I be forced to give up my room and move to another room?
- What kind of protection do I have against rate increases?

Main Types of Alternative Living

The main alternatives to nursing homes are retirement communities, continuing-care retirement communities, assisted-living facilities, and home health care. These alternatives differ in the range of medical and personal service they provide to you. Each of these will be discussed in greater detail in this chapter, as well as a few other types of alternative living arrangements that are becoming more popular.

Problems with the Alternatives

The companies that are building these alternative living arrangements usually focus on more affluent people. While some states allow you to use government funding toward living in these alternatives, many states do not.

One of your great concerns must be whether you are selecting a facility or program that accommodates effectively your possible need for nursing care in the future. If so, do you have the resources to cover the costs? Some institutions do not accept Medicaid; so if you run out of funds, you have to find one that does and then move. That will be disruptive.

 **CHECK IT OUT**

Do not be fooled by flashy brochures and other marketing techniques. Talk with the other residents and their families, and call the references for the service you are considering.

RETIREMENT COMMUNITIES

What Are They?

Retirement communities are groups of houses or apartments where you must reach a certain age before you are allowed to move in. This minimum age is usually somewhere between 55 and 65 years of age.

What Do They Offer?

Retirement communities often offer transportation to grocery stores, shopping malls, doctors' offices, and community events such as plays and movies. Your fee might include one or more meals a day in the main dining room and exercise classes.

Retirement communities differ a great deal in the range of services and amenities they offer, from a few social and recreational amenities on the one extreme, to meals, personal care, medications supervision, and even nursing home care at the other extreme. The costs and payment structures also differ a great deal.

ASSISTED LIVING FACILITIES

What Are They?

Assisted-living facilities are good alternatives for older persons who can care for themselves but need some help. They are sometimes called residential care facilities, personal care homes, or homes for adults. This is one of the fastest growing types of housing in the country. One of the leaders in the assisting-living industry opened 92 assisted-living facilities in 1998. The same company plans to open 300 more assisted-living facilities by the year 2002.

Should You Live There?

Assisted-living facilities are for you if you need help with some of your day-to-day activities, such as preparing meals, getting dressed, or bathing. Some may also supervise your taking of medications. Unlike nursing homes, which are highly regulated by your state department of health, assisted-living facilities are usually licensed by your state social services department.

 PROFILE OF A RESIDENT

The average assisted-living resident is an 84-year-old single or widowed woman who needs help with at least three of her daily activities, such as preparing meals and getting dressed.

What About Cost?

Before signing any contracts with an assisted-living facility, make sure you are clear on what type of care is covered. The facility may offer a basic package of services. If you use any other services, you could be charged an additional fee. Or you may be on your own in finding a particular service. For example, your facility may offer housekeeping services and food preparation for two meals a day. If you need health care services such as physical therapy or help with your medication, that may cost you extra.

Any contract that you are asked to sign as part of the entrance into any facility or program is an important legal document, with consequences that you might later regret. It should be reviewed by your lawyer before you sign it.

Pay special attention to the deposit you are asked to make. Will you or your family be entitled to get it back if you die prematurely? Can you sell your new place of residence and make a profit, or is your interest limited to the investment you have made?

How Do I Pay for It?

When assisted-living facilities were first built, the residents were not allowed to use Medicaid to pay for their costs within the facilities. During the past few years, however, the states began to realize that many people lived in nursing homes because there was no other choice and that assisted-living facilities were less costly than nursing homes. Letting people pay for assisted-living facilities with Medicaid would actually save money for Medicaid. About two-thirds of the states now let qualified individuals use Medicaid to live in an assisted-living facility.

What Kind of Services Should an Assisted-Living Facility Provide?

These can vary from one facility to the next, but in general an assisted-living facility will provide more services than a retirement community. Residents in a retirement community tend to be younger and more physically able than those in an assisted-living facility. Some services that you should look for include:

- help with bathing, dressing, preparing meals, and taking medication;
- laundry;
- shopping;
- housekeeping;
- transportation, such as to and from the grocery store;
- physical therapy;
- nursing care;
- meal service.

CONTINUING-CARE RETIREMENT COMMUNITIES (CCRC)

What Are They?

In a continuing-care retirement community, also known as life-care facilities, you move from independent living to more supervised living as your needs change. It differs from other alternatives in that it combines aspects of retirement communities with nursing home care. In effect, you could move into your own apartment within the community when you are 55 and progress through several levels of care until moving into the nursing home when you are in your nineties.

TALKING TO A LAWYER
When Services Are Reduced

Q. At the time we moved into our community, the association provided a security guard in the parking garage and in the main areas of the building. The security protection is now reduced to video cameras in the hallways and parking garage. Can we force them to bring back the services we were promised when we moved in?

A. In practical terms, that depends on the language of the contract you signed before you moved in. Oral promises are very hard to prove. Check and see what the contract says.

Answer by Jeff Atkinson, Professor of Law,
DePaul University School of Law, Chicago, Illinois

Cost

The original CCRCs charged a one-time fee when you moved in that covered all the services that would be available to you. It did not matter whether you wanted or needed those services. Today a CCRC would more likely ask for a one-time initiation fee followed by a monthly fee or rent. After that you may be charged for any service that you use within the facility.

Something to Watch Out For

Some CCRC contracts state that you are guaranteed care for your lifetime, even if you run out of money. This is part of what your initiation fee covers. Other CCRC contracts reserve the right to make you leave if you can no longer pay. Be sure you find out whether you have guaranteed lifetime care. If you will be asked to leave when you can no longer pay, what kind of notice will you receive? How much time will you have to move?

The Benefit for Couples

The apartment complex of the CCRC will often be connected by a hallway to a nursing home. If your spouse goes into the nursing home, you would be able to stay in your apartment and walk down the hall to visit your spouse. Even if the nursing home is in a separate building on the campus, you will be quite close to your spouse.

HOME HEALTH CARE

Why Is It a Good Alternative to a Nursing Home?

Like most of the other alternatives, home health care is almost always less expensive than a nursing home. (An exception is when you need 24-hour care or other treatment that is unusually costly.) Plus, you get to stay in your own home, which gives you more independence and privacy.

How Do I Pay for It?

This is one of the few alternatives for which Medicaid will pay. If you are receiving skilled nursing care (as opposed to help with day-to-day activities such as housekeeping) in your home, Medicaid may pay for part of the care you receive if you meet income and asset tests.

Medicare also pays for more home care than is generally

presumed. But it takes a sophisticated advocate to navigate through the definitions of "homebound," "part-time or intermittent care," and "skilled care."

Problems with Home Health Care

Because you are getting care in your home, there is little supervision unless your doctor makes home visits. There is no way for you, your doctor, or even the home health care agency to know for sure that you are getting the care you need. Your doctor may not be aware of some of your health concerns or of some of the problems that may arise unless you tell him.

This puts more responsibility on your family to make sure you have a regimen of health care at home. However, there are reputable, licensed agencies that provide this type of care and may be bonded regarding the persons assigned to provide your care.

If you choose home health care, you should address other concerns, such as the security of your valuables, as you will have strangers in your home on a regular basis. You may need the assistance of your family to make sure you do not become the victim of elder abuse, which can occur when people become careless regarding their own security and the security of their property.

OTHER ALTERNATIVES

Home Sharing

Approximately 400 groups, many of them nonprofit, offer to help elderly people find younger people to share their homes. Home sharing works like this: The older person provides a room or shares the whole house with a younger person. The younger person takes care of the housekeeping and meals and provides company for the older person. In exchange, the younger person pays little or no rent.

The Benefits for the Older Person

You get to stay in your own home much longer, and you have someone to help with the upkeep. You stay independent and connected with the community. Your family gets peace of mind, knowing that you are not alone and that there is someone there to help care for you. You have the added security of a stronger person with a clearer mind being there for you if someone tries to take advantage of you or to break into your home.

The Downside for the Home Owner

If you have lived in your house for decades, it may be difficult for you to adjust to someone new living in your home. You may feel as if a stranger is invading your privacy. Even small adjustments, such as moving the furniture around or cooking a food you have never tried before, may seem like a big deal at first.

How to Choose a Person for Home Sharing

There are hundreds of groups that offer this service. These groups are a better option than putting a classified ad in the newspaper. The service you choose should find out—in great detail—the lifestyle habits of any person the service is considering putting into your home. The person's references should be checked, as should yours. If the service finds a person that might be a good match for you, a meeting should be arranged. Then it should be up to the two of you whether you want to live together. Some of these services will also act as a go-between if you and your new roommate are having trouble adjusting to living together.

How to Find These Services

Begin by asking friends and neighbors in your church and community. Nursing homes, geriatric doctors, and associations for retired people may also be able to provide you with information on these services. Check with your local senior center or center on aging or with the state center on aging. Do an Internet search by asking your favorite search engine to search on "home sharing elderly" plus your state.

Cooperative Shared Housing

Cooperative shared housing is living with other older people in a family-style house that is owned by an agency. This house is in a residential neighborhood.

The Benefits to You

You would have your own room, as would several other older people. You would be responsible for your own personal care. Cooperative shared housing is usually less expensive than a retirement community. It gives you a chance to be independent and still have companionship. You are free to come and go as you would in your own home. If you want privacy, you can simply go into your own room and shut the door.

What the Agency Provides

A manager that works for the agency would have a room in the house as well. The manager would prepare all your meals and take care of all the housekeeping. The agency might also provide other services, such as visits from a nurse.

Intergenerational Homes or Communities

When people from several age groups live together in one housing complex or community, that is an intergenerational home or community. For instance, an apartment complex may include families with young children, college students, and one or more floors that are equipped as assisted-living areas for the elderly. The students and families pay less rent because they spend part of their week working in the assisted-living areas. In this way you remain a part of the larger community.

The Benefits for the Older Person

People who miss their own families or who enjoy being around young children like the interaction that intergenerational living provides. The residents look out for one another and create a stable sense of family that many older people find comforting.

Residents can become like grandparents to the children in the building.

What You Might Not Like
Not everyone likes being around young children. If you are easily bothered by the sound of babies crying, balls bouncing, or children playing, this is not for you.

The Intergenerational Community

There is a growing trend toward the intergenerational community. Instead of selling your house and moving into an apartment, you would buy a smaller home (sometimes called a villa) in a development that is geared for several different age groups. The housing association would take care of your landscaping. The exterior of your house would be maintenance free. Your neighbors would be other retirees and families of all age groups.

 A REPRESENTATIVE COMMUNITY

A New York intergenerational community includes 175 single-family homes, 50 townhomes, 48 villas, and an apartment building with 168 apartments for retirement-age people only. There is an on-site health coordinator for the residents. All of the apartments are equipped with a push-button emergency-response system.

These developments usually offer a clubhouse, a pool, and exercise facilities. It gives you the feeling of a close-knit community while allowing you to keep a high level of privacy. These communities do not offer the health care services that some retirement homes and assisted-living facilities provide. This type of housing is growing in demand as our population ages, though, and some builders are beginning to offer those services to entice you into their development.

THE WORLD AT YOUR FINGERTIPS

- The AgeNet Information and Referral Network offers advice on long-term housing choices for seniors, as well as links to other resources and information. You can find them online at *http://www.agenet.com/housing_options.asp*.
- The Administration on Aging offers advice on how to find transportation services in your area for the elderly, allowing seniors to live more independently. The site is at *http://www.aoa.dhhs.gov/aoa/eldractn/transp.html*.
- The Administration on Aging also offers insight on how to remodel or modify a house to enable an elderly person to live there with minimal assistance. That site is *http://www.aoa.dhhs.gov/aoa/eldractn/homemodf.html*.
- For more available alternatives, go to *www.seniorresource.com* and click on "Housing Choices." This can also lead you to alternatives available in your particular state.

YOU MUST REMEMBER THIS

- Alternatives to nursing homes are usually less expensive than nursing home care.
- The alternatives discussed in this chapter offer you more privacy and independence than a nursing home.
- These alternatives are generally paid for by you or your family. Medicaid and Medicare do not usually include these types of living arrangements.
- Be sure to find out exactly what is included in any fees you pay.

PART SIX

Regulating Medical Professionals

The Law Tries to Protect You from

Incompetence and Malpractice

It seems as though there are laws and regulations for everything related to health care—doctors, nurses, insurance companies, health maintenance organizations, and hospitals. How do those laws protect you? This section will look at those laws and regulations and how they safeguard you, the patient.

In Chapter 23 we cover the licensing of doctors, nurses, and hospitals. You will learn who is required to be licensed and the effect of these regulations on the quality of health care. We will also tell you how to find out if your doctor's license is valid and steps to take to file a complaint against a licensed professional.

Chapter 24 discusses medical malpractice and the steps to take if you think you suffered an injury at the hands of your doctor. We will also explain why some states put a limit on the money you can collect for medical malpractice.

Research on humans is considered in Chapter 25. This chapter explains the protections the law imposes on research programs. We will make clear the steps that a researcher must follow before you can be subjected to certain types of experimental treatment, and we will fill you in on how you can protect your individual rights as a research subject.

If you would like more information on these and other topics, please check at the end of the guide for additional resources and websites regarding these issues.

CHAPTER 23

Licensing of Doctors, Nurses, and Hospitals

It's One of the Ways the State Tries to Protect You

Glenn knows she is overweight and needs to lose about 100 pounds. She feels desperate until she sees an advertisement in a newspaper about a medication that helps people lose weight. She calls the number at the bottom of the advertisement and makes an appointment with the weight loss clinic. When she goes to the clinic, she is seated in the doctor's office. Glenn is a smart woman. She looks closely at the framed certificates on the wall until she finds the doctor's license. If the doctor is licensed, he must know what he is doing. Or does he?

LICENSING REQUIREMENTS

Who Licenses Health Care Professionals and Facilities?

Each state government sets its own requirements for the licensing of doctors, nurses, hospitals, and other health care professionals and facilities. The state does this to protect the health and safety of you and your neighbors. Once a doctor is licensed to practice medicine, that doctor is licensed to practice any type of medicine. In theory, a dermatologist can deliver a baby, an obstetrician can perform liposuction, and a plastic surgeon can perform brain surgery. In reality, hospital regulations, fear of malpractice claims, and disciplinary actions discourage doctors from giving medical care outside their fields of expertise.

The states began to pass laws in the 1870s and 1880s requiring doctors to be licensed. Before that, doctors did not need a license to practice medicine. These laws usually required that a doctor pass a state's licensing examination in order to receive a license. In the early part of the 1900s, the American Medical Association (AMA) set standards for medical schools and lobbied for laws that would allow only graduates of those schools that met those standards to take the licensing examination. That is how the AMA came to oversee the accreditation of medical schools, a power it retains to this day.

Who Needs a License?

That varies by state. In general, states will license chiropractors, dentists, doctors, surgeons, physical therapists, nurses, optometrists, psychologists, physician assistants, respiratory therapists, pharmacists, and clinical social workers. Some states may also decide to license hearing aid dispensers, eyeglass and contact lens dispensers, clinical laboratory technologists, and midwives.

Why Do Doctors Need a License?

The state legislators believe that by requiring a license for doctors, they can help ensure that you will receive quality medical care. A license means they can make sure that doctors graduated from medical schools that taught them what they need to know to treat you. These laws can prevent you from being cared for by a person who has a criminal history or a character defect. It means that if a doctor does not care for you in medically acceptable ways, the doctor may be disciplined by license revocation or suspension.

On the other hand, licensing requirements are not favored by everyone. Some commentators argue that the licensing requirements discriminate against minorities or raise the price of your medical care. Others suggest that licensing requirements impose a stifling conformity on medicine, because all doctors attend strictly regulated medical schools that teach the same classes and do not encourage other ways of thinking or treating patients.

THREE LONG STEPS

In most states, to become a licensed doctor a person must:

- graduate from college;
- complete four years of medical school; *and*
- complete an internship.

A state may use the licensing standards as a way to promote public policy. For example, when the California legislature determined that many doctors knew less about human sexuality than most nondoctors, the California Medical Licensing Board added training in human sexuality as a requirement for licensing.

Who Actually Does the Licensing?

The state legislature enacts laws regarding who may receive (and sometimes lose) a license. The laws are then used by state medical boards to regulate doctors, nurses, facilities, and other health care professionals. For example, a board of doctors will use the laws to decide what new doctors must know or do to receive their licenses, as well as how the doctors must perform once they are licensed. The state medical board will also use the laws when deciding whether to discipline a doctor. Note that it

MINIMUM REQUIREMENTS

For a health professional to be licensed, he or she must usually:

- graduate from an approved program, such as a medical or nursing school;
- pass a standardized licensing examination; *and*
- undergo a review of his/her personal history.

is the profession of medicine—the doctors—that carries the regulatory burden. In general, a hallmark of a profession—as opposed to a vocation—is self-regulation.

NURSES AND PHYSICIAN ASSISTANTS

What About Nurses?

The profession of nursing really got its start on bloody battlefields. The heroic contributions of Florence Nightingale and other nurses in the Crimean War and of Clara Barton and her colleagues in the American Civil War established the value of nursing.

The first nursing school was founded in 1873. The early nursing schools were based in hospitals and provided unpaid labor by student nurses to the hospitals. In the 1890s, many of the first nursing students, particularly those from well-to-do families, were now nurses and teaching the next nursing classes their profession. At the same time, there were women from the lower classes of society who did not attend nursing schools but who nevertheless held themselves out as nurses. The teaching nurses began to press for licensing of nurses so that they could improve patient care. By 1923, forty-eight states required nurses to be licensed. To be licensed, the nurses had to attend a nursing school.

 THE BAD OLD DAYS

In the 1800s, women were considered to be better suited to nursing because they were considered compassionate and reassuring to patients and were expected to clean the wards and make the beds. Nurses worked 60 to 70 hours a week for little pay, living in the hospital or school, and were subjected to harsh discipline, such as room inspections at any time of the day or night.

Today, professional nursing associations continue to push for more education in order for nurses to be licensed. In many states, nurses are not required to attend college to take the standardized test and receive a license. A diploma from a hospital-based nursing school is enough. Many nursing associations believe a college degree is needed for nurses to be fully trained. Hospital-based nursing schools and nurses without college degrees disagree; they oppose adding a further educational requirement.

Are Physician Assistants Licensed?

Usually. Most states allow physician assistants to be licensed, certified, or registered in some way in order to make physician assistants meet professional standards. Being licensed, certified, or registered requires the physician assistants to meet the standards set by the state for their profession.

Physician assistants do certain things that are delegated to them by the doctors they assist. What a doctor may delegate to a physician assistant depends on the law of each state and the customs of the medical profession. All physician assistants must be supervised by a licensed doctor, but each state differs as to how much supervision is required. In some states, physician assistants may prescribe medication. In others, the practice is strictly forbidden.

WHEN CAN A LICENSE BE REVOKED?

It is difficult to get a doctor's or a nurse's license revoked. A professional license is considered "property" under the Constitution, so the person must be told the reason for the revocation and given a fair hearing. The most common ground for suspending a license is unprofessional conduct.

COMPLAINING TO LICENSING AUTHORITIES ABOUT A HEALTH CARE PROFESSIONAL

Where Do I File a Complaint?

Each state has a medical board and other boards in charge of licensing, investigating complaints, and disciplining doctors and other health care professionals. You can look in the telephone book, or you can do an online search, using a search such as the name of your state + medical + board. The medical board or other board will tell you how to get a complaint form to begin the process. Some boards put this form on their website, and you can print it from there. Be sure to fill out the form completely and clearly. This form will ask you to sign a release allowing the board to look at your medical records. You are not required to sign this; but without looking at your records, the board may not be able to investigate your complaint fully. Some states require that your complaint form be notarized, which would require your name on the form.

What Happens Then?

Usually the board will examine the complaint form and decide whether the complaint should be investigated. In some situations the board will not have the authority to investigate. For example, if you complain that your doctor kept you waiting too long for your examination, the board may decide that complaint does not have merit and will inform you that it will not be investigated.

Following are some types of complaints that would probably be investigated by a medical board:

- substandard medical care,
- illegal sale of drugs,
- professional misconduct,

- a criminal conviction,
- sexual misconduct,
- neglect or abandonment of a patient,
- alcohol or substance abuse,
- mental or emotional illness that impairs the doctor's judgment,
- discrimination,
- billing for services not provided,
- false advertising,
- fraud,
- failure to provide medical records,
- overcharging for medical records,
- failure to supervise staff.

How Is the Complaint Investigated?

The medical board will notify the doctor of the complaint and ask your doctor to respond. When the board receives the doctor's response, it will decide whether to continue the investigation. If an investigation is needed, the board will look at your medical records (and others as deemed necessary) and interview witnesses.

How Long Does the Investigation Take?

An investigation can take anywhere from a few weeks to several years, depending on the complexity of the complaint and the difficulty of the investigation. You can check on the status of your complaint by contacting the medical board.

What Happens After the Investigation?

If the board finds that the complaint is unwarranted, it will dismiss it. If it finds that the complaint is justified, it may request that the complaint be investigated further. In some cases, the complaint will be dismissed, but the board will notify the doctor that certain methods or actions must be changed in the future. It may order your doctor to take more training or to stop performing particular treatments. It may require that the doctor enter into treatment for substance or alcohol abuse. If the board finds that the doctor should be disciplined, there will be an administrative hearing, at which time the doctor may be disciplined in some way, including having his or her license revoked or suspended.

Do I Have to Give My Name When I Complain?

Some medical boards will not investigate a complaint that is anonymous. It would be nearly impossible to investigate a complaint without access to the complaining patient's medical records. On the other hand, medical boards will often keep your name confidential if you so request. In other words, your doctor will not find out directly from investigators that it was you who complained, even though the medical board knows your name and sees your medical records. However, the doctor may be able to infer that it was you when the board requests your records.

What Happens to My Complaint After It Is Either Dismissed or the Doctor Is Disciplined?

These documents typically become part of the doctor's file kept by the medical board. In some states this is available to the public because it is considered a public record.

Can I Appeal If My Complaint Is Dismissed?

No. There is no appeals process through the medical board. When a complaint is dismissed by the medical board, it may mean only that an investigation would not provide enough proof to discipline the doctor.

If the Board Does Not Take Action, Do I Have Other Options?

Yes. The dismissal of your complaint by a medical board does not affect your right to bring a legal action, such as for medical malpractice, against your doctor. Medical malpractice is discussed in the next chapter.

HOSPITALS, NURSING HOMES, AND OTHER HEALTH CARE FACILITIES

Quality Control

Just as doctors must be licensed and meet certain standards, so must hospitals, nursing homes, and most other types of health care facilities. Unlike doctors though, health care facilities (including hospitals and nursing homes) are regulated by a combination of state and federal laws, including Medicaid and Medicare. These regulations dictate the type of care that may be provided, the way that the professional staff may be selected and trained, and the maintenance and sanitation of the buildings and equipment. In addition, health care facilities may choose to meet the standards of private accreditation organizations to boost their public image or to increase their competitive edge.

Who Does Not Need a License?

There are some health care facilities that do not fit the legal definition of a hospital or a nursing home or a clinic. Depending on the state and where those facilities are located (such as separate from a hospital), those facilities may not need to be licensed unless they fall under some other legal definition that requires licensing. Examples of facilities for older persons that may offer some level of medical care but not be licensed are board-and-care facilities, continuing-care retirement communities, residential-care facilities, homes for the aged, and assisted-living facilities.

Hospitals

Although every hospital must be licensed and is regulated by both state and federal governments, hospital standards are largely set by a private group, the Joint Commission on Accreditation of Healthcare Organizations (JCAHO). Both state and federal regulations defer to JCAHO for enforcing those standards.

JCAHO is the leading accreditation organization for hospitals, and it also accredits nursing homes and other types of health care facilities. When a hospital joins JCAHO, it agrees to comply with the organization's standards of quality and agrees that JCAHO may enforce the standards against the hospital.

The benefit of having a private organization such as JCAHO perform this function is that it saves the government millions of dollars. In addition, JCAHO is able to change and to enforce its standards much more quickly than the government, which must follow lengthy procedures to alter its standards or rules. In fact, most states incorporate JCAHO standards into their licensing requirements for hospitals, and the Medicare law considers JCAHO-accredited hospitals to meet the standards for Medicare certification. Although JCAHO is not the only hospital accreditation organization in the country, it is by far the largest.

Nursing Homes

Nursing homes can be accredited by JCAHO as well, but nursing homes have not participated in accreditation programs to the extent of hospitals. Nursing homes are required by every state to be licensed, but the quality of care may leave something to be desired. Most states require a registered nurse to supervise nursing care, but nursing care is often offered by nurses' aides with little or no training. Compare this with licensed nurses who take care of patients in hospitals. Several scandals over poor care in nursing homes have caused an uproar in both the public and state legislatures.

As a result, nursing homes are more stringently regulated by the government, and those regulations are more rigorously enforced than those for hospitals. With hospitals regulating themselves through JCAHO, state and federal agencies are able to concentrate their efforts on making sure that nursing homes are following the requirements set out in the licensing standards.

PRACTICING WITHOUT A LICENSE
State Medical Practice Acts

Each state has laws that forbid anyone but licensed doctors from practicing medicine. Practicing without a license is known as the unauthorized practice of medicine. How these laws define medicine varies from state to state, with most states using a broad definition. For example, the Pennsylvania medical practice act defines *medicine* as "the art and science of which the objectives are the cure of diseases and the preservation of the health of man, including the practice of the healing art with or without drugs, except healing by spiritual means or prayer."

Usually *medicine* does not include the sale of books that discuss healing nor the sale of vitamins or nutritional substances, as long as those activities do not involve making a diagnosis of the patient. It does not include home remedies, the self-injection of insulin, or tattooing.

However, *prescribing* vitamins to cure an illness is practicing medicine, and someone would need a license to do that. The same is true of taking blood or urine samples for analysis in order to diagnose or treat an illness or injury.

What Is the "Unauthorized Practice of Medicine"?

The **unauthorized practice of medicine** occurs when an unlicensed person does something that is part of the legal definition of *medicine*. This does not include simply offering general advice (as, for example, in a magazine article for the general public) or offering informal advice about a co-worker's cold, but it does involve holding yourself out as a licensed doctor when in fact you do not have a license to practice medicine. For instance, if you diagnose a person as having cancer, but you are not a doctor, you engaged in the unauthorized practice of medicine and you may be prosecuted in a criminal court. If you prescribe a healing salve for a skin condition or give obstetrical examinations but you are not a licensed health professional, you engaged in the unauthorized practice of medicine and you may be prosecuted in a criminal court.

LEARNING THE LINGO

Unauthorized practice of medicine: This occurs when someone holds herself out as being a licensed doctor when in fact the person has no license, or when the person does something that is considered "medicine," such as diagnosing or treating a patient.

Even a person who is licensed may commit an unauthorized practice of medicine. If a licensed nurse sells her services as a midwife in a state that does not allow midwives, that nurse may be subject to discipline by a nursing board or in a criminal court. Physician assistants are allowed to provide medical care only under the supervision of a licensed doctor. If the doctor does not provide the required supervision, the doctor may be disciplined by a medical board for knowingly aiding, assisting, or advising an unlicensed person to practice medicine.

What If I Want to Be Treated by That Person Even Though I Know the Doctor or Health Care Professional Is Not Licensed?

In most states it does not matter if you have *agreed* to be treated by a health care professional whom you know is not licensed. The medical practice acts of each state are intended to protect your health and safety. Those acts allow the states to make the unauthorized practice of medicine illegal regardless of your consent to the treatment.

Who Decides What Is the Practice of Medicine?

That usually falls to the medical board within the state. As mentioned earlier, the law defines medicine very broadly, which leaves the board room to make flexible decisions depending on available medical technology and the custom of the medical profession. Sometimes a state may try to be more specific in its definition of medicine, but that can backfire. When the Medical Association of Georgia wanted to keep optometrists from using lasers on patients to correct vision problems, the Georgia legislature passed a law that only doctors, dentists, podiatrists, and veterinarians were allowed to perform any surgery or invasive procedure in which tissue would be cut, pierced, or otherwise altered. An unintended side effect of the law was that it was suddenly illegal for nurses to insert intravenous lines. It was suddenly illegal for diabetics to inject themselves with insulin. Even ear piercing and tattooing was suddenly illegal unless performed by a doctor, dentist, podiatrist, or veterinarian. While the legislature did not intend to make those activities illegal, the new law did just that. The Georgia courts soon struck down the law as unconstitutional.

Naturopathy and Homeopathy

A handful of states allow the practice of naturopathy and homeopathy. In other states naturopathy and homeopathy are considered the unlicensed practice of medicine.

LEARNING THE LINGO

Naturopathy: A method of treating an illness with natural processes, such as nutritional science.

Homeopathy: System of medical practice that treats a disease by the administration of minute doses of a remedy that would in healthy persons produce symptoms of the disease treated.

Currently only Arizona and Nevada allow for the practice of homeopathy. In Utah, Oregon, Washington, and Kansas, the practice of naturopathy is legal and regulated by the states. Even in states that allow alternative forms of medical treatment, doctors may hesitate to use them if those forms of treatment are not accepted by the mainstream medical profession.

What Is the Corporate Practice of Medicine Doctrine?

The corporate practice of medicine doctrine makes it illegal for corporations and other businesses to practice medicine. This prevents corporations from hiring doctors to treat employees, insurance companies from providing medical care, and partnerships between doctors and people who are not doctors. Most states do not allow corporations to control doctors' practices because it is considered an unauthorized practice of medicine. The reasoning behind the doctrine is that doctors need to be able to treat patients according to the patients' needs rather than according to the rules set up by corporate management. The fear is that corporations will commercialize the practice of medicine to the point that patients will lose confidence in doctors and medical care.

NOT EVEN A NONPROFIT

In the 1970s a group of San Antonio, Texas, residents created a nonprofit corporation to hire doctors to serve people who did not have access to medical care. The Texas Medical Society took the group to court and had the corporation shut down because state law did not allow doctors to work for organizations controlled by people who are not doctors.

The corporate practice of medicine doctrine seems distinctly out of step in these days of managed care, where health maintenance organizations directly affect how doctors practice medicine. Managed care, in theory at least, makes health care more affordable and efficient, which in turn increases the quality of care for the patient. Although few states have decided to abandon the corporate practice of medicine doctrine outright, it looks as if that is the direction in which health care is moving.

To Find Out If a Doctor Is Licensed

To find out if your doctor is licensed, call the licensing board in your state. This is usually in the phone book under your state's name, followed by "medical examination" or "licensing board." Or check out the website for the Association of State Medical Board Executive Directors at *http://www.docboard.org/*. This website will link you to your state's licensing board. Many of the states give you instructions on the Internet for lodging complaints against your doctor in addition to checking on a license. There are also resources at the end of this chapter that you can use to find out whether your doctor is, in fact, licensed.

What Should I Do If I Find Out My Doctor Is Not Licensed?

First of all, double check the information—you don't want to make a false report. If you're certain, report that person to the medical board in your state. Earlier in this chapter we explained how to find the medical board in your state and how to file a complaint. The person practicing without a license may be subject to criminal penalties and will face trial. Depending on the situation, you may have a civil action against the person for *battery*—wrongful physical action, usually a beating or something similar, but possibly a wrongful physical examination—and you may be able to bring a lawsuit seeking monetary damages against the person.

THE WORLD AT YOUR FINGERTIPS

- To find the website for the medical licensing board in your state, go to your favorite search engine and try the following search: [your state] + medical + licensing board.
- The Medical Board of California licenses doctors and investigates complaints. If you live in California, you can check to make sure your doctor has a valid license or if your doctor has been sued for malpractice. Go to the medical board's website at *http://www.medbd.ca.gov/*. You can search on either the doctor's name or license number.
- Massachusetts patients can get background, licensing, and disciplinary information about their doctors from the Massachusetts Board of Registration in Medicine at *http://www. massmedboard.org/*.
- The American Medical Association offers the Online Doctor-Finder. This service provides information on more than 650,000 licensed doctors in the United States. Use this site to get background information on your doctor. The site, *http://www.ama-assn.org/aps/amahg.htm*, does not give information on disciplinary actions or malpractice suits.
- The American Board of Medical Specialties offers a physician locator and information service at *http://www.certified doctor.org/*. Use this service to find out if your doctor is truly certified within one of twenty-four specialty areas.

YOU MUST REMEMBER THIS

- Every state requires that doctors, nurses, and hospitals be licensed.
- A license ensures that your doctor, nurse, or hospital meets the minimum standards for providing medical care.
- A license is no guarantee that your doctor, nurse, or hospital is competent. Ask your friends and family about their health care providers, or get references from your doctor.
- Call the state licensing board to find out if your doctor is licensed.

CHAPTER 24

Medical Malpractice

You Have Legal Recourse When
Bad Medical Care Harms You

*Jackie thought she had a cold. It started in February with a cough.
When it did not go away by March, Jackie went to see her doctor. The
doctor prescribed an antibiotic and told Jackie that if her cold did not
get better within the next two weeks to make another appointment.
Jackie took the antibiotics off and on for a couple of weeks. Her cold
did not clear up, but she did not make another appointment for several
months. By that time her cough was worse. When she finally returned
to the doctor's office, the doctor ordered a CT scan of Jackie's upper
chest. The scan showed that Jackie had a tumor that turned out to be
Hodgkin's Disease. Jackie starts chemotherapy the next week.
Her prognosis is good, but it would be better if she had returned to the
doctor sooner rather than later. Jackie is angry that the doctor did
not tell her it could be something other than a cold. She wants to
know if she can sue for malpractice. Can she?*

IN GENERAL

What Is Medical Malpractice?

The goal of a medical **malpractice** suit is to recover funds to
compensate you if a doctor injures you. Malpractice lawsuits are
time-consuming and costly for doctors, even if the doctor is
insured or wins the case. The fear of malpractice is meant to
keep doctors from making medical mistakes and from acting
carelessly. In this way, the law can control the quality of health
care. Malpractice puts responsibility on doctors to act in a way
that will not result in an injury to you. If doctors are forced to

pay for the costs of their medical mistakes, they will be more careful to make sure that mistakes do not happen in the first place. (Note, though, that some observers think that fear of malpractice does not so much improve medical care as make doctors more defensive in how they treat you. The result may be more tests and other measures to establish a solid record of care—good for defense in a malpractice case, but a factor in making health care more time-consuming and expensive.)

LEARNING THE LINGO

Malpractice: Medical care that does not meet the standard of care that other doctors would have given you in the same or similar situation and that results in an injury to you.

Can a Doctor Go to Jail for Medical Malpractice?

Not for ordinary malpractice, though sometimes prosecutors have succeeded in getting criminal sanctions levied for gross deviations from the standard of care. In all but these extraordinary cases, medical malpractice has a civil penalty. In a criminal case, the state prosecutes the accused person, and the person may go to jail if found guilty. In a civil case such as medical malpractice, you, the patient, would bring a lawsuit against a doctor. If a jury finds that the doctor acted negligently and that you were injured as a result of that act, the doctor (or the doctor's insurance company) will have to pay you an amount that is determined by either the jury or the judge to compensate you for your injury. Being sued for malpractice may cause the doctor's insurance rates to go up. That cost is then passed on to you and other patients. Typically a medical malpractice lawsuit is not reported to the state licensing agency and has no effect on the doctor's license. It is, however, reported to the National Practitioners DataBank, which, though not open to the public, is open to hospitals and health plans.

How Would a Jury Decide If My Doctor Committed Malpractice?

A jury will compare your doctor's conduct with that of doctors faced with the same or similar circumstances. The doctor is not compared to a person in the general population. Instead, the doctor is compared to other doctors with the same type of medical training and skills.

For example, if you are a 30-year-old woman who runs marathons and you tell your doctor you have chest pains, the actions your general practitioner doctor takes will be compared with what other general practitioners would have done if a 30-year-old female marathon runner came in complaining of chest pains.

If a jury finds that your doctor did not act with the same level of care that other doctors would have used in a similar situation, the jury will find that your doctor committed malpractice.

As shown in the example that began this chapter, other factors can also be important. Did Jackie, the woman with the cough that turned out to be a symptom of cancer, contribute to her problem by not making another appointment with the doctor, as the doctor had recommended? **Contributory negligence** is often an issue in medical malpractice cases.

But What About All Those Huge Malpractice Awards I Read About in the Paper?

Many times those awards are greatly reduced on appeal or by subsequent settlement.

Some medical mistakes may have catastrophic consequences, crippling a patient for life. The costs of permanent care for a person totally paralyzed in an operating room blunder, for example, could be staggering—and these costs would be reflected in **compensatory** damages.

Sometimes a doctor not only makes a mistake but also acts so recklessly or carelessly toward you that a jury may decide to punish the doctor. A jury does that by awarding **punitive** damages. Punitive damages are damages above and beyond the amount of money it will take to compensate you for your injury. Punitive damages are used to punish doctors for bad behavior and to give you solace for mental anguish. These damages are not meant to compensate you for your injury. Punitive damages set an example by telling doctors that if they conduct their medical care in a way that is outrageously wrong, they will be punished. Not all states allow for punitive damages in medical malpractice cases.

LEARNING THE LINGO

Punitive damages: A money award that is used to punish someone for outrageous conduct.

So If My Doctor Makes a Mistake, I Can Sue for Malpractice?

It is not automatically malpractice when something bad happens as a result of medical care given to you by your doctor. As long as your doctor uses reasonable care and skill in treating you, your doctor did not commit malpractice. Five doctors can examine and diagnose the same person and come up with five different opinions as to what medical care is needed. That does not mean that four of the doctors are wrong or incompetent. It means that there are many ways to treat that person. The key is that all the doctors acted according to acceptable medical standards and treated you as any reasonable doctor would have treated you.

Keep in mind that at the very least, the doctor's mistake has to be the cause of your injury. If your doctor makes a mistake but you are not injured as a result of it, there is no malpractice.

What Do I Need to Do to Prove Malpractice?

First, you will need to prove that your doctor had a duty to you. This means you must have a doctor-patient relationship. Then you will have to establish for a jury that the medical profession itself has a standard of care for your illness or injury—in other words, that doctors are supposed to treat your type of medical condition in a certain way. After that you will need to show that you suffered an injury and that the injury was a result of the doctor's failure to give you appropriate medical care.

PROVING MALPRACTICE

In a medical malpractice case, you will need to prove that:

- there was a doctor-patient relationship;
- other doctors in the same or similar situation would have provided different medical care;
- you suffered an injury; *and*
- your injury was the result of your doctor not giving you appropriate medical care.

SUING FOR MALPRACTICE

What Will Happen the First Time I Meet with a Malpractice Attorney?

The attorney will ask you questions about what happened and take a look at your medical records. An experienced attorney should be able to tell you at the end of this meeting whether your claim is worth pursuing. This does not mean that malpractice did or did not occur. Sometimes it would cost you so much to sue your doctor that you are better off not suing at all. Other times patients do not have strong cases, and the attorney knows that the patient would not win, even though the doctor may have acted improperly.

If I'm Willing to Take the Risk of Losing, Shouldn't My Attorney Pursue the Case?

Legal battles are complex. Attorneys are bound by ethical rules—and in some states, laws—that require attorneys to only bring cases that are worthwhile and will not waste the court's time. A number of states require that an attorney discuss the malpractice claim with a qualified doctor who, in turn, decides whether any malpractice did occur. Then there is the matter of how your attorney gets paid. Most malpractice lawsuits are paid on a *contingent fee* basis—your attorney gets a percentage of the amount of money you are awarded. If you do not win your case, your attorney does not get paid. In some cases, the attorneys pay for the court costs for which you are responsible. Those costs—which are separate from the fee your attorney will receive—also come out of your monetary award. If you lose the case, your attorney gets stuck with those bills as well—unless you have agreed to pay them.

What Are Contingency Fees?

If a lawyer represents you for a contingency fee, your lawyer gets a percentage of any money that you are awarded by a jury. In many states, this percentage ranges from 33 1/3 to 50 percent. The actual percentage will depend on the agreement you reach with your attorney when he takes your case. A number of states now have laws that limit the percentage of your award that your attorney may claim. In California a contingency fee cannot be more than 40 percent of the first $50,000 of your jury award, 33 1/3 percent of the second $50,000, 25 percent of the following $500,000, and 10 percent of any award beyond $600,000. Another thing to keep in mind is that this percentage applies to settlement agreements, too.

Do I Have to Agree to Arbitration or Mediation?

Yes, if your state laws require you to do so. Even if your state does not require you to agree to arbitrate or mediate your claim, it may require that your malpractice claim go through a screening process. The panel that screens your claim may have the authority to put a limit on the amount of money you can receive from a jury, or it may decide that your claim does not have merit and dismiss it.

What Factors Will an Attorney Look For in Deciding Whether to Take My Case?

First and foremost, was there, in fact, malpractice? The attorney will determine whether your case has merit. The road to the courthouse is long and arduous. If, for example, you are lying, you will cost your attorney and the court vast amounts of time and money. No attorney wants that. Your attorney will also consider your injury. Visible, permanent injuries bring higher jury awards than injuries that are temporary. The same is true of the shock value of your injury. If your injury is unique in some way, you are more apt to get a bigger jury award.

What If I Tell My Attorney the Truth, but She Does Not Believe Me?

Find another attorney. You know that old saying that truth is stranger than fiction? You would not believe some of the bizarre injuries that patients have suffered. An inexperienced attorney may find your story far-fetched and think that you must be making it up. An experienced malpractice attorney will know that weird things happen to patients everyday and will be able to find out whether you are exaggerating. In one case a patient went to the hospital to have his cancerous right kidney removed. Unfortunately the doctors removed his left kidney instead. The first attorney consulted by the patient did not believe the patient's story and refused the case. The second attorney checked into the patient's story and found out it was true. The case is proceeding.

TALKING TO A LAWYER
As Time Goes By

Q. If I bring a malpractice lawsuit against my doctor, how long will it be before the case is heard and I find out whether I've won?

A. Assuming that you have a claim that supports a lawsuit, it may take anywhere from three to seven years. If the verdict is appealed for some reason, it will take even longer. The time frame for your case will depend on how complicated your claim is, as well as the number of cases that were scheduled for trial before yours. It is because of factors like these, and the uncertainties of litigation, that many malpractice cases are settled before trial.

Answer by Salvatore J. Russo,
Executive Senior Counsel,
New York City Health & Hospitals Corporation,
New York, New York

THE PATIENT'S RESPONSIBILITY

What Part Do I Play in All This?

The court will look at your actions to determine whether you played a part in your own injury.

How Could I Possibly Play a Part in My Own Injury?

Let's pretend that you are a 30-year-old marathon runner complaining of chest pains. The doctor tells you that it probably is not a heart attack considering your age and activity, but that you should stop running for the next few days while the doctor runs some tests. You leave the doctor's office, drive to the gym, and run 5 miles before dropping to the floor with a heart attack. Even if you could prove that other doctors would have diagnosed you as having a heart attack when you first walked into the doctor's office, the fact that you ignored your doctor's warning will be taken into account when a jury is deciding a malpractice case. Your actions probably contributed to your injury, and you may either lose the malpractice case altogether or receive less compensation.

Another way you can play a part in your injury is by failing to come back for the treatment your doctor recommends. If your doctor recommends that you schedule a CT scan to see if you have a tumor and you decide not to do that, you cannot claim that the doctor committed malpractice if a later scan shows that you have a tumor. On the same note, if your doctor recommends that you take medication every four hours but you decide to take it every two hours, your doctor is not responsible for the consequences.

What If I Did Not Know That What I Was Doing Would Contribute to My Injury?

That is a factor that will be considered by the court. Just as the doctor must act reasonably, so must you. If a reasonable person would have taken the doctor's advice and not run 5 miles, then it was unreasonable for you to ignore the doctor's advice. The same goes for medication. If the doctor prescribes medication for you but does not tell you that you should avoid dairy products while you are taking it, you do not play a part in your injury if you drink a glass of milk. If your doctor tells you to avoid dairy products while you are taking the medication and you drink a glass of milk anyway, you contributed to your injury. If a reasonable person would have decided to not drink the milk, your doctor has a defense to a malpractice claim and you could lose your lawsuit.

THE PATIENT'S RESPONSIBILITY

You, as a patient, have a duty to act reasonably when it comes to your health and well-being. That includes following your doctor's instructions in order to prevent injuring yourself.

What If I Forget to Tell the Doctor About a Preexisting Condition?

This is a tricky area and courts disagree on how it should affect a malpractice case. The court will take into account whether you knew that the information was important. If you know that you are allergic to penicillin but you do not tell that to your doctor, even when your doctor tells you that you need penicillin or some other antibiotic, you probably realize that your allergy is something important that your doctor needs to know. If you do not share that information, it probably will not be considered malpractice if your doctor prescribes penicillin.

In a Louisiana case, though, a court found that a patient did not have a duty to repeat her medical history to every person who gave her medical care. Instead, the second doctor should have asked for her medical history before examining her. In New York, a woman told a doctor that she had taken an overdose of barbiturates but did not tell the doctor that she was a drug addict. The doctor treated the woman for the overdose but did not treat her for drug addiction, and she later died. The doctor was found to have committed malpractice because the doctor should have gotten the woman's medical history to treat the addiction.

BIG BUCKS OR BIG BLUNDER?

How Much Can I Win?

Forget about those huge sums you read about in the newspaper. It may seem that people are walking out of courtrooms with wheelbarrows full of money. In reality, those cases are few and far between. In the majority of malpractice cases, the doctor wins.

 NOT A GET-RICH-QUICK PROPOSITION

The doctor wins most malpractice lawsuits. Very few patients receive large sums of money. Media attention in those cases, however, may make it seem as though winning a malpractice claim is as easy as hitting the jackpot.

Moreover, many states put a limit, known as a **damages cap,** on the amount of punitive damages that may be awarded and on noneconomic damages such as pain and suffering.

While those caps may still sound like a lot of money, remember that you will have large legal fees to get to that point and that there is a good chance you will get less than the amount of the cap. The doctor may appeal if you win, or the judge may reduce the amount of your award. Do not think of medical malpractice as a way to hit the jackpot. Think of it as a way to *possibly* be *minimally* compensated if, in fact, you are injured by the actions of your doctor.

What Exactly Is a Damages Cap?

A damages cap limits the amount of money a jury may award to you in a malpractice case. The damages cap varies by state. Indiana caps damages at $500,000. California caps damages at $250,000. Some states do not cap damages at all, claiming that to do so would violate that state's constitution. The states may put a limit on punitive damages only or on both punitive damages and any money that compensates you for your injury alone. Putting caps on damages is a hot topic in legal and political circles. The type of cap may vary from state to state, but look for more states to put a cap on damages in the coming years.

 LEARNING THE LINGO

Damages cap: A limit on the amount of money you may recover in a malpractice lawsuit. These vary by state.

Why Would a State Put a Cap on Damages?

Many juries are sympathetic to people who are injured, regardless of whether the doctor caused that injury. The jury may believe that the doctor makes a lot of money and can afford to pay thousands of dollars to someone less fortunate, or the jury might think that the doctor's insurance will cover the award. It is easy to take money from a faceless company and give it to the injured person you see every day in a courtroom.

By putting a cap on damages, states discourage people from bringing lawsuits simply because they think they can win a lot of money. When there are fewer lawsuits, the cost of your health care goes down because doctors are not passing on the legal costs to you.

Can the Jury Get Around the Damages Cap?

Usually. For that reason some states do not allow lawyers or judges to tell the jurors that there is a damages cap. That way the jurors will not be tempted to change their decision about other compensation for the victim. The point is to keep the legal process fair for both you and your doctor. For instance, let's say you live in a state where the cap is $100,000. The jury knows about the cap and decides that you suffered a minor injury. The jury may start with the $100,000 and decide that you deserve a quarter of that because your injury was minor. That leaves you with $25,000. If the jury had not known about the cap, they might have started with a figure of $500,000 and awarded you a quarter of that, which is $125,000. Because of the cap, you will only get $100,000 of that award, but it is still much more than the $25,000 you would have gotten if the jury knew of the cap.

On the other hand, it is not fair for the jury to award you $1 million simply because they think the doctor's insurance will cover it, regardless of whether the doctor actually caused your injury. A sympathetic jury is not always a fair jury. The damages cap may protect the doctor from a jury with a distorted view of the facts.

THE WORLD AT YOUR FINGERTIPS

- Dr. Timothy McCall explains how to determine whether your doctor is providing you with the correct medical care in *Examining Your Doctor: A Patient's Guide to Avoiding Harmful Medical Care* (Birch Lane Press, 1995).
- *Damages: One Family's Legal Struggles in the World of Medicine* by Barry Werth (Berkley Publishing Group, 1999) chronicles one family's struggles in a seven-year court battle on a malpractice claim.
- *Harmful Intent* by Blaine Kerr (Scribner, 1999) is a legal thriller centered on a medical malpractice lawsuit. This is a fictional account, but the concepts are sound and the average reader may find it more interesting than many nonfiction books.
- In *Suing for Medical Malpractice* (University of Chicago Press, 1993), the authors—Frank A. Sloan, Penny B. Githens, David F. Partlett, and Gerald B. Hickson—take on the notion that too many patients are winning huge awards in malpractice lawsuits. It is based on a survey of 200 malpractice cases in Florida.

YOU MUST REMEMBER THIS

- Just because your doctor made a mistake or you had a bad result from medical treatment does not mean that your doctor committed malpractice.
- Those big jury awards you read about in the newspaper are few and far between.
- Doctors win most malpractice cases—not because doctors have more power than patients, but because the juries do not believe that the doctors caused the patients' injuries.
- If your state has a damages cap, there will be a limit on the money you can be awarded in a malpractice case.

CHAPTER 25

Research on Humans

Medical Advances Are Good—but How Can We Ensure That People Are Protected?

Jesse is a teenager with an inherited liver disease. He is invited to participate in a gene therapy experiment to help determine whether an injection of genes might correct the problem. Before he agrees to participate, he and his father ask about the risks and possible side effects. Should he go forward with the experiment? How can he know the information he's being given by researchers is complete and accurate? How will his safety be protected during the experimental procedure?

PROGRESS THROUGH EXPERIMENTATION

The advances in medicine that we take for granted today—dialysis, organ transplantation, the artificial heart, amniocentesis—are only available because someone was the first patient to use the experimental treatment. Without experimentation and research on humans, medical technology could not improve.

At the same time, it is essential that the patients' rights to confidentiality and privacy be observed and that their informed consent be obtained before experimentation begins. Unfortunately, in the past some of that experimentation was forced on patients who either were unable to say no or did not know that they were being used as research subjects.

The Nuremberg Code

Concentration Camps

During World War II, Nazi doctors used concentration camp prisoners as research subjects. At the Dachau concentration camp, doctors were experimenting on the best way to treat persons who had been severely chilled or frozen. Doctors put prisoners in tanks of ice water for hours at a time or put naked prisoners outside in temperatures below freezing. At the Ravensbrück concentration camp, wounds were inflicted on prisoners so that the doctors could infect the wounds with bacteria. The goal was to create wounds similar to those found in the battlefield and then figure out how to better treat German soldiers. At the Buchenwald concentration camp, doctors secretly put poisons into the prisoners' food. The prisoners would be studied as they died, or they would be immediately put to death so that Nazi doctors could do autopsies.

THE NUREMBERG CODE SETS STANDARDS

The Nuremberg Code continues to set guidelines for research on humans. The following paraphrases it:

1. A person must volunteer to be a research subject and his or her consent must be informed.

2. The experiments must be scientifically and socially necessary.

3. The experiments should be based on the results of nonhuman experimentation (i.e., tried out on animals first).

4. The doctors should avoid unnecessary burdens and suffering on the subject.

5. Research should be conducted only by scientifically qualified persons.

6. Research should not be conducted if there is reason to believe death or disabling injury will occur.

7. The researchers must take precautions to protect the subject from harm.

8. The subject must have the right to quit the experiment at any time.

9. The researchers must terminate the experiment if they believe that its continuation is likely to result in harm to the subject.

The "Doctors' Trial"

When the war ended, three United States judges presided over the "Doctors' Trial" at Nuremberg. Twenty-three Nazi doctors were found guilty of war crimes and crimes against humanity, and seven were executed. The Nuremberg War Crimes Court devised the Nuremberg Code, which sets ethical standards for appropriate experimentation on humans.

Research on Americans

Americans were quick to condemn the Nazi doctors for their actions. Yet many Americans, for decades after World War II ended, were subjected to medical experiments without their knowledge. In the Tuskegee Syphilis Study, hundreds of low-income African American men in the South were denied treatment for syphilis so that the "natural history" of the disease could be studied. The study went on for 40 years. There were other instances of experimentation without consent as well.

WHO PROTECTS YOU?

Congress

Congress enacted the National Research Act in 1974 to protect the public when taking part in medical research and experiments. The Act does not mean that doctors cannot experiment on you. Rather, the National Research Act set up standards for research on humans that must be followed if the researchers want to receive federal funds for their programs. These standards require the following:

• You must give informed consent to take part in experimental treatment. This means the doctors must tell you about the procedure and about the risks, side effects, and benefits associated with it. They must also tell you about any alternative procedures available to you.

- You must volunteer to take part in the research. Your doctor cannot force you or pressure you into being part of an experiment.

Institutional Review Boards

The National Research Act required that Institutional Review Boards (IRBs) be established at every program conducting research funded by the U.S. Department of Health and Human Services or carried out on products regulated by the Food and Drug Administration (FDA). Because the federal government is a major source of research funds, IRBs have been set up at virtually all medical schools, universities, and hospitals where research on humans is conducted.

The IRBs review the research plans or experiments that are requested and either approve or deny the request. They review the plans to make certain that they provide subjects with adequate opportunity to provide informed consent and do not expose them to unreasonable risks. After the research is approved, they provide continuing oversight to ensure that protections remain in force.

 WHO CAN BE ON AN IRB?

An IRB must have at least five members (but may have dozens) of

- varying racial and cultural backgrounds;
- scientific, legal, and professional competence to understand the proposed research;
- both genders;
- at least one nonscientist;
- at least one member that is not affiliated with the institution doing the research.

How an IRB Makes Its Decision

The IRB must make seven findings in order to approve a research program:

1. The risk to subjects must be minimized as much as possible.
2. The risk to subjects must be reasonable compared to the benefits.
3. The selection of the subjects must be unbiased.
4. Potential subjects must be given adequate information to determine whether they wish to participate (informed consent will be explained further in a moment).
5. The informed consent must be documented.
6. The data must be adequately monitored.
7. Subjects' privacy must be protected, and their personal data must be kept confidential.

YOUR CONSENT TO BEING A RESEARCH SUBJECT

Your Consent Must Be "Informed"

Informed consent is a legal doctrine governed by the laws of each state. While each state may require something a little different, the basic concept for human research remains the same: you must be given sufficient opportunity to decide whether you want to be part of the research. When the research is explained to you, the researchers must use language that you understand. If they do not, your consent is not informed because you do not have all the information necessary to make your decision.

How You Give Informed Consent

Your informed consent to be a research subject will most likely be in written form and include eight parts:

1. An explanation of the research, including how long you would be expected to participate, a description of the procedures to be done, and which of the procedures are experimental.
2. A description of any risks or discomfort you might be expected to experience.
3. A description of any possible benefits to you or to others that may come out of the research.
4. An explanation of any other procedures or treatments that are available to you for your particular medical condition.
5. A description of how your privacy will be protected.
6. A description of any medical treatments that are available if you are injured if the research involves more than minimal risk to you. (In this case the researcher should tell you whether you would be entitled to financial assistance for your injury. The researcher is not required to pay you, only to tell you whether compensation will be available.)
7. The names of persons to contact for answers about the research or your rights as a research subject.
8. A statement that your participation is voluntary and that you can withdraw as a research subject at any time.

If You Decide to Withdraw from the Research

You have the right to leave the research program at any time. If you do so, your doctor or hospital cannot refuse to treat you simply because you left the program. You are still entitled to receive treatment from your doctor as would any other patient who did not take part in the research.

PROBLEMS SPUR CHANGES

Many persons battling illness wish to get into clinical trial programs in the hope of benefiting from drugs or procedures not generally available. This predisposes many of them to trust their hopes and not their fears and to give consent to some possibly dangerous experiments. In addition, a presidential advisory committee reported in 1996 that as many as a third of research studies had problems with informed consent, including consent forms that are overly optimistic about the benefits of research, that inadequately explain the impact of the treatment, and that are difficult for laypeople to understand.

Some celebrated experiments gone wrong have also raised widespread public concern. This chapter began with a paragraph about a teenager contemplating entering a research study. In real life, that story had an unhappy ending. Eighteen-year-old Jesse Gelsinger died four days after being injected with genes at a University of Pennsylvania Hospital. Gelsinger's father later testified before a Senate subcommittee, saying that they were not told that a monkey had died in a similar experiment and that another patient had serious side effects. The university later announced that its gene therapy institute would no longer perform research on humans and announced a systemwide review of its policies and procedures regarding research on humans.

The federal government has also become more active in monitoring research. Federal investigators greatly increased their number of site visits in the late 1990s. They suspended some programs because of lax safety oversight, including almost all government-funded research involving humans at Duke University Medical Center.

In addition, the Inspector General of the Department of Health and Human Services issued several reports analyzing the Institutional Review Board system and making recommendations for improvements.

What does all this mean to you if you're contemplating entering a research program? Problems haven't been found at most programs, and problems are probably taken a good deal more seriously at other programs. Still, you are your own best defense. Make sure you investigate any possible research study as carefully as you can. Ask questions until you are sure you fully understand the consent form and your concerns have been addressed.

OTHER ISSUES

What Can I Do If My Doctor Subjected Me to an Experimental Procedure Without My Consent?

In that situation you may be able to sue your doctor for medical malpractice. You might be required to demonstrate the extent of any injury you suffered during the procedure. Malpractice is discussed in the previous chapter.

Can I Get Insurance Coverage for Experimental Treatment?

Whether a health plan should cover experimental treatment is a common cause of disputes between patients and their insurance companies. Expensive new treatments and technologies can drive up medical costs, which in turn drive up insurance costs for you and everyone else. Insurance companies review these experimental treatments on a case-by-case basis. While laws give insurance companies great leeway in denying coverage for experimental treatment, courts tend to be sympathetic toward the patient, particularly if the patient's life is at stake. A court can force an insurance company to pay for the treatment if the court reviews the policy and determines that the policy does not clearly state that it won't pay for that treatment.

One of the factors the court will consider is whether the treatment is widely accepted within the medical and scientific community. If it is widely accepted, you stand a better chance of having your insurance company pay for the treatment. If it is not widely accepted, your chances are fifty-fifty. In contrast, the current majority of states do not require insurance companies to cover infertility treatments, in part because infertility is not a life-threatening illness. Rather, it is considered an elective procedure.

Can I Get Medicare Coverage for Experimental Treatment?

In the past, the answer was generally no. Medicare typically did not pay for treatment that was experimental, looking instead to whether the treatment is safe, effective, cost-effective, appropriate, and accepted by the medical and scientific community. However, in June 2000, President Bill Clinton directed the government to begin paying for "routine patient care" of Medicare recipients who volunteer for experimental medical treatments. The change was made to bring more older people into clinical trials, especially those dealing with conditions most common in the elderly.

RESEARCH ON CHILDREN, PRISONERS, AND THE ELDERLY

A Rock and a Hard Place

There is a catch-22 when it comes to finding new medical treatments for children and the elderly. Research must be done to better understand diseases that affect those groups in particular, such as cystic fibrosis and Alzheimer's disease. That means research must be done on children and the elderly, which are two of the most vulnerable groups in society. Neither a child nor an elderly person suffering from a mental illness such as Alzheimer's has the legal capacity to consent to being part of a research study. So how can researchers study people who cannot consent to being studied?

Researchers must get consent from the parents or guardians of the people they wish to study in order to proceed with the research. The goal is to allow researchers to study children and the elderly while at the same time protecting them from abuse and mistreatment.

Prisoners

Using prisoners for medical testing is highly controversial and generally not allowed. One school of thought holds that an inmate may not be a true "volunteer." Consider this: The prisoner is told when to wake up, when to eat, when to work, when to go to bed. Because he is confined in a prison, he can easily be forced into "volunteering" in exchange for privileges not given to other inmates. There is an inherent inequality between his position as inmate and that of the people running the prison. The inmate cannot be expected to make a decision about being a test subject without feeling some pressure. Thus, his consent is not voluntary, and he cannot be a research subject.

The counterargument is that experimentation is permissible if prisoners volunteer and provide informed consent. Prisoners retain some rights of self-determination and autonomy. Moreover, participating in such experiments might be a legitimate way for them to help society. Those making this argument caution, however, that prisoners should never receive a reduction in sentence for participating.

Fetal Research

One of the biggest controversies in human research is the use of fetuses (either still in the uterus or aborted) and embryos. Research is allowed on fetuses within the uterus as long as the risk is minimized and the mother gives her consent. This is only done in situations where the fetus needs the medical treatment or procedure to continue developing until birth.

Federal regulations severely limit the research that may be done on aborted fetuses. For those who oppose abortion, the regulations do not limit the research enough. Others believe that the regulations should allow more testing on aborted fetuses so that other fetuses can benefit from the research, which would possibly lead to fewer miscarriages, stillbirths, and severe birth defects. In general, research on aborted fetuses is allowed only when needed to develop important biomedical knowledge that cannot be obtained in any other possible way. In addition, the mother must consent to the research.

Embryo Research

Most research on embryos is aimed at increasing the rate of pregnancy in women seeking in vitro fertilization or other means of assisted reproduction. Other research focuses on gene therapy or on understanding how embryos develop. Couples who undergo fertility treatment and do not want to have the embryos transferred sometimes donate the embryos for research. This type of research brings religious and political controversy. Current federal law prohibits research on embryos, as well as the creation of embryos for the sole purpose of research. At present embryos are not legally considered "life," but embryos do get special respect in the law because of their potential for human life.

The issue of research using tissue from embryos and fetuses took on heightened importance in December 1998, when two groups of scientists announced that they had successfully isolated and cultured human pluripotent stem cells. According to an article by Susan Lee (*Journal of Law, Medicine & Ethics* 28, no. 1: 81-83),

> This news was greeted with both tremendous enthusiasm and concern. Because these cells can develop into most types of cells or tissues in the human body, they hold great promise for scientific research and medical advances. For example, stem cells can potentially be used to:
>
> - generate cells and tissues for transplantation and therapy for conditions such as Parkinson's disease, spinal cord injury, stroke, burns, heart disease, diabetes, and arthritis;
>
> - improve scientists' understanding of the complex events that occur during normal human development, as well as

the abnormal events that cause conditions such as birth defects and cancer. . . .

At the same time, the advent of laboratory-ready human pluripotent stem cells provokes pressing legal and ethical concerns. The derivation of stem cells from human embryos and fetal tissue raises legal issues in light of the federal ban on human embryo research and federal regulations on fetal tissue research. There is also considerable ethical disagreement on the appropriate level of respect for human embryos and fetal tissue as sources of stem cells. Finally, some fear that stem cell research sits at the brink of a slippery slope that may lead to human cloning practices (p. 81).

Lee goes on to note that the National Institutes for Health (NIH) has come up with guidelines to apply to publicly funded research involving pluripotent stem cells. Attempting to walk a fine line, the guidelines require scientific investigators to show that stem cells originating from human embryos must come from excess embryos created for the purposes of infertility treatment, not expressly for research. If stem cells originate from fetal tissue, the research must be in compliance with all laws and regulations governing human fetal tissue research and the fetal tissue transplantation research statute. Excess embryos and fetal tissue must be obtained with the donor's informed consent.

THE WORLD AT YOUR FINGERTIPS

- *Acres of Skin: Human Experiments at Holmesburg Prison: A True Story of Abuse and Exploitation in the Name of Medical Science* by Allen M. Hornblum (Routledge, 1999) chronicles medical experiments on Philadelphia prisoners. The experiments, which ended in 1974, tested the effects of chemicals on the skin and of mind-altering drugs such as LSD on the brain.
- *The Plutonium Files* (Dial Press, 1999) earned author Eileen Welsome a Pulitzer Prize. In the 1940s the government

subjected unsuspecting men, women, and children to radiation and then secretly studied them to learn the long-term
effects of radiation poisoning.

- *Children of the Flames: Dr. Josef Mengele and the Untold
Story of the Twins of Auschwitz* (Penguin, 1992) is a chilling
account of Auschwitz's "Angel of Death," who experimented
on thousands of twins, as told by the few survivors of
Mengele's experiments.
- For more on Institutional Review Boards and recent
attempts to reform them, go to *www.hhs.gov* and search for
the term.

YOU MUST REMEMBER THIS

- Subjects of human research must be volunteers.
- You must be informed of the type of research being done and
agree to be a part of it.
- The researchers must explain the risks to you.
- Be sure to ask the researchers how your privacy will be pro-
tected.
- You have the right to withdraw from the research at any
time.

PART SEVEN

Death and Dying

How We Die Is Changing—and the Law

Is Growing More Important in

End-of-Life Choices

I t is inevitable—all of us are going to die. Perhaps what frightens us is not the thought of death itself but the dying process. The preferred way to die is to simply go to sleep and not wake up. For most of us, though, the process will include a chronic illness or a sudden serious illness or injury. For many, it may include a period of living in a debilitated state. This section will help you prepare yourself, and your family, for that process.

Your right to refuse life-sustaining treatment is the subject of Chapter 26. This chapter explains the importance of advance directives, such as living wills and durable health care powers of attorney. We will spell out what information needs to be included in those advance directives and how they can benefit you and your family.

We will then explore hospice in Chapter 27. What is it and is it covered by Medicare? We will also fill you in on how an advance directive or "Do Not Resuscitate" (DNR) order affects your hospice care.

Chapter 28 discusses organ donation. Can your family or your doctor override your wishes and decide whether to donate your organs? Even if you sign a donor card, your family may need to consent to the donation before the hospital or doctor will proceed with your wishes. This chapter explains why you should not include organ donor information in your will and what to do if you change your mind about donating your organs.

Finally, in Chapter 29 we will discuss assisted suicide. This is a controversial topic in health care and ethics and in political and religious circles. We will take a look at the legislation that is enacted or proposed in several states to give patients the legal right to decide when, where, and how they want to die.

If you would like more information on these and other topics, please check at the end of the guide for additional resources and websites regarding these issues.

CHAPTER 26

Your Right to Refuse Life-Sustaining Treatment

You Clearly Have the Right—
Know How to Use It

Elizabeth is a healthy 35-year-old mother of two. She and her husband agree that quality of life is very important. One day Elizabeth is in a car accident. When her husband arrives at the hospital, he is told that Elizabeth suffered severe brain injuries and is being kept alive by artificial life support. After several weeks of treatment, it is clear that there is no hope for recovery. Elizabeth would be in a vegetative state for the rest of her life. Her distraught husband wants the doctors to remove all artificial life support and "let nature take its course." Should the doctors remove the machines and let Elizabeth die? What if the doctors refuse?

Charlotte, 76 years old, is relatively healthy. She entered the hospital for hip replacement surgery. Charlotte did not react well to the surgery, and her health began to fail. Worse, she became confused and lost. Now she lacks the capacity to make decisions for herself, and her husband must decide whether to allow the doctors to operate again or to give Charlotte medication with serious side effects. The surgery and the medication would prolong her life, but neither would help her to actually recover. Charlotte's husband does not want the doctors to operate or to give her medication because Charlotte always told him that she did not want extraordinary measures taken to prolong her life. Can Charlotte's husband stop the doctors from prolonging her life when he knows that she will never recover her health?

YOUR RIGHT TO REFUSE TREATMENT

You clearly have a legal right to refuse treatment, even if that treatment would prolong your life. In fact, with a few narrow exceptions, you can refuse any treatment, at any time, as long as you are competent. Contrast that with assisted suicide, to which you have no right, at any time, in all states but Oregon.

Since 1914, courts have recognized the right of adults of sound mind to make decisions affecting the integrity of their bodies. This right includes the right to refuse medical treatment that may save or prolong life.

In 1957 Pope Pius XII announced that a Catholic person was not required to agree to extraordinary medical treatment, even if death would result from refusing it. The Pope also stated that it was acceptable to administer pain-relieving drugs to a patient in unbearable pain even if the drugs would shorten the patient's life. According to the Pope, neither the doctor nor the patient would be committing a sin or a crime as long as the primary purpose of the drugs or the decision was to relieve pain and suffering.

Put It in Writing—the Written Advance Directive

The dilemma comes when you are unable to tell your doctor whether you wish to continue with life-sustaining treatment such as artificial life support. In that case your parent, spouse, child, or sibling may need to implement or to make that decision for you. This is a difficult burden for any of your loved ones, but you can make it easier for them by putting your wishes in writing. These documents are often known as **advance directives**, which include **living wills** and **durable health care powers of attorney**. Oral statements of your wishes can also serve as an advance directive, but you should make sure that you've discussed your wishes with your personal physician and that your oral statements are documented in your medical record.

While advance directives are unpleasant to think about, they are necessary. In one case a husband and wife agreed that if one of them ended up in a vegetative state, the other one would refuse to let artificial life support prolong life. They did not put their wishes in writing. When the husband suffered an accident and ended up on life support, his wife sought to have the machines removed. The husband's sister did not want to stop life support. Because the husband's wishes were not in writing, his sister was able to stop the wife from having the life support removed. The husband remained in a vegetative state for years, while his wife was drained emotionally and financially. While this is an unusual result—laws in most states would permit the wife to speak for the husband (act as a **surrogate decision maker**)—it would not have happened had there been a written directive.

 A LANDMARK CASE

In 1975, 21-year-old Karen Quinlan collapsed and ceased breathing for at least two fifteen-minute periods. This left her in a chronic persistent vegetative state with no hope of recovery. Her parents wanted doctors to remove artificial life support. The doctors refused. The New Jersey Supreme Court held that a terminally ill patient or the patient's surrogate decision maker has a constitutionally protected right to make doctors withdraw life-sustaining medical treatment. This right is grounded in the right to privacy. The case is *In re Quinlan*, 355 A.2d 647 (NJ 1976).

If you spell out in writing what you want to happen in case you end up on artificial life support with no hope of recovery, your doctor will be much more confident that it is your wish that is being carried out. While most states give great deference to the decision that would be made by your family, the only sure way for your family to know what you would have wanted is to put it on paper.

TALKING TO A LAWYER
Suicide?

Q. Is it suicide to refuse life-sustaining treatment?

A. No. All of the court opinions that look at this issue have clearly distinguished suicide from the refusal of treatment, including life-sustaining treatment. Suicide is a self-inflicted death. When treatment is withdrawn or withheld, if death then results, it is primarily the result of the underlying disease.

Answer by Lois Snyder, Director,
Center for Ethics and Professionalism, American College of Physicians-
American Society of Internal Medicine, Philadelphia, Pennsylvania

TALKING TO A LAWYER
Refusal of Life-Sustaining Treatment
(Part 1)

Q. My mother is terminally ill, and she wants to die. Still, there are new treatments that could extend her life. Following her wishes, her doctor refuses to go ahead with the treatment, even though my mother will surely die without it. Can I take legal action to make the two of them agree to the treatment?

A. A competent adult has the right to refuse medical treatment, including life-sustaining treatment. This is now well established in law and medical ethics. If there is good reason to challenge your mother's ability to make decisions, you could try to have a court declare her incompetent. But refusal of life-sustaining treatment is not an indication of incompetence.

Answer by Lois Snyder, Director,
Center for Ethics and Professionalism, American College of Physicians-
American Society of Internal Medicine, Philadelphia, Pennsylvania

TALKING TO A LAWYER
Refusal of Life-Sustaining Treatment
(Part 2)

Q. I want to pursue this further. What is the process of becoming my mother's guardian? If I succeed, can I order the new treatment for her?

A. If your mother lacks capacity to make health care decisions for herself, you may petition the court to be her guardian to make these decisions. The court will appoint a lawyer to represent your mother at a hearing concerning her capacity. Should your mother be found unable to make such decisions, the court will consider a variety of factors concerning your appointment. Among the factors that the court will consider is her terminal prognosis even with treatment, her wishes, and the invasiveness and consequences of the treatment. Additionally the probability of success and the potential side effects of the new therapy will be considered by the court.

Should you lose the hearing, as a practical matter you will not have any further recourse. If you win and are appointed guardian, you could not compel your mother's physician to provide the new therapy. However you could obtain the services of another physician who was willing to provide the treatment to a terminally ill unwilling patient.

Answer by Salvatore J. Russo, Executive Senior Counsel,
New York City Health & Hospitals Corporation,
New York, New York

Safekeeping Your Advance Directive

It is understandable to safeguard your private papers, but you should remember that your family will need these papers in order to carry out your wishes. It is not uncommon for family members to know that the person in the hospital has an advance directive and then not be able to find the document. Tell your family where to find your advance directive and give them a copy of the document.

You should also give a copy to your personal physician and your lawyer and have a copy with you while traveling.

Proving That These Are Your Wishes

States also vary in the type of proof needed to remove life-sustaining treatment. If you executed a health care advance directive appointing an agent to make decisions for you when you are no longer able to do so and you granted your agent authority to remove life-sustaining equipment, that should suffice. In other circumstances, the person making the decision for you may have to prove that you clearly wanted the treatment to be discontinued under the circumstances. Remember, although you have a constitutional right to forgo medical treatment, you (or your loved one) will have to prove that you wanted to assert that right. This is easier to prove if you put your wishes in writing; but, as noted above, oral instructions can be effective, especially if there is some written record to verify them, as in a physician's notes.

If you don't put anything in writing, your wishes might not be followed unless all of the members of your immediate family agree to removal of treatment. In most cases doctors will abide by the wishes of your family as long as your family can reach an agreement on whether the treatment should be stopped. If even one person disagrees, doctors will usually err on the side of caution and continue treatment, unless your family can prove that you would want the treatment to stop. A number of states, though, have laws to cover this type of situation. In those states, such as Illinois, there is a legal hierarchy of relatives who can make health care decisions for you if you do not have an advance directive. Some of these states even recognize a close friend as a potential surrogate in the absence of family.

Until you have something in writing (and even after), be sure to talk to your doctor and family members about what you would want them to do if you were placed on life-sustaining treatment. This may or may not be enough to convince a court of your wishes, but it will help in guiding your doctor and family in making decisions regarding your care and may help avoid a trip to court altogether.

TALKING TO A LAWYER

No Next of Kin

Q. I have a patient who is incapacitated and unable to make decisions for himself. He has no family or close friends. Whom do I turn to when decisions about his medical care need to be made?

A. In states that have them, you can contact the state guardianship office to set in motion the process of obtaining a guardian for your patient. If your patient is hospitalized, a hospital social worker can do this. In a few states, including Alabama and Arizona, ethics committees, in cooperation with the physician, are authorized to act as decision makers about certain kinds of treatment when there is no family member or friend to do so.

Answer by Bethany Spielman,
Department of Medical Humanities,
Southern Illinois University School of Medicine,
Springfield, Illinois

Why Doctors Need Proof

There is a good reason for you to have to prove that you do not want life-sustaining treatment. First and foremost, doctors want to make sure that it is their patients' wishes that are being carried out, and also doctors want to protect themselves from liability. Proof of your wishes is needed to assure the doctors that they are in fact carrying out your desires and not those of others who may not have your best interests at heart.

WHY YOU NEED AN ADVANCE
HEALTH CARE DIRECTIVE

Many states allow for **living wills, durable powers of attorney for health care,** or some other type of formal recognition of the right of someone else to make medical decisions for you if you are unable to make those decisions for yourself. These forms vary from state to state, but the common goal is to help your family make the decision you would make if you were able to have a say in whether to continue treatment. These directives let you decide in advance about life support and/or pick someone to make decisions for you about medical treatment.

HEALTH CARE ADVANCE
DIRECTIVE—SAMPLE

Appendix C contains a model advance directive prepared by AARP, the ABA, and the AMA. It combines a living will and a durable power of attorney for health care. This is a general form that meets the requirements of most states. Even if it does not meet the requirements of your state, it may provide an effective statement of your wishes if you cannot speak for yourself.

The sample health care advance directive included in this book permits you to avoid any possible confusion caused by having both a living will and a durable health care power of attorney. It simply encompasses both in a single document. If you do have both in separate documents, you might be heading for difficulty in some states because the two documents might conflict given the facts of a particular case. For example, the living will is often vague or unclear and could potentially thwart the legitimate powers of your health care agent, who is trying to carry out your wishes as reflected in the health care power of attorney. Check with an attorney or other information source to find out what the law requires in your state. You can also get more specific information about your state's laws by contacting Partnership for Caring, 1035 9th St. NW, Washington, DC 20007 (800-989-9455).

LIVING WILLS

As noted in the preceding section, we recommend wherever possible that you execute a comprehensive health care advance directive, as we consider it to be superior in flexibility and usefulness to a living will. Nonetheless, because so many Americans are familiar with the concept of a living will and may have one, we discuss them in this section.

A **living will** is not actually a will because it does not dispose of property and because it takes effect while you are still alive. It is your written statement about your feelings regarding the use of life-sustaining medical care if you become terminally ill and unable to communicate, if you are in a persistently vegetative state, or if you become irreversibly comatose.

LEARNING THE LINGO

Living will: A document that tells doctors and family members whether you want to be placed on life support in the event that you are unable to tell them yourself because of illness or injury. It is not an actual will and does not require a lawyer's help to execute, but it is often drafted at the same time as a real will. Many lawyers include living wills or other advance directives as part of their estate planning services for clients.

If the living will is properly prepared and clearly states your wishes, the hospital or the doctor will be immune from criminal prosecution or malpractice for withholding treatment. Do not be afraid that writing a living will means your doctor will abandon you too soon. You can specify in your living will that you want your doctor to try all possible treatment until there is no hope of recovery. Whatever your wishes, put them in writing so that your doctor and loved ones are able to carry them out.

These days you can walk into any office supply store and buy a general living will form. Laws vary by state, though, so these forms may not be tailored according to the laws in your state. Your lawyer can help you draft one that meets your state's requirements.

If you decide to write a living will yourself, be specific. One of the biggest problems with living wills is that many are either too vague (i.e., "extraordinary treatment") or so specific as to be inflexible. Writing a living will is much like a riddle. There are simply so many gray areas and changing circumstances when it comes to the end of life that it is impossible to predict every possible situation that may arise. That is one reason why more people are turning to health care advance directives that incorporate a durable health care power of attorney. That power gives your agent more room to deal with other kinds of disabilities, injuries, or illnesses that you might suffer.

DURABLE POWER OF ATTORNEY FOR HEALTH CARE

A **durable power of attorney for health care** is a written document whereby you appoint another person to act for you as your agent if you become disabled and can no longer make medical decisions for yourself. This power of attorney applies only to health care decisions.

As noted earlier, such a power is incorporated in our sample health care advance directive. This discussion will help you understand how it works as part of that document or standing alone.

How It Differs from a Living Will

Durable power of attorney differs from a living will in that it *designates a person* to make decisions for you regarding life-sustaining treatment. This power of attorney applies only to decisions regarding health care. *Durable* means that it remains in effect after you become incapacitated. It ends when you die or when you cancel it (which you can do at any time while competent).

DURABLE POWERS OF ATTORNEY FOR HEALTH CARE

In all states you will definitely want to have a durable power of attorney for health care, preferably as part of an overall health care advance directive, as long as there is someone you trust to make decisions for you.

- A health care power of attorney appoints someone (an agent) to act for you. A living will does not always include an agent.

- A health care power of attorney applies to all medical decisions unless you specify otherwise. Many living wills apply only to decisions near the end of your life and are limited to when you have a "terminal illness" or are in "persistent vegetative state," which are open to interpretation.

- Your health care power of attorney can include specific instructions to your agent about your values or what you want that person to do in particular circumstances. It can encompass organ donation, for example.

The Advantages over a Living Will

A durable power of attorney for health care offers three advantages over a living will.

1. Living will laws are constantly changing, while the concept of power of attorney is fairly stable. Your living will can quickly become outdated, while a power of attorney will not.

2. A living will cannot anticipate every possible event or treatment that could occur. Should all treatment be stopped or just artificial respiration? What about nutrition or hydration that keeps your body alive although you are comatose? Power of attorney lets a trusted friend or relative make the call.

3. Some hospitals and doctors are still reluctant to withdraw or to withhold treatment based on your living will alone. Only a durable power of attorney will let your agent require the doctor or the hospital to abide by your wishes.

How a Durable Power of Attorney for Health Care Is Created

The laws on creating a durable power of attorney for health care vary by state, but usually it has to (1) be signed, (2) witnessed or notarized, (3) specify that it is durable, and (4) name the person you want to be your agent. This person can be your spouse or child or anyone else you choose. A durable power of attorney for health care can limit your agent to decisions about life-sustaining treatment, or it can give your agent the authority to make decisions about things such as nursing homes or surgeries.

A durable power of attorney for health care is much more flexible than a living will. Keep in mind that this is a tool for your agent. Be sure to discuss your values and wishes with the person you appoint as your agent. He or she will need this information to carry out your desires if you should become incapacitated. Another point to consider is that being an agent is entirely voluntary. In other words, the person you choose to be your agent must agree to act in that role for you. It's a good idea to name an alternative agent in case your agent will not or cannot serve. If there is no one you trust to act for you, perhaps you should content yourself with a living will.

SELF-TEST

Questions to ask yourself before making advance directives:

What are my values?

- How important is independence and self-sufficiency in my life?
- What role should doctors and other health professionals play in medical decisions that affect me?
- What kind of living environment is important to me?
- What role do religious beliefs play in these decisions?
- How should my family and friends be involved (if at all) in these decisions?

Who should be my agent?

- Which person would I like to have make decisions about health care for me if I become incapacitated?
- Whom can I trust to know what I would want if unexpected circumstances arise?
- Who will be able to handle the stress of making such decisions?

Keep in mind that in some states health care providers who are treating you are not allowed to act as your agent.

What guidelines should I impose?

You need to leave your agent some flexibility if the unexpected happens. If you have specific wishes, however, you should write them down to help guide your agent in making decisions on your behalf.

THE WORLD AT YOUR FINGERTIPS

- *Planning for Uncertainty: A Guide to Living Wills and Other Advance Directives for Health Care* by David Doukas and William Reichel (John Hopkins University Press, 1993) explains why you should decide now about what you want to happen at the end of your life. It explains the types and the purposes of advance directives and uses a question-and-answer format to help you determine your values and preferences.

- *www.partershipforcaring.org/* is the website for Partnership for Caring, a nonprofit organization that provides advance directives, counsels patients and families, and offers a range of educational publications and services.
- "Shape Your Health Care Future with Health Care Advance Directives," a booklet and form published by the ABA, the AMA, and AARP, is available in abbreviated form in Appendix C of this book and in full on the Web at *www.abanet.org/elderly.*
- For more information on advance directives and on what you should include in yours, check out *http://www.ama-assn.org/public/booklets/livgwill.htm.* You can read it online or print out the free booklet. This site includes a section on some of the topics that should be covered in an advance directive.
- "Five Wishes," an advance directive published by Aging with Dignity, is available online at *www.agingwithdignity.org* or by writing to them at P.O. Box 11180, Tallahassee, Florida 32302.

YOU MUST REMEMBER THIS

- Always put your wishes regarding life-sustaining treatment in writing, or consult with your doctor and have him or her document your wishes in your medical record.
- A living will is your written statement about your feelings regarding the use of life-sustaining health care if you become unable to communicate.
- Durable power of attorney for health care differs from a living will in that it designates a person to make decisions for you regarding life-sustaining treatment.

- A durable power of attorney for health care is much more flexible than a living will but gives more authority to someone else (your agent) to make decisions on your behalf.
- Let your agent know your wishes and values regarding the end of your life.
- A health care advance directive enables you to encompass a living will and durable power of attorney for health care in one document.

CHAPTER 27

Hospice

How the Law Affects Care for the Terminally Ill

Florence is in the advanced stages of cancer. Her doctor estimates she will live about six more months, if she is lucky. Florence feels anything but lucky. She does not want to die in a sterile hospital room, surrounded by strangers. She wants to die at home, but she worries that her husband will not be able to take care of her and that it would be too much of a burden for him. He is already distraught at the thought of losing his wife. Who will be there for him when he needs relief? Florence's children say they will help, but she knows that they are busy with their jobs and families. Florence's doctor tells her that she should consider a hospice program. Florence needs to know what a hospice is and whether Medicare covers it.

WHAT IS HOSPICE CARE?

Hospice care is **palliative care.** That means that the care is aimed at pain relief and control of the disease's symptoms, rather than at curing the illness. Hospices are a lot like midwives. Just as midwives lend support and wisdom during childbirth, hospices provide support and specialized knowledge during the dying process.

LEARNING THE LINGO

Palliative care: Care that is aimed at pain relief and control of the disease's symptoms, rather than at curing the illness.

Hospices come in many forms. A hospice may be a facility where patients go to live out their final days. It may be a network of health care providers that allows you to remain in your home through the use of home health care aides and other caregivers. It may be part of a hospital or a separate nonprofit organization.

Part of the appeal of hospice care is the autonomy. Hospice care may allow you to stay in your own home much longer than you could if you had no home health care, in which case you might be hospitalized, perhaps for weeks or even months. Hospice care will not help you die. Hospice care is intended to help you live as full a life as possible until you die.

Some form of hospice care has been around for centuries. The modern day philosophy of hospice took root in England. Cicely Saunders was a nurse and a medical social worker in 1948 when she met a man who was dying from complications of rectal cancer. David Tasma, an agnostic, asked Saunders to explain spirituality to him. He asked her to tell him what was in her mind and heart.

During the next three months, Saunders told Tasma about her desire to care for the terminally ill in a special place. When Tasma died, his will left Saunders five hundred pounds sterling and a note that said: "I'll be a window in your new home." Saunders went on to become a doctor. In 1967, Dr. Saunders opened the first freestanding hospice of the modern day, St. Christopher's. The hospice has a window dedicated to Tasma. Saunders is credited with creating the concept of "total pain," encompassing physical, psychological, social, and spiritual distress. Queen Elizabeth later named her a Dame of the British Empire.

The first hospice to open in the United States was the Connecticut Hospice in 1973. Its medical director, Dr. Sylvia Lack, had trained under Dr. Saunders at St. Christopher's. Today there are almost two thousand hospices in the United States. The majority of these are home-care programs that send home health care aides to patients' homes.

By law it is your decision—and yours alone, as long as you are competent to make your own decisions—whether to seek hospice care once you are considered terminally ill. It is always a good idea, though, to discuss your options with your doctor and family members.

WILL MEDICARE PAY FOR HOSPICE CARE?

Medicare Part A

Medicare Part A pays for medically necessary hospice care if Medicare certifies your hospice. *You must be enrolled in Part A of Medicare to qualify for the hospice benefit.* Medicare requires that hospice patients be **terminally ill.** Some states have laws that only Medicare certified hospices may be licensed. That allows your state to make sure that the hospice is following appropriate guidelines for your care. The goal is to prevent unethical people from setting up hospices and then giving patients substandard care.

LEARNING THE LINGO

Terminally ill: Under the Medicare hospice benefit, a patient is terminally ill if the patient's attending doctor or a hospice medical director certifies that the patient has less than six months to live if the illness follows its expected course.

As a terminally ill patient, your medical supplies and medications will be provided to ease your pain and suffering in your final days rather than to bring about a recovery from the illness. The hospice may not discontinue or diminish your care if you become unable to pay for that care.

Your Hospice Team

Medicare requires that the hospice provide care by an interdisciplinary team. This team must include at least one doctor, one registered nurse, a social worker, and a spiritual counselor. The team will create a care plan for you. This plan is based on your medical condition and the services you will require. The team will include a review process for certain intervals in your

TALKING TO A LAWYER
Miraculous Recovery

Q. *My father received hospice care, paid for by Medicare. Against all odds he is doing better now and no longer requires hospice while in remission. When the disease attacks again, will he be eligible for hospice benefits under Medicare?*

A. Medicare approves hospice coverage for specific time periods—two periods of 90 days, followed by successive periods of 60 days. If you are no longer considered "terminal" after a period, hospice coverage will be denied. But if the condition again becomes diagnosed as terminal, coverage can be resumed. Predicting when someone is likely to die is a very uncertain task, so more often than not, physicians wait longer than they should before certifying someone as terminal. To get early and full coverage of a hospice often takes some pushing by the patient and family.

Answer by Charles Sabatino,
ABA Commission on Legal Problems of
The Elderly, Washington, DC

plan. The team is required by law to review your plan and to document the review process.

Volunteers

Medicare also requires that volunteers provide at least 5 percent of your direct care. These volunteers can be your friends, members of your family, or anyone else you know who is willing to assist you. Your Medicare benefits allow for home health care workers and members of your team to provide the rest of your care. Medicare allows for hospitalization when required and for most other counseling that you may need. At times your team may consider it necessary for these services to be provided for you 24 hours a day.

Medical Supplies

Medicare will cover durable and consumable medical supplies for you when your hospice team considers it necessary to your care. *Durable medical equipment* includes such things as a hospital bed brought into your home, which makes it easier for your caregiver and you. *Consumable medical supplies* include items such as oxygen and diapers for adults. Your hospice provider can help you make arrangements to get any equipment you need. The hospice is there to help you in any way it can to make staying in your own home as convenient and safe as possible.

Medication

The Medicare hospice benefit will pay for most medications for pain relief and those medications needed to relieve the symptoms of your disease. To be in hospice care, the illness will have progressed to the point at which there is no hope for recovery. Thus, the Medicare hospice benefit will not cover medications to "treat" your disease.

Respite Care

Medicare requires hospices to make arrangements for hospitalization or **respite care** when needed. Respite care is short-term in-patient care (less than five consecutive days) that gives family caregivers some relief. If your hospice does not have the facilities necessary to provide this type of care, it may contract with another hospice or a hospital to provide in-patient or respite care.

Length of Benefits

When you choose the Medicare hospice benefit, you are covered for 90 days. After 90 days, you can choose to continue in hospice care for another 90 days if you are still considered terminally ill. After the second 90-day period, you can choose to stay in hospice care for an unlimited number of 60-day benefit periods, as long as your condition remains terminal.

You may revoke your hospice care at any time during a benefit period. When you revoke hospice care, your regular Medicare benefits will resume immediately. You are still allowed to go back to hospice care at a later date.

Revoking Your Hospice Care

To revoke your hospice care, you write a statement to the hospice that says you are revoking your election for Medicare coverage of hospice care for the remainder of that election period. Include the date that the revocation is to be effective. Sign the statement and give it to your hospice provider.

Grief Counseling for Your Family

Hospices provide care to people other than patients. Medicare covers training and counseling for your family as well as for you (the patient). Hospices will also offer bereavement counseling for your survivors after your death.

LEARNING THE LINGO

Bereavement counseling: Grief counseling services provided by the hospice to the patient's family after the patient's death.

Reimbursement

Medicare hospice benefits provide coverage for the aforementioned items, but Medicare does not typically reimburse hospices for the full cost of the services they provide. Hospices make up the difference between the cost of services and the reimbursement rate by relying on fundraising, memorial gifts from the patient's family, or, if the hospice is part of a larger health care facility, with profits from other areas of the facility.

HOSPICES, ADVANCE DIRECTIVES, AND ASSISTED SUICIDE

If a hospice receives payment from Medicare, it is required to tell you about your right to execute an advance directive (such as a living will or a durable power of attorney for health care). An advance directive tells the hospice about your wishes regarding life-sustaining treatment if you become incompetent or unable to communicate. The hospice cannot tell you what to put in the directive.

A hospice cannot refuse to treat you based on your decision to execute an advance directive. Some hospices do require that patients agree to have their doctors issue *do-not-resuscitate* (DNR) orders. A DNR order states that you will not receive cardio-pulmonary resuscitation (CPR) or other aggressive treatment if your heart stops beating. Commentators are doubtful that hospices can legally require a DNR order, but this has not been tested in the courts. The basic concept of hospice care is to let the patient's death come naturally. A DNR order is consistent with the concept of letting nature take its course.

If you choose hospice care, it is still a good idea to get a DNR order. Your family members or caregivers may be unsure about how to handle a medical emergency. If you go into cardiac arrest, their first instinct will be to call 911. If you keep a DNR order in a place where it may be easily found during an emergency, the emergency medical staff will know they are faced with a terminal patient who has executed a DNR order. (But be aware that they may not be required to follow the order. The requirement that the emergency staff follow a nonhospital DNR order varies from state to state.)

Letting death come naturally does not mean that you will not be given medications to ease your pain. You will still be prescribed appropriate medication for pain management. The dosage required to ease your suffering may be high, and it may shorten your life. However, hospice organizations do not endorse the taking of medications in doses that cause the patient's death. In other words, pain management is not the same as committing suicide by taking large doses of painkillers.

AFTER DEATH OCCURS

Many hospice patients will die at home. If your loved one is in hospice care, there is no need to call 911 after death occurs. Call the hospice. A nurse or a doctor will come to the home to pronounce the patient dead and to sign a death certificate. In some cases a hospice worker will call the funeral home and arrange for the body to be removed from the home. If you are in hospice care, it may be helpful to your family to be given the telephone number of the funeral home and the name of the funeral director before you die.

FOR MORE INFORMATION
ABOUT HOSPICES

Your doctor can most likely offer you information on hospice care in your area. You can also contact the National Hospice Helpline at 1-800-658-8898. Organizations such as the American Cancer Society, the American Association of Retired Persons, and the Social Security Administration also offer information on hospices.

THE WORLD AT YOUR FINGERTIPS

- *All Kinds of Love: Experiencing Hospice (Death, Value, and Meaning Series)* by Carolyn Jaffe and Carol H. Ehrlich (Baywood Publishing Company, 1997) provides insight into hospice care through the eyes of a hospice nurse.
- *At Home with Terminal Illness: A Family Guide to Hospice in the Home* by Michael Appleton (Prentice Hall, 1994) is an easy-to-follow guide to caring for your loved one at home. It leaves out the medical jargon and concentrates on how the patient's caregivers can take care of their loved one while not becoming emotionally devastated in the process.

- *Caregiving: The Spiritual Journey of Love, Loss, and Renewal* by Beth Witrogen McLeod (John Wiley & Sons, 1999) is one woman's account of her parents' death and how what she learned may help others deal with facing the loss of someone special.
- For more on the laws and other issues regarding hospice care, go to the Hospice Patients Alliance at *http://www. hospicepatients.org/*.
- The National Association for Home Care provides information on searching for hospice care, as well as on laws and regulations governing hospice, at *http://www.nahc.org/home. html*.

YOU MUST REMEMBER THIS

- Hospice care is aimed at making the rest of your days as comfortable as possible.
- Medicare Part A provides benefits for hospice care.
- Medicare requires that a patient be terminally ill (have six months or less to live) in order to qualify for hospice benefits.
- It is a good idea for the hospice patient to choose a funeral home and to provide family members with its telephone number.
- If your loved one dies while in hospice care, call the hospice first. Then call the funeral home.

CHAPTER 28

Donating Your Organs

Your Opportunity to Make the Gift of Life

Steve and Judy are married with one child. Although they are in their early twenties, they have already executed a will and advance directives for health care. Neither their wills nor the advance directives mention whether Steven and Judy want their organs, corneas, or tissue donated to a patient in need or to research. Instead, Steven and Judy checked the box on their driver's licenses indicating that they are organ donors. Steve and Judy wonder if this is enough. Will doctors abide by the checkmark in this box if either Steve or Judy dies in an accident? Can they specify that they only want to be organ donors for other patients, rather than for research? What if Steve and Judy are injured and become "brain dead" but could be kept alive for years on artificial life support? Steve and Judy are thinking about including in their wills the fact that they want to be organ donors, but they do not want the hassle of changing their wills if they should change their minds later on.

Organ donation is known in legal circles as an **anatomical gift,** which includes organs, tissue, and even bones. For the purpose of this chapter, though, we will use *organ* as a general term to include any part of the anatomy that can be donated.

WHO CAN BE AN ORGAN DONOR?

Age and Physical Condition

Almost anyone can be an organ donor, depending on a person's medical condition and the circumstances surrounding death.

Donors need to be at least 18 years old (with a few exceptions), but there is no maximum age. Some donors are over age 70.

All, Part, or None

You can donate your entire body for anatomical study, or you can specify organs and tissues. The most needed organs are kidneys, hearts, livers, lungs, and pancreases. Tissue donations include eyes, skin, heart valves, bone, and bone marrow. You can donate bone marrow and a kidney while you are still living.

Can I Sell an Organ?

No. The National Organ Transplant Act, a federal law, makes it illegal to buy or sell organs for profit. You can be sentenced to five years in prison or a $50,000 fine, or both. It is also illegal under the law of most states to sell organs for profit. If you donate your organs, though, you can be reimbursed for some of the costs involved. For example, if you donate one of your kidneys, it is most likely legal for you to accept payment for your lost wages and medical expenses. The amount of these payments must be reasonable. Anything outlandish would be considered profit, which is not legal.

May a Living Child or an Incompetent Person Be an Organ Donor?

Sometimes, but only if there is some benefit to the child or incompetent person. Legally a child or an incompetent person is not able to consent to being an organ donor. The fear is that people needing organs will prey on vulnerable people. There are rare situations when the guardians of children or incompetent persons will be allowed to let them be organ donors.

In one example, a young man, Tommy, was suffering from a fatal kidney disease. His parents and many relatives had themselves tested to see if any of them could provide Tommy with one of their kidneys. None of them were medically acceptable. As a last resort, Tommy's parents had his brother, Jerry, who was mentally disabled and institutionalized, tested. Jerry was a match. The parents asked a court to allow them to have one of Jerry's kidneys removed and transplanted into Tommy.

The court had a difficult decision to make. In the end, it found that Tommy and Jerry were very close and that Jerry relied on Tommy emotionally and psychologically. To lose his brother would devastate him. The parents had made every possible effort to find another donor, but to no avail. Tommy's time was running out. Jerry's parents were getting older. If Jerry lost Tommy, he would also lose his financial support. The court allowed the parents to have one of Jerry's kidneys removed and transplanted into Tommy because giving Tommy the chance to live provided a benefit to Jerry.

In another instance, the parents of seven-year-old twins were allowed to have a kidney transplanted from one twin into the other. Courts will not always allow this, though. The child or the incompetent person must be the only available option for a court to even consider it. In Wisconsin, a family wanted a kidney taken from their son, an institutionalized schizophrenic, and transplanted into their daughter, a mother of six. Other family members were acceptable matches, but none of them wanted to donate a kidney. The court did not allow the family to take a kidney from their son.

SHOULD YOU BE AN ORGAN DONOR?

Consider Your Values

Your decision on whether to become an organ donor will be based not on legal concepts, but on your culture, religion, and values. The law does affect how your family or doctors carry out your decision. Nearly all of the world's major religions consider organ donation a gift of life to others. You may wish to ask your pastor whether your religion endorses organ donation.

Consider Your Community

Survey after survey shows that the vast majority of us are in favor of organ donation. Yet very few of us donate our organs. It is a very personal decision, but you should consider this: at this time there are more than 60,000 people on the waiting list for organs with the United Network for Organ Sharing (UNOS), which is the national organ waiting registry. About one-third of the people who need lifesaving organs such as hearts or livers will die before an available organ is found.

 ## THE LAW MAKES IT POSSIBLE

Every state has some form of a law called the Uniform Anatomical Gift Act (UAGA). This law allows you, if you are at least 18 years old and of sound mind, to:

- donate all or part of your body at your death;
- designate that you are donating your organs for transplantation into someone else or for medical research;
- name a hospital, doctor, person, or educational institution as the donee.

Consider Your Family

Now consider the possibility that one day you—or your spouse or child—could be on that waiting list. One concern of donors is whether donating their organs will affect how their bodies will appear at open-casket funerals. Removal of organs is a surgical procedure and will rarely interfere with funeral or burial arrangements. The law requires that hospitals and doctors treat the body with the utmost care when removing organs and tissue. Any unnecessary damage or injury to the body is forbidden.

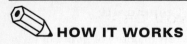

HOW IT WORKS

Once the organs are removed, the body is returned to the family so that funeral or burial arrangements may be made.

TALKING TO A LAWYER
Hospitals and Organ Donations

Q. Why did the hospital ask me if I was an organ donor when I was admitted for a minor procedure?

A. Almost every state requires hospitals to ask you, when admitted, whether you are an organ donor. If you say yes, the hospital is required to get a copy of your donor card, driver's license, or advance directive indicating that you wish to donate your organs. If you say no, the hospital is required to tell you about your options for deciding whether to become an organ donor.

　　If you are near death and the hospital has no record of your decision about being an organ donor, the hospital is required to ask your next of kin to donate your organs. The purposes of these laws is to find out and to document your wishes, as well as to increase the number of organs available for transplant. Your doctor will make every effort to save your life even if you are an organ donor. Medical and legal standards require that organ donation only becomes an issue after all efforts to save your life are exhausted and you are declared brain dead.

Answer by Cindy J. Moy,
attorney and author,
Golden Valley, Minnesota

WHEN ARE YOU DEAD?

Sounds like a silly question, doesn't it? Medical technology is advancing at breakneck speed, and *death* is being redefined. Death used to occur when your heart stopped beating. Then artificial life support was developed for people with severe brain injuries. Suddenly there was a new form of death—brain death. Doctors and hospitals were afraid to stop treatment on a brain dead person because that person's heart was still beating with the help of artificial life support.

LEARNING THE LINGO

Brain dead: A patient is considered brain dead when brain function has stopped, including that which controls breathing and heart activity. All circulatory and respiratory functions are maintained by artificial life support. In essence, brain dead is the same as "dead."

In 1980, death received a new definition. You are dead when either your circulatory and respiratory functions stop for good or when your entire brain, including the brain stem, irreversibly stops functioning. Most states legally define death in this way. If you are an organ donor, circulatory and respiratory functions will be kept going by artificial life support if you are brain dead to preserve your organs until they can be harvested for transplantation.

LEARNING THE LINGO

Death: Death occurs when a person either sustains irreversible cessation of circulatory and respiratory functions or suffers irreversible cessation of all functions of the entire brain, including the brain stem.

HOW TO BE SURE THAT YOUR ORGANS WILL, OR WILL NOT, BE DONATED

A Will Is Not Enough

It is not a good idea to include your wishes regarding organ donation in your will. Doctors will need to remove your organs or tissue under very specific and delicate timelines and procedures. By the time your will is read, the opportunity to donate your organs will have passed. Instead, include your wishes regarding donation of organs in your advance directives on health care, and tell your family what you want them to do in that situation.

 ## WITNESSES USUALLY NOT NECESSARY

At one time the law required that an organ donor card be signed in the presence of two witnesses. Today the law does not require you to have witnesses, unless you do not intend to put your wishes in writing. In that case, if you want to be an organ donor, make your wishes clear in front of at least two people.

If you do include organ donation in your will, be sure your family knows of your wishes so that they can bring the will to the hospital in the event of your death. Removal of organs is considered by law to be a gift that becomes effective at your death. The hospital does not have to wait for the will to clear probate in this instance.

Your Family Needs to Know

Your doctor will almost always require your family's consent in order to remove organs, regardless of your wishes or whether you filled out an organ donor card. Even if you include your donation in your will and advance directive, it is customary for doctors to ask your family to agree to the donation. In some states hospitals are required by law to abide by the deceased person's wishes regardless of the family's consent. In practice, though, in order to avoid malpractice lawsuits, hospitals and doctors are reluctant to go against the wishes of the family members.

WHAT HAPPENS IF YOU DO NOT MAKE A DECISION ABOUT ORGAN DONATION?

Your Family Makes the Decision

If you did not indicate whether you want your organs donated, then your family will make that decision for you when you die. Your family will decide whether to donate all or part of your body. Usually your doctor will seek a decision from your spouse first. If you do not have a spouse, the doctor will turn to your adult son or daughter. If you do not have children, the doctor will get a decision from your parent, your adult brother or sister, a grandparent, or your guardian.

TALKING TO A LAWYER

If You Change Your Mind

Q. *What should I do if I change my mind about being, or not being, an organ donor?*

A. You can change your decision at any time. To revoke your decision to be an organ donor, write a statement to that effect and put it with your driver's license and your advance directive. You can also revoke your decision orally, but this is not as surefire as a written statement. In either case, tell your family and loved ones about your decision so that there is no confusion about your wishes.

Answer by Cindy Moy,
attorney and author,
Golden Valley, Minnesota

WHO GETS YOUR ORGANS?

Organ Procurement Organizations

In 1984, Congress enacted the National Organ Transplant Act (NOTA). As part of NOTA, organ procurement organizations (OPOs) were established. These organizations are divided into separate service areas. When you die, they coordinate the procurement of your organs with the transplantation process. This includes keeping a list of possible recipients and training hospital staff in getting the family's consent.

There is no cost to the organ donor for donating organs. The OPO assumes all the expenses associated with organ recovery. This does not include funeral and burial expenses, which are still the responsibility of the donor's family.

How It Works

When your doctor declares you dead and your family consents to organ donation, the OPO staff is called into the hospital to organize the process. OPO makes the arrangements to harvest your organs. This involves removing your organs surgically, testing your tissue for disease and to determine its type, comparing your gift to the list of potential recipients, and transporting your organs to the transplant center.

Who Chooses the Recipients?

The United Network for Organ Sharing keeps a national computer list of patients waiting for transplants. This list is used to match your organs with patients who might receive them through a transplant. Information about you, such as your blood type, is entered into the computer-match program. Possible recipients are listed according to the time they have been on the waiting list, their age, and their degree of compatibility with the characteristics of the donor's organs. Organs are offered to local patients first. If there is no patient locally that is a good match for the organ, the organ will

NEEDED: THE WISDOM OF SOLOMON

Choosing an organ recipient means that only one of two or more patients will have a chance of survival. So which person should get the organ? Several decades ago the decision was made by organ screening committees that used personal information about patients to make their choices. Today, more objective methods for determining recipients are used, for good reason. For example, consider what a member of a Seattle organ screening committee stated about having to choose between possible recipients:

> The choices were hard. . . . I remember voting against a young woman who was a known prostitute. I found I couldn't vote for her, rather than another candidate, a young wife and mother. I also voted against a young man who, until he learned he had renal failure, had been a ne'er-do-well, a real playboy. He promised he would reform his character, go back to school, and so on, if only he were selected for treatment. But I felt I'd lived long enough to know that a person like that won't really do what he was promising at the time.

be offered on a regional or national level. When transplants first became an option, committees would receive personal information about patients such as their race, income, gender, family status, and job before making a decision. The UNOS computer-match program makes every effort to select patients regardless of their race, gender, religion, or other personal information.

THE WORLD AT YOUR FINGERTIPS

- *Organ Transplants: A Patient's Guide* was written by the Massachusetts Organ Transplant Medical Team with the help of journalist H. F. Pizer (Harvard University Press, 1991). The book goes into great detail about the history of organ transplantation as well as about the process of removing and transplanting organs.

- *I'm Glad You're Not Dead: A Liver Transplant Story* by Elizabeth Parr (Journey Publishing, 1996) is her account of her struggle with liver disease and the process she went through while waiting for a transplant. Parr, a former nun and teacher, puts the stressful process of organ transplantation into comforting perspective.
- *The Ethics of Organ Transplants: The Current Debate* (Prometheus Books, 1999) is a series of essays on the ethical, legal, political, and religious aspects surrounding organ transplantation. Topics include the use of animal organs in humans and ways to increase the number of organs available for transplantation.

YOU MUST REMEMBER THIS

- To be an organ donor, you must be at least 18 years old and of sound mind.
- Removal of organs is a surgical procedure and will rarely interfere with funeral or burial arrangements.
- Your doctor or hospital will ask your next of kin for permission to take your organs, even if you sign an organ donor card or name organ donation in your advance directive. If your next of kin refuses, the hospital probably will not remove your organs.
- Do not put your organ donation only in your will. A better plan is to put it in your advance directive and to discuss your wishes with your family and doctor. By the time your will is located, it will be too late to donate your organs.
- You are dead when your brain ceases functioning.

CHAPTER 29

Assisted Suicide

The Law Addresses a Highly Controversial Topic

Karl is 54 years old, suffering from advanced colon cancer. He is in constant pain and well aware that there is no chance for recovery. Karl can no longer care for himself. Every day he watches as the strain of his disease takes its emotional and physical toll on his wife and children. Then there is the financial strain. He worries that with the mounting medical bills, there will be nothing left for his family after he is gone. Karl wishes to spare himself the increasing ravages of his disease and to protect his family from emotional and financial ruin. Karl wants to control the end of his life. Karl asks his doctor to prescribe barbiturates so that he can decide when and where to die. Karl's doctor does not want to give him the medication. Does Karl have a right to die by having his doctor help him to commit suicide?

SUICIDE AS AN OPTION

Is It Legal to Commit Suicide?

It is not against the law to commit, or to attempt to commit, suicide. The rationale is that suicide is usually prompted by a mental illness and people should not be criminally punished for being mentally disabled.

Helping Someone *Else* Commit Suicide

It *is* against the law in most states to aid or assist someone *else* in committing suicide. For instance, in Illinois and Ohio it is considered homicide to help someone else commit suicide. This is where **physician-assisted suicide** comes in. Physician-assisted suicide is legal in only one state—Oregon. In 1997, Oregon enacted the Death with Dignity Act. This law allows, but does not require, doctors to prescribe medication to competent, terminally ill patients, knowing that the medication is going to be used by the patient to end his life. The law is highly controversial.

During Oregon's first year of legalized assisted suicide, a study of all the patients who chose physician-assisted suicide showed that they based their decisions to commit suicide on the loss of autonomy and control of bodily functions. They were less concerned with the fear of uncontrollable pain or with putting a financial burden on their families. This may be in part due to the progress medicine has made in dealing with pain.

 EUTHANASIA VERSUS ASSISTED SUICIDE

Euthanasia (Greek for "good death") is the act of putting to death painlessly a person suffering from an incurable and painful disease or injury. It is sometimes called **mercy killing. Suicide** is the taking of one's own life.

Physician-assisted suicide is different from euthanasia. In a physician-assisted suicide, a patient asks a doctor to prescribe a lethal substance and the patient self-administers it. In euthanasia, the doctor administers the lethal substance to the patient. Physician-assisted suicide is currently legal in only one state; euthanasia is illegal in all states.

Recent Attempts to Legalize Physician-Assisted Suicide

In recent years, physician-assisted suicide bills have been introduced in many states, including Iowa, Maine, Michigan, Illinois, and New Hampshire. In New Hampshire's Death with Dignity bill, a patient who wished to end her life had to be examined by two doctors. After the patient was determined to be terminally ill, the attending doctor could give the patient a prescription for medication. The patient could then end her life by taking the medication at the time and place and in the manner she chose. None of the physician-assisted suicide bills passed.

The Federal Assisted-Suicide Funding Restriction Act of 1997 prohibits the use of federal funds in physician-assisted suicide.

What Doctors Think

Today physician-assisted suicide, while illegal in 49 states, is sometimes practiced. In one study, 53 percent of doctors treating AIDS patients in the San Francisco Bay area admitted to assisting patients with suicide. Another survey, this one by the *New England Journal of Medicine,* found that at least one in five doctors had prescribed medication with the intent of helping their patients end their suffering by ending their lives. Thus, even under current law, some doctors are willing to help terminally ill patients end their lives.

Is There a Constitutional Right to Physician-Assisted Suicide?

In 1997, three terminally ill patients, four doctors, and a non-profit group that counsels patients considering physician-assisted suicide filed suit in federal court, claiming that Washington State's ban on such physician-assisted suicide is unconstitutional. They asserted that the "right" to assistance in committing suicide is a liberty protected by the Due Process Clause of the Fourteenth Amendment. They prevailed at the district court and appellate court levels, but ultimately lost in the U.S. Supreme Court.

The Court stated that Washington's ban on physician-assisted suicide did not infringe on a fundamental liberty under the Due Process Clause. Rather, an examination of U.S. history, legal practices, and legal traditions shows that there are no exceptions to the assisted-suicide ban for those near death. To find such a right in the Fourteenth Amendment, the Court would have had to overturn centuries of legal practice and doctrine and go against the public policy of nearly every state in the country. Rather, the Court held, the ban was rationally related to legitimate government interests, such as prohibiting intentional killing and preserving human life, protecting the medical profession's integrity and ethics, maintaining physicians' role as their patients' healers, and preventing harm to those people who are the most vulnerable, including the poor, the elderly, disabled persons, and the terminally ill.

In a companion case decided the same day, the Court also held that New York State's ban on assisted suicide did not violate the Equal Protection Clause of the Fourteenth Amendment. Physicians and gravely ill patients filed suit, claiming that New York violated the equal protection of the laws by permitting patients to hasten their deaths by refusing life support systems, but not permitting them to hasten their deaths by self-administered prescribed drugs. An appellate court agreed with them, but the Supreme Court held that the distinction between letting a patient die and making a patient die is important, logical, rational, and well established: "[T]he two acts are different, and New York may, therefore, consistent with the Constitution, treat them differently."

The Court's rulings leave states free to decide to enact laws allowing physicians to assist patients who wish to end their lives. The Court's rulings simply mean that the states are not *required* by the Constitution to do so.

THE FUTURE OF PHYSICIAN-ASSISTED SUICIDE

The Argument in Favor of Physician-Assisted Suicide

While the Supreme Court has plainly stated that people do not have a constitutional right to assisted suicide, many people believe that current medical practices and public opinion are at odds with laws that always and in every situation outlaw physician-assisted suicide.

Many patients are demanding more say in their treatment, including their care at the end of their lives. They want to make their own decisions about their progress. They want to keep their dignity. They are worried that doctors will "play God" and keep their bodies alive long past the time when they or their families wish to let them die. No one wants to be a living corpse, and people around the country are calling for more freedom in their medical choices.

People in favor of making physician-assisted suicide legal propose several ways of ensuring that physician-assisted suicide is not abused. One suggestion is that the patient must be suffering from severe pain or indignity and that the patient repeatedly requests assistance in committing suicide. Another proposal is to require the doctor to consult with another doctor about whether assisted suicide would be appropriate in that situation. There are also proposed requirements that the doctor must be convinced that the patient is seeking assisted suicide without any coercion or incentive from others, that the patient must be able to understand what she is requesting, and that all other alternatives, including palliative care and hospice, must be explored.

The Argument Against Physician-Assisted Suicide

If physician-assisted suicide becomes the norm for those with certain types of illnesses, such as cancer, a misdiagnosis could lead a person to kill himself before finding out that the test results were incorrect or that his particular type of cancer is highly treatable.

Then there is the problem of knowing if you want to take your own life to avoid pain and suffering or if your children or spouse is pressuring you to kill yourself so that you will not be a financial or emotional burden to your family. There is also the concern that severely disabled people will be more apt to seek physician-assisted suicide than other groups of patients. There is some fear that assisted suicide would be the same as telling the disabled that their lives have no value. Some people fear that if the terminally ill are allowed to kill themselves, then somehow this will be expanded to euthanasia—the *involuntary* killing of the uneducated, the unemployed, and any other group considered undesirable by society. In fact, surveys show that many people, especially those belonging to minority groups, worry that they will be denied care and left to die against their wishes if physician-assisted suicide becomes an accepted practice.

These are some of the questions and arguments that must be addressed before physician-assisted suicide is made legal throughout the country.

THE WORLD AT YOUR FINGERTIPS

- The book *Euthanasia and Physician-Assisted Suicide (For and Against)* (Cambridge University Press, 1998) discusses the moral issues at the heart of the right-to-die movement. Gerald Dworkin and R. G. Frey argue for legalization of physician-assisted suicide, while ethicist Sissela Bok makes the case against physician-assisted suicide.

- *Euthanasia and Physician-Assisted Suicide: Killing or Caring?* by Michael Manning (Paulist Press, 1998) provides historical background and the framework that surrounds the controversy over euthanasia and physician-assisted suicide.

- *Regulating How We Die: The Ethical, Medical, and Legal Issues Surrounding Physician-Assisted Suicide* by medical ethicist Dr. Linda Emanuel (Harvard University Press, 1998) provides testimony from leading experts to provide clear arguments for and against physician-assisted suicide and euthanasia, as well as historical and legal perspectives on this issue.

- To follow legal developments regarding assisted suicide, visit the website for the Choices in Dying organization at *www. choices.org*.

- The Hemlock Society advocates giving patients the right to assisted suicide. The organization does not endorse suicide but rather supports giving terminally ill patients the right to legally prescribed medication and the choice of when to use it to end their lives. You can learn more about this organization at *www.hemlock.org*.

YOU MUST REMEMBER THIS

- It is not illegal to commit suicide.
- It is illegal in every state but Oregon for a doctor to assist a patient in committing suicide.
- The U.S. Supreme Court ruled that there is no constitutional right to physician-assisted suicide.
- States are free to enact laws allowing or prohibiting physician-assisted suicide.
- While there is some support for laws allowing physician-assisted suicide, only Oregon has passed such a law.

CHAPTER 30

Where Do You Go from Here?

The Best Places to Turn for More Information

*Throughout this book, we've given you resources, resources, and still
more resources to help you find more information on certain topics.
We're not done yet. Here are even more resources for you to check out.
(A few of these may have been mentioned in previous chapters, but we
think they're your best places to start.) Also included are some reminders
and tips you can use to go about getting more information.*

GENERALLY SPEAKING: TEN WEBSITES TO GET YOU STARTED

Some of these websites are housed within search engines, but they do contain rather lengthy sections on health law topics. You're bound to find what you're looking for at one of these sites or from one of their links. (*Note:* These are not arranged in any order of preference.)

Healthfinder® is a gateway provided by the United States government to health-related websites. It links to online journals and free information services. You can find it at *http://www. healthfinder.gov/aboutus/selection.htm*.

The People's Medical Society is a nonprofit organization dedicated to educating consumers about their medical rights and other health issues. Their online address is *www.peoplesmed.org*.

The National Health Law Program serves legal services programs and other organizations that provide health care for uninsured or underinsured low-income people. You can visit them online at *www.healthlaw.org*.

The Center for Public Representation offers information about health care issues at *www.law.wics.edu/pal/health/htm*.

The online site for the American Civil Liberties Union

(ACLU) provides information and resources on various health law issues. Their website can be found at *www.aclu.org/*.

The American Association of Retired Persons (AARP), *www.aarp.org*, is a good place to find information on issues, including health care issues, that affect older Americans.

To learn more about improving the quality of health care for immigrant and ethnically diverse communities, visit Diversity Rx at *www.diversityrx.org*.

Every Child by Two, *www.ecby.org*, focuses their efforts on reducing infant mortality through timely immunization.

The Long-Term Care Campaign seeks decent health care for older Americans. Their online address is *www.ltccampaign.org*.

The National Black Women's Health Project, *www.nbwhp.org*, seeks to better the medical care received by women of color.

SOME GOOD BOOKS

Each of these books makes for informative and valuable reading. They're on a variety of topics having to do with health care. Don't forget to check out what your local library has to offer and to visit amazon.com and other online bookstores.

Outsmarting Managed Care: A Doctor Shares His Insider's Secrets to Getting the Health Care You Want by Bruce A. Barron (Times Books, 1999)

The Complete Idiot's Guide to Managed Health Care by Sophie M. Korczyk and Hazel A. Witte (Macmillan Distribution, 1998)

Prescription for Profit: How Doctors Defraud Medicaid by Paul Jesilow and Gilbert Geis (University of California Press, 1993)

The Clone Age: Adventures in the New World of Reproductive Technologies by Lori B. Andrews (Henry Holt & Company, Inc., 1999)

Back to the Asylum: The Future of Mental Health Law and Policy in the United States by John Q. La Fond and Mary L. Durham (Oxford University Press, 1992)

The FMLA Handbook: A Practical Guide to the Family & Medical Leave Act for Union Members & Stewards by Robert M. Schwartz (Work Rights Press, 1996)

Medicare Rules and Regulations: A Survival Guide to Policies, Procedures, and Payment Reform by Maxine Lewis (Practice Management Information Corporation, 1999)

The Medicare Answer Book by Connacht Cash (Race Point Press, 1999)

Enough Already! The Overtreatment of Early Breast Cancer with Chapters on the Law of Informed Consent and Medical Malpractice by George Goldberg (Paracelsus Press, 1996)

PATIENT TO PATIENT

Whether you're taking care of elderly parents, trying to keep up with the latest viruses your kids are bringing home, or just doing some basic research about health care, it always helps to talk to someone who's been that route before. Speak to your friends, associates, family members, or professional acquaintances to get an idea of how to look out for your family's health care and what pitfalls to avoid. Learning from others' experiences can aid you in the long run.

Don't know any folks like this to speak to? Log on to the Internet, where countless posting boards, user groups, mailing lists, and chatrooms exist to help you in your quest for knowledge. Most of the health sites we've included in this book feature the aforementioned ways to communicate either with professionals or with other folks like yourself. Check out some of the sites featured above to get started right away.

If face-to-face is more appealing than cyberspace, check out your library or other public arenas where open lectures are held to see if any health law attorneys are speaking. Call the local bar association and find out who is on the health law committee.

Another good idea is getting in touch with local associations for retired persons.

That's about all we have for you right now, but please visit us on the Web at *http://www.abanet.org/publiced/*. You can also drop us a line to let us know what you think of this book or to make suggestions for future editions. E-mail us at: abapubed @abanet.org

Good luck!

APPENDIX A

Getting Help with Medicare Questions

ORDERING FREE INFORMATION

Medicare can be very confusing. Fortunately there are several places you can call for help. For free booklets on the different aspects of Medicare, call the Medicare Hotline at 1-800-638-6833.

HELP WITH MEDICARE QUESTIONS

For questions about choosing a Medicare plan, submitting your bills, buying a supplemental insurance policy, or filing a complaint about your care or treatment, call your state health insurance assistance program.

Alabama
1-800-243-5463

Alaska
1-800-478-6065

Arizona
1-800-432-4040

Arkansas
1-800-852-5494

California
1-800-434-0222

Colorado
1-800-544-9181

Connecticut
1-800-994-9422

Delaware
1-800-336-9500

District of Columbia
1-202-676-3900

Florida
1-800-963-5337

Georgia
1-800-669-8387

Hawaii
1-808-586-7299

Idaho
1-800-247-4422 (Boise)
1-800-488-5725 (Lewiston)
1-800-488-5731 (Twin Falls)
1-800-488-5764 (Pocatello)

Illinois
1-800-548-9034

Indiana
1-800-452-4800

Iowa
1-800-351-4664

Kansas
1-800-860-5260

Kentucky
1-502-564-7372

Louisiana
1-800-259-5301

Maine
1-800-750-5353

Maryland
1-800-243-3425
TTY: 1-410-767-1083

Massachusetts
1-800-882-2003

Michigan
1-800-803-7174

Minnesota
1-800-333-2433

Mississippi
1-800-948-3090

Missouri
1-800-390-3330

Montana
1-800-332-2272

Nebraska
1-402-471-2201

Nevada
1-800-307-4444

New Hampshire
1-800-852-3388

New Jersey
1-800-792-8820

New Mexico
1-800-432-2080

New York
1-800-333-4114
1-212-869-3850
(New York City)

North Carolina
1-800-443-9354

North Dakota
1-800-247-0560

Ohio
1-800-686-1578

Oklahoma
1-800-763-2828

Oregon
1-800-722-4134

Pennsylvania
1-800-783-7067

Puerto Rico
1-800-981-4355

Rhode Island
1-800-322-2880

South Carolina
1-800-868-9095

South Dakota
1-800-822-8804

Tennessee
1-800-525-2816

Texas
1-800-252-9240

Utah
1-800-439-3805

Vermont
1-800-642-5119

Virginia
1-800-552-3402

Washington
1-800-397-4422

West Virginia
1-800-642-9004

Wisconsin
1-800-242-1060

Wyoming
1-800-856-4398

OTHER USEFUL TELEPHONE NUMBERS
FOR QUESTIONS ABOUT MEDICARE

Social Security Administration: If you lose your card, change your address or want your Medicare premium deducted from your Social Security check, call 1-800-772-1213.

Health Care Financing Administration Regional Offices: To find out about local seminars that are offered to explain your new Medicare health plan choices or to make a complaint about your Medicare coverage, call:

Boston Office (if you live in Connecticut, Maine, Massachusetts, New Hampshire, Rhode Island, Vermont) 1-617-565-1232

New York Office (New York, New Jersey, Puerto Rico, Virgin Islands) 1-212-264-3657

Philadelphia Office (Delaware, District of Columbia, Maryland, Pennsylvania, Virginia, West Virginia) 1-215-861-4226

Atlanta Office (Alabama, Florida, Georgia, Kentucky, Mississippi, North Carolina, South Carolina, Tennessee) 1-404-562-7500

Chicago Office (Illinois, Indiana, Michigan, Minnesota, Ohio, Wisconsin) 1-312-353-7180

Dallas Office (Arkansas, Louisiana, New Mexico, Oklahoma, Texas) 1-214-767-6401

Kansas City Office (Iowa, Kansas, Missouri, Nebraska) 1-816-426-2866

Denver Office (Colorado, Montana, North Dakota, South Dakota, Utah, Wyoming) 1-303-844-4024

San Francisco Office (Arizona, California, Hawaii, Nevada) 1-415-744-3602

Seattle Office (Alaska, Idaho, Oregon, Washington) 1-206-615-2354

APPENDIX B

Getting Help with Medicaid Questions

HELP WITH MEDICAID QUESTIONS

If you have questions about applying for Medicaid or submitting a bill to Medicaid, call your state Medicaid office:

Alabama
1-800-362-1504

Alaska
1-800-770-5650

Arizona
1-602-417-4680

Arkansas
1-501-682-8487

California
1-800-952-5253

Colorado
1-303-866-2993

Connecticut
1-860-424-5008

Delaware
1-302-577-4901

District of Columbia
1-202-727-0735
1-202-724-5506

Florida
1-850-487-4382

Georgia
1-800-282-4536

Hawaii
1-808-586-5391

Idaho
1-208-334-5747

Illinois
1-800-252-8635

Indiana
1-317-232-4966

Missouri
1-573-751-3425

Iowa
1-515-281-8621

Montana
1-406-444-5900

Kansas
1-785-296-3349

Nebraska
1-402-471-9147

Kentucky
1-502-564-6885

Nevada
1-702-687-4775

Louisiana
1-504-342-3885
    (questions about bills)
1-504-342-5716
    (questions about applying)

New Hampshire
1-603-271-4344

New Jersey
1-609-588-2600

Maine
1-207-624-5277

New Mexico
1-505-827-3100

Maryland
1-410-767-1432

New York
1-518-486-4803

Massachusetts
1-800-841-2900

North Carolina
1-800-662-7030

Michigan
1-800-642-3195

North Dakota
1-800-755-2604

Minnesota
1-800-657-3739

Ohio
1-800-324-8680

Mississippi
1-601-359-6056

Oklahoma
1-405-530-3439

Oregon
1-503-945-5811

Pennsylvania
1-717-787-1870

Puerto Rico
1-787-765-1230

Rhode Island
1-401-464-2121

South Carolina
1-803-253-6100

South Dakota
1-605-773-3495

Tennessee
1-615-741-0213

Texas
1-512-438-3219

Utah
1-801-538-6155

Vermont
1-802-241-2880

Virginia
1-809-774-4624

Washington
1-800-562-3022

West Virginia
1-800-642-3607

Wisconsin
1-608-266-2522
Wyoming
1-307-777-5500

APPENDIX C

Health Care
Advance Directive

SECTION 1.
HEALTH CARE AGENT

Print your full name in this spot as the principal or creator of the health care advance directive.

Print the full name, address, and telephone number of the person (age 18 or older) you appoint as your health care agent. Appoint *only* a person with whom you have talked and whom you trust to understand and carry out your values and wishes.

Many states limit the persons who can serve as your agent. If you want to meet all existing state restrictions, *do not* name any of the following as your agent, since some states will not let them act in that role:

- **your health care providers, including physicians;**

- **staff of health care facilities or nursing care facilities providing your care;**

This appendix is adapted from the booklet *Shape Your Health-Care Future with Health-Care Advance Directives.*

- guardians of your finances (also called conservators);
- employees of government agencies financially responsible for your care;
- any person serving as agent for 10 or more persons.

SECTION 2.
ALTERNATE AGENTS

It is a good idea to name alternate agents in case your first agent is not available. Of course, only appoint alternates if you fully trust them to act faithfully as your agent and if you have talked to them about serving as your agent. Print the appropriate information in this section. You can name as many alternate agents as you wish, but place them in the order in which you wish them to serve.

SECTION 3.
EFFECTIVE DATE AND DURABILITY

This sample document is effective if and when you cannot make health care decisions. Your agent and your doctor determine if you are in this condition. Some state laws include specific procedures for determining your decision-making ability. If you wish, you can include other effective dates or other criteria for determining that you cannot make health care decisions (such as requiring two physicians to evaluate your decision-making ability). You also can state that the power will end at some later date or event before death.

In any case, you have the *right to revoke*, or take away, the agent's authority at any time. To revoke, notify your agent or health care provider orally or in writing. If you revoke, it is best to notify in writing both your agent and physician and anyone else who has a copy of the directive. Also destroy the health care advance directive document itself.

SECTION 4.
AGENT'S POWERS

This grant of power is intended to be as broad as possible. Unless you set limits, your agent will have authority to make any decision you could make to consent to or to stop any type of health care.

Even under this broad grant of authority, your agent still must follow your wishes and directions, communicated by you in any manner now or in the future.

To specifically limit or direct your agent's power, you must complete Part II of the advance directive, section 6, on page 408.

SECTION 5.
MY INSTRUCTIONS ABOUT
END-OF-LIFE TREATMENT

The subject of end-of-life treatment is particularly important to many people. In this section, you can give general or specific instructions on the subject. The four main paragraphs are options—**choose only one.** Write your desires or instructions in your own words if you choose paragraph four. If you choose paragraph two, you have three additional options, from which you can choose one, two, or all three. If you are satisfied with your agent's knowledge of your values and wishes and you do not want to include instructions in the form, initial the first option and do not give instructions in the form.

Any instructions you give here will guide your agent. If you do not appoint an agent, they will guide any health care providers or surrogate decision makers who must make a decision for you if you cannot do so yourself.

Directive in Your Own Words: If you would like to state your wishes about end-of-life treatment in your own words instead of choosing one of the options provided, you can do so in this section. Since people sometimes have different opinions on whether nutrition and hydration should be refused or stopped under certain circumstances, be sure to address this issue clearly in your directive. Nutrition and hydration means food and fluids given through a nasogastric tube or tube into your stomach, intestines, or veins, and *does not include* non-intrusive methods such as spoon feeding or moistening of lips and mouth.

Some states allow the stopping of nutrition and hydration only if you expressly authorize it. If you are creating your own directive and you do not want nutrition and hydration, state so clearly.

SECTION 6.
ANY OTHER HEALTH CARE
INSTRUCTIONS OR LIMITATIONS
OR MODIFICATIONS OF
MY AGENT'S POWERS

In this section, you can provide instructions about other health care issues that are not end-of-life treatment or nutrition and hydration. For example, you might want to include your wishes about issues such as nonemergency surgery, elective medical treatments, or admission to a nursing home. Again, be careful in these instructions not to place limitations on your agent that you do not intend. For example, while you may not want to be admitted to a nursing home, placing such a restriction may make things impossible for your agent if other options are not available.

You also may limit your agent's powers in any way you wish. For example, you can instruct your agent to refuse any specific types of treatment that are against your religious beliefs or unacceptable to you for any other reasons. These might include blood transfusions, electroconvulsive therapy, sterilization, abortion, amputation, psychosurgery, or admission to a mental institution. Some states limit your agent's authority to consent to or to refuse some of these procedures, regardless of your health care advance directive.

Be very careful about stating limitations because the specific circumstances surrounding future health care decisions are impossible to predict. If you do not want any limitations, simply write in *"No limitations."*

SECTION 7.
PROTECTION OF THIRD PARTIES
WHO RELY ON MY AGENT

In most states, health care providers cannot be forced to follow the directions of your agent if they object. However most states also require providers to help transfer you to another provider who is willing to honor your instructions. To encourage compliance with the health care advance directive, this paragraph states that providers who rely in good faith on the agent's statements and decisions will not be held civilly liable for their actions.

SECTION 8.
DONATIONS OF ORGANS
AT DEATH

In this section you can state your intention to donate bodily organs and tissues at death. If you do not wish to be an organ donor, initial the first option. The second option is a donation of any or all organs or parts. The third option allows you to donate only those organs or tissues you specify. Consider mentioning the heart, liver, lung, kidney, pancreas, intestine, cornea, bone, skin, heart valves, tendons, ligaments, and saphenous vein. Finally, you may limit the use of your organs by *crossing out* any of the four purposes listed that you do not want (transplant, research, therapy, or education). If you do not cross out any of these options, your organs may be used for any of these purposes.

SECTION 9.
NOMINATION OF GUARDIAN

Appointing a health care agent helps to avoid a court-appointed guardian for health care decision making. However, if a court becomes involved for any reason, this paragraph expressly names your agent to serve as guardian. A court does not have to follow your nomination, but normally it will honor your wishes unless there is good reason to override your choice.

SECTION 10.
ADMINISTRATIVE PROVISIONS

These items address miscellaneous matters that could affect the implementation of your health care advance directive.

Required state procedures for signing this kind of document vary. Some require only a signature, while others have very detailed witnessing requirements. Some states simply require notarization.

The procedure in this book is likely to be far more complex than your state law requires because it combines the formal requirements from virtually every state. Follow it if you do not know your state's requirements and you want to meet the signature requirements of virtually every state.

1. **Sign and date the document** in the presence of two witnesses and a notary. Your witnesses should know your identity personally and be able to declare that you appear to be of sound mind and under no duress or undue influence.

   In order to meet the different witnessing requirements of most states, do *not* have the following people witness your signature:

- Anyone you have chosen to make health care decisions on your behalf (agent or alternate agents).

- Your treating physician, health care provider, health facility operator, or an employee of any of these.
- Insurers or employees of your life/health insurance provider.
- Anyone financially responsible for your health care costs.
- Anyone related to you by blood, marriage, or adoption.
- Anyone entitled to any part of your estate under an existing will or by operation of law or anyone who will benefit financially from your death. Your creditors should not serve as witnesses.

If you are in a nursing home or other institution, a few states have additional witnessing requirements. This form does not include witnessing language for this situation. Contact a patient advocate or an ombudsman to find out about the state's requirements in these cases.

2. **Have your signature notarized.** Some states permit notarization as an alternative to witnessing. Doing both witnessing and notarization is more than most states require, but doing both will meet the execution requirements of most states. This form includes a typical notary statement, but it is wise to check state law in case it requires a special form of notary acknowledgment.

HEALTH CARE ADVANCE DIRECTIVE

PART I
APPOINTMENT OF HEALTH CARE AGENT

1. Health Care Agent

I, _____, hereby appoint

PRINCIPAL

_____

AGENT'S NAME

_____

ADDRESS

_____

HOME PHONE #   WORK PHONE #

as my agent to make health and personal care decisions for me
as authorized in this document.

2. Alternate Agents

If
- I revoke my Agent's authority; or
- my Agent becomes unwilling or unavailable to act; or
- my agent is my spouse and I become legally separated or
  divorced,

I name the following (each to act alone and successively, in the
order named) as alternates to my Agent:

A. First Alternate Agent _____

    Address _____

    Telephone _____

B. Second Alternate Agent _____

Address _____

Telephone _____

3. Effective Date and Durability

By this document I intend to create a health care advance directive. It is effective upon, and only during, any period in which I
cannot make or communicate a choice regarding a particular
health care decision. My Agent, attending physician, and any
other necessary experts should determine that I am unable to
make choices about health care.

4. Agent's Powers

I give my Agent full authority to make health care decisions for
me. My Agent shall follow my wishes as known to my Agent
either through this document or through other means. In inter-
preting my wishes, I intend my Agent's authority to be as broad
as possible, except for any limitations I state in this form. In
making any decision, my Agent shall try to discuss the proposed
decision with me to determine my desires if I am able to communicate in any way. If my Agent cannot determine the choice I
would want, then my Agent shall make a choice for me based
upon what my Agent believes to be in my best interests.

Unless specifically limited by Section 6, below, my Agent is
authorized as follows:

A. To consent to, to refuse, or to withdraw consent to any
   and all types of health care. Health care means any care,
   treatment, service, or procedure to maintain, diagnose,
   or otherwise affect an individual's physical or mental
   condition. It includes, but is not limited to, artificial

respiration, nutritional support and hydration, medication, and cardiopulmonary resuscitation;

B. To have access to medical records and information to the same extent that I am entitled, including the right to disclose the contents to others as appropriate for my health care;

C. To authorize my admission to or discharge from (even against medical advice) any hospital, nursing home, residential care, assisted-living facility, or similar facility or service;

D. To contract on my behalf for any health care related service or facility on my behalf, without my Agent incurring personal financial liability for such contracts;

E. To hire and fire medical, social service, and other support personnel responsible for my care;

F. To authorize or refuse to authorize any medication or procedure intended to relieve pain, even though such use may lead to physical damage or addiction or hasten the moment of (but not intentionally cause) my death;

G. To make anatomical gifts of part or all of my body for medical purposes, authorize an autopsy, and direct the disposition of my remains to the extent permitted by law;

H. To take any other action necessary to do what I authorize here, including (but not limited to) granting any waiver or release from liability required by any hospital, physician, or other health care provider; signing any documents relating to refusals of treatment or the leaving of a facility against medical advice; and pursuing any legal action in my name at the expense of my estate to force compliance with my wishes as determined by my Agent, or to seek actual or punitive damages for the failure to comply.

PART II
INSTRUCTIONS ABOUT HEALTH CARE

5. My Instructions About End-of-Life Treatment

(Initial only ONE of the following FOUR main statements):

1. _____ NO SPECIFIC INSTRUCTIONS. My Agent knows my values and wishes, so I do not wish to include any specific instructions here.

2. _____ DIRECTIVE TO WITHHOLD OR WITHDRAW TREATMENT. Although I greatly value life, I also believe that at some point life has such diminished value that medical treatment should be stopped, and I should be allowed to die. Therefore, I do not want to receive treatment, including nutrition and hydration, when the treatment will not give me a meaningful quality of life.

(If You Initialed this Paragraph, Also initial Any or All of the Following Three Statements With Which You Agree):

By this I mean that I do not want my life prolonged . . .

_____ . . . if the treatment will leave me in a condition of permanent unconsciousness, such as in an irreversible coma or a persistent vegetative state.

_____ . . . if the treatment will leave me with no more than some consciousness and in an irreversible condition of complete, or nearly complete, loss of ability to think or communicate with others.

_____ . . . if the treatment will leave me with no more than some ability to think or communicate with others, and the likely risks and burdens of treatment outweigh the expected benefits. Risks, burdens, and benefits include consideration of length of life, quality of life, financial costs, and my personal dignity and privacy.

3. _____ DIRECTIVE TO RECEIVE TREATMENT. I want my life to be prolonged as long as possible, no matter what my quality of life.

4. _____ DIRECTIVE ABOUT END-OF-LIFE TREATMENT IN MY OWN WORDS:

_____

_____

_____

_____

_____

6. Any Other Health Care Instructions or Limitations or Modifications of My Agent's Powers

_____

_____

_____

_____

_____

7. Protection of Third Parties Who Rely on My Agent

No person who relies in good faith on any representations by my Agent or Alternate Agent(s) shall be liable to me, my estate, or my heirs or assigns for recognizing the Agent's authority.

8. Donations of Organs at Death

Upon my death:
(Initial one)
_____ I do _not_ wish to donate any organs or tissues, OR
_____ I give _any_ needed organs, tissues, or parts, OR
_____ I give _only_ the following organs, tissues, or parts:
(_please specify_)

_____

_____

_____

My gift (if any) is for the following purposes:
(Cross out any of the following you do not want)

- Transplant
- Research
- Therapy
- Education

9. Nomination of Guardian

If a guardian of my person should for any reason need to be appointed, I nominate my Agent (or his or her alternate then authorized to act), named above.

10. Administrative Provisions

(All apply)
- I revoke any prior health care advance directive.
- This health care advance directive is intended to be valid in any jurisdiction in which it is presented.
- A copy of this advance directive is intended to have the same effect as the original.

Signing the Document

BY SIGNING HERE, I INDICATE THAT I UNDERSTAND THE CONTENTS OF THIS DOCUMENT AND THE EFFECT OF THIS GRANT OF POWERS TO MY AGENT.

I sign my name to this Health Care Advance Directive on this _____ day of _____, 20_____.

My Signature_____

My Name _____

My current home address is _____

_____

_____

Witness Statement

I declare that the person who signed or acknowledged this document is personally known to me, that he/she signed or acknowledged this health care advance directive in my presence, and that he/she appears to be of sound mind and under no duress, fraud, or undue influence.

    I am not:

- **the person appointed as agent by this document;**
- **the patient's health care provider;**
- **an employee of the patient's health care provider;**
- **financially responsible for the person's health care;**
- **related to the principal by blood, marriage, or adoption; and,**
- **to the best of my knowledge, a creditor of the principal or entitled to any part of his/her estate under a will now existing or by operation of law.**

Witness #1:

_____
SIGNATURE   DATE

_____
PRINT NAME

_____
RESIDENT ADDRESS

_____
TELEPHONE

Witness #2:

_____

SIGNATURE   DATE

_____

PRINT NAME

_____

RESIDENT ADDRESS

_____

TELEPHONE

Notarization

STATE OF _____.)   My Commission Expires:

) ss.

COUNTY OF _____.)

On this _____ day of _____, 20 _____,

the said _____, _____

known to me (or satisfactorily   NOTARY PUBLIC
proven to be the person named
in the foregoing instrument)
personally appeared before me,
a Notary Public, within and for
the State and County aforesaid,
and acknowledged that he or she
freely and voluntarily executed
the same for the purposes stated
therein.

INDEX

Experimentation. *See* Research on humans

Immunizations. *See* Vaccinations
Income cap, 263–64
Income tests, 78, 263
Infertility. *See* Assisted
    reproductive technology
Information sources (books and
    journals), 385–86
  abortion, 148–49
  advance directives, 353
  assisted suicide, 382
  hospice care, 364–65
  human research, 337–38
  long-term care, 259
  malpractice, 324
  managed care, 63
  mandatory testing, 202
  Medicaid, 83
  midwifery, 138
  nursing homes, 239
  organ transplantation,
    375–76
  privacy, 21
  quarantine, 223
  reproduction, 108
  sterilization, 128
  tort liability, 215
  See also Websites
Informed consent, 1–2, 36–47
  changing mind on, 45
  definition of, 36–37
  of disabled or non-English-
    speaking patients, 37
  forms, 42–43, 44
  on human research, 330–31,
    334–35
  origins of, 37–38
  proper, 39
  questions on, 42, 43–45
  requirements, 40–42
  right to refuse treatment, 46
  on vaccination, 190
Inheritance laws, 106–7
Injunctive relief, 205, 206

Institutional Review Boards
    (IRBs), 329–30, 332
Insurance. *See* Health insurance
Intergenerational
    homes/communities,
    290–91
In vitro fertilization, 97, 99
IRBs. *See* Institutional Review
    Boards
Irrevocable trusts, 274

J

JCAHO. *See* Joint Commission
    on Accreditation of
    Healthcare Organizations
Joint Commission on
    Accreditation of Healthcare
    Organizations (JCAHO),
    10–11, 304–5
Judicial bypass option, 146

K

Kansas, naturopathy in, 308

L

Labor and delivery. *See*
    Childbirth
Lack, Sylvia, 357
Law enforcement officers, 14,
    199
Lee, Susan, 336–37
Liability, 205
Licensing, 295–311
  complaints to authorities,
    300–303
  of doctors, 295–97, 299–303,
    309–10
  of health care facilities, 303–5
  of midwives, 134–35
  of nurses, 298–99

ABOUT THE AUTHOR

Cindy J. Moy is an attorney, writer, and speaker based in Golden Valley, Minnesota. Her practice specializes in intellectual property and employment issues. She is a former television and newspaper journalist who anchored television news broadcasts and hosted a radio program entitled *Speak Out,* which covered current-interest topics. She currently contributes to many publications, including writing several chapters for the *ABA Legal Guide for Small Business* and contributing articles to the ABA's *Preview of U.S. Supreme Court Cases.*